the

shared

journey

An Introduct
to Encounter

DATE DUE			

TERRY O'BANION

University of Illinois, Champaign

APRIL O'CONNELL

Santa Fe Junior College, Gainesville, Florida

the
shared
journey

An Introduction
To Encounter

Prentice-Hall, Inc., *Englewood Cliffs, New Jersey*

PRENTICE-HALL INTERNATIONAL, INC., London
PRENTICE-HALL OF AUSTRALIA, PTY. LTD., Sydney
PRENTICE-HALL OF CANADA, LTD., Toronto
PRENTICE-HALL OF INDIA PRIVATE LTD., New Delhi
PRENTICE-HALL OF JAPAN, INC., Tokyo

© 1970 by Prentice-Hall, Inc., Englewood Cliffs, N.J.

Current printing (last digit):

10 9 8 7 6 5 4 3

13-807834-3

Library of Congress Catalog Card Number: 76-108563

Printed in the United States of America

to   JOSEPH W. FORDYCE,
       A visionary,
       Who dared to put into practice
       What this book is all about

                    and

to   ALL "OUR" STUDENTS,
       Those we've known in the past,
              And who became part of this book,
       Those we will one day
              In some way encounter,

                    and

       Those whom we will never meet face-to-face,
                              . . . But who journey with us now
                                    through these pages.

foreword

I walked barefoot on the mile of dirt streets between home and school every day as a boy. I remember a dog. He was not a spaniel, terrier, or hound; he was a dog. Every morning and afternoon he sat in front of his owner's house at the half point of my trip. When he caught first glimpse of me he ran toward me greeting me with his tail. We spent only a brief time together each day. Even though our relationship was hampered by the fact I was not a dog, this encounter somehow made me feel more like me. There was an elderly woman confined to a wheel chair who always waved to me as I passed. I never knew her name. But somehow her daily recognition of me made me feel more like me.

As a star gazing adolescent, the dog and the woman and others who shared my being a child were no longer there to greet me as I walked to high school with shoes on paved streets. But I remember the English Literature teacher for whom I wrote an essay about my nightly walks home. She read it and then we looked at each other. It was a brief, nonverbal encounter but somehow it made me feel more like me. And the band director gave me many tangible rewards such as awards for most outstanding band student, the title of assistant director, and rides home after summer band practice. Even then I realized I couldn't play that clarinet very well. His interest in more than my musical performance, his interest in me somehow made me feel more like me.

In college there was a girl who would wait for me between classes although we could spend only a minute. Her smile, her gaze, her caring somehow made me feel more like me.

And there was a Dean who believed in me and asked me to help him. We would meet dozens of times each day but each time he greeted me with a smile and handshake as though it was our first discovery of each other. Somehow he made me feel more like me.

As an Assistant Dean I visited men confined to the Infirmary and would occasionally run errands for them picking up their books from their residence or telling a friend they were ill. The way they looked when they said thank you somehow made me feel more like me.

A girl walked into my counseling office and said I feel as though I am floating through clouds. Every time I reach out nothing is there. Can you help me? The psychiatrist diagnosed her as schizophrenic and said she was in serious condition. We spent only two months seeing each other before she had to drop out. She would sometimes bring her guitar and sing plaintive folk songs. Other times she would read me poems she had written. Other times we would talk or just sit with each other. She said that during our encounters she felt for the first and only times a little like she was herself. I know that those encounters somehow made me feel more like me.

These moments of encounter, these brief, fleeting moments of discovering my own identity through the being of others help me realize that I probably can't find my being by doing but by being with others. And perhaps these others gain fleeting glances of their own identity, their own being, themselves during these moments.

Perhaps the organizational castles, the castles of brick and activities —all of my professional doing is only significant if it allows me to truly encounter a student so that somehow he feels more like him.

I realize that most moments of encounter in my past were not consciously planned, but must encounters be accidental? Must I wait passively for a meaningful union with another to occur? Behavior can be learned, and behavior called encounter is no exception. Yet to be able to learn behavior, I must be able to know what it is. We tend to view encounter in a mystical sense that is elusive to scholarly analysis.

Terry and April have accomplished in this book what many have termed an impossibility. They describe the human encounter. And they use all modes of human expression. They do use the cognitive approach which is the most natural in writing. But they also have been able to blend the emotional, imaginative, and practical which makes their description of encounter as whole as the human experience itself.

The use of this book should make the teaching and learning of encounter behavior in college and other settings a more effective and efficient experience. Because of its mystical aura, many colleges have looked upon encounter as not an appropriate behavior to be a concern of an academic institution. At the same time there is a clear awareness of the need to respond in a scholarly and meaningful way to the need for identity students express today. The skills involved in the human encounter are also valued behavior in virtually all professions and occupations. Hopefully, this contribution of Terry and April will facilitate the college in fulfilling its responsibility to teach behaviors necessary for adequate human functioning.

To attempt an encounter with us through the medium of this book took courage. The risk involved is complex and continuing. But behavior is risky. One cannot risk success without risking failure. In my judgment, Terry and April's risk has resulted in a great success. Reading it made me feel more like me.

W. HAROLD GRANT
MICHIGAN STATE UNIVERSITY
DECEMBER 8, 1969

to

the student

The authors struggled long and hard in deciding how to write this book. Not only did we want to introduce encounter as an exciting and rewarding experience, but also we wanted the book itself to be an experience—the way a novel can be exciting, or the way a discussion between two people can be stimulating, or the way a course can challenge you to do some deep thinking when you have a dynamic teacher.

How could we do this? We thought for many hours about this question. We had a lot of ideas and a few of them seemed fairly good. But one factor for us seemed to stand out above all the others. We wanted to be as open and as honest with you as we could. We wanted to meet you not as two authors of a book, or two "experts" in the area of encounter, but as real people who have ourselves lived out some of our own real problems, and who are still struggling with other problems of living. We wanted to talk *to* you, not *at* you. We should have liked to talk with you over a cup of coffee, or in your office, or in your home, or wherever you may be reading this, but we will settle for at least talking *to* you.

You will notice that the term "encounter" occurs again and again. Encounter is what this book is all about. And by this time, you are probably wondering *just what is encounter*? Well, it's a lot of things. It's a way of meeting people. It's a way of knowing people more deeply and profoundly than you have perhaps ever thought possible. Encounter is like having a set of extraordinary friends, or a very special and understanding family. As a new philosophy and a methodology for living, this new approach to relating to each other has the possibility, we believe, of cementing our rapidly fragmenting society.

Encounter is also a way of being real, of being yourself and just yourself. Every so often, for example, you will come to a chapter that is an actual dialogue between the two of us (Terry and April), a meeting in which we just sat down together and tried to get to know each other. That is what is called encounter.

As you read our dialogues we hope *you* get to know *us*. We hope you come to see us in our very human totalities—with all our strengths and all our limitations.

But we want you to do more than that. We really want you to experiment with encountering other persons in the world. Encounter is an opportunity for you to establish very special relationships with those other persons who make up your world: your friends, your classmates, your business associates, your family—and to share with them the process that is living.

The task of finding out who you are is perhaps the most agonizing and beautiful task of your life. It is your lifetime journey, and encounter is a way of sharing this journey with others in all its depth and wonder.

We risk ourselves in this book. And because we do, we anticipate criticism. This book may be the "impossible dream." It may be that encounter is too nebulous to be captured in words and definitions. It may also be that some will be shocked by our openness and self-revealment, and that others will be confused by the several ways we have presented the concept of encounter to you. Even the ways we disagree with each other may be unsettling. But out of unsettling experiences shared together there is the possibility of something new. And that was true for us. For we both were different people at the end of the book than we were at the beginning (as you will see).

So, yes, we have risked ourselves in this book. We dared to do so because we wanted a book that tries to do things a book is supposed to do, but sometimes doesn't—to stimulate you to think, to respond, and to participate, yourself, in the world we all share together. We wanted a book that would be serious in intent but not dull. We dared because we want you to be more willing to risk yourselves and to make this everyday world of ours—with all its laughter and tears and sweat and joy and pain—a more exciting and rewarding place in which to live. Our hope is that we have succeeded. . . .

TERRY O'BANION
APRIL O'CONNELL

contents

I

what is human encounter?

It is probably impossible to describe any kind of human experience to the satisfaction and understanding of all. It is particularly difficult to describe and define the human encounter, for the experience is as varied as people are. Moreover, very little has been written about the human encounter until quite recently.

As two authors we share many common areas of experience and agreement regarding the human encounter. We have worked as a team with classes of students and as co-facilitators of faculty encounter groups. We have worked on many committees together to implement our ideas in an educational institution. In our personal lives we have encountered each other in our struggle to know the other and to be known by the other; we have on occasion stood face to face in confrontation. As we have moved closer, we have become more aware of our separateness—of our distinctness—of what makes each of us different from the other. We have come to appreciate each other in that recognition of separateness—and that has given us more to appreciate in what we share together.

As we discuss the human encounter, therefore, the discussion most often reflects shared ideas. But since our approach is not always the same you will have opportunities to move toward an understanding of the human encounter through our various perceptions and experiences. In this way we hope you will come to choose your own direction to the human encounter, that through your own experience you will discover your own meaning, your own definition. When you have experienced the human encounter more thoroughly you may wish to return to this first chapter and write your own "why" of human encountering.

In the next two chapters we talk about what the human encounter is *not* and offer some descriptions that may help lead you to a definition. In one chapter we "point toward" the definition of the human encounter; in the Dialogue we explore some further aspects of the encounter process as we discuss what it means to us.

1

the why
of human
encountering

THE STATE OF MAN

All of us have experienced the pain and loneliness that comes with being human. Most of us live inside ourselves in a world of loneliness. Our existence seems meaningless, and we experience the joy of living only on rare occasions. This condition of man has been noted by poets, psychologists, and even by our major entertainers. From the words of "Within You Without You," the Beatles express the common state of modern man:

We were talking . . . about the space between us all.
And the people . . . who hide themselves behind a wall of illusion.[1]

Each man is alone, often alienated from himself and from others. There is little meaningful communication between people, as each of us hides behind a mask and remains unknown. We receive nothing, and we have nothing to give.

. . . the chief problem of people in the middle decade of the twentieth century is *emptiness*. By that I mean not only that many people do not have any clear idea of what they feel. When they talk about lack of autonomy, or lament their inability to make decisions—difficulties which are present in all decades—it soon becomes evident that they have no definite experience of their own desires or wants.[2]

Man has become empty though he appears to have much. We own things (or they own us), and our world is one of plastics, cosmetics, conveniences, and comfort.

We live well
In our tri-level shell
In the very latest hell.

In our well-constructed shells, however, we know that all is not right. When the television is silent and we listen to the static of our own minds we become aware that we are trapped in the very latest hell. W. H. Auden has called this the *Age of Anxiety* and has characterized the feeling in one of his poems:

. . . this stupid world where Gadgets are gods and we go on
  talking,
Many about much, but remain alone,
Alive but alone, belonging where?
Unattached as tumbleweed.[3]

Students know these feelings of loneliness and emptiness perhaps too well. They have felt keenly the difficulties of living in the world and have expressed these feelings, often dramatically, in outbursts at Berkeley, Columbia, the Sorbonne, and on college campuses throughout the world. Students do not want to settle for the delusions that come with age; they are demanding examination and change in hopes of building a better world. But it is a difficult struggle. One student expressed his feelings to one of the authors:

[1] The Beatles, "Sgt. Peppers Lonely Hearts Club Band," Capitol Album 2653 (London, Eng.: Northern Songs Ltd.). Reprinted with permission.   Copyright © 1967 Northern Songs Limited.
[2] Rollo May, *Man's Search for Himself* (New York: W. W. Norton & Company, Inc., 1953), p. 14.
[3] W. H. Auden, *The Age of Anxiety* (New York: Random House, Inc., 1947), p. 44.

The hopeless human comedy, cynicism abounds, and rightly so, for whom can we really trust, and what is worthwhile?

So we retreat and withdraw. We do not reach out because to reach out is to get hurt. We hide ourselves from ourselves and from others. We trust no one. We are afraid to reveal ourselves, to share ourselves with others; to do so makes us vulnerable to attack and suspicion. What is more frightening is that there may be no response from others at all. In *The Transparent Self* Sidney Jourard describes our state of being:

> We conceal and camouflage our true being before others to foster a sense of safety, to protect ourselves against unwanted but expected criticism, hurt, or rejection. This protection is purchased at a steep price. When we are not truly known by the other people in our lives, we are misunderstood. When we are not known, even by family and friends, we join the all too numerous lonely crowd! Worse, when we succeed too well in hiding our being from others, we tend to lose touch with our real selves, and this loss of self contributes to illness in its myriad forms.[4]

In the lonely crowd we can remain alone and unnoticed. We do not have to encounter other human beings. We are safe, painfully safe. Rollo May says that we lose the ability to communicate:

> What has been lost is the capacity to experience and have faith in one's self as a worthy and unique being, and at the same time, the capacity for faith in, and meaningful communication with, other selves, namely one's fellow-men.[5]

We do not really need poets and psychologists, however, to describe these feelings for us. Each of us has experienced loneliness, alienation, the awareness that we have lived less than we can or want to.

To feel and know that we are empty and alone, however, is not enough. To feel and know may lead only to despair and to more intense anguish. We cannot survive long periods of such anguish.

WHAT DOES MAN NEED?

When each of us experiences the agony of our despair, when we recognize that we are ultimately alone in the world, when the pain of our being human is greatest—we ask for salvation not as defined by the organized religions but salvation in terms of being saved from our loneliness and despair. We wish for direction, for answers,

---

[4] Sidney Jourard, *The Transparent Self* (Princeton, N.J.: D. Van Nostrand Co., Inc., 1964), Preface.

[5] Rollo May, *The Meaning of Anxiety* (New York: The Ronald Press Company, 1950), p. 6.

for help, for understanding, for involvement, for meaning; in short, we wish to share love.

Man is love; he needs to give love to others and he needs to have others give love to him. Without love we have no meaningful existence. Without love we die.

Love is the very reason for living, yet we seldom if ever talk about it in our society. When we do talk about love we do so in very guarded ways. In religious terms love becomes a mysterious concept existing outside of man. In the family love becomes confused with respect, responsibility, and duty. In the marketplace love is a commodity wrapped in sex-colored cellophane. In education, if love is considered at all, we assume that it is something to be analyzed rather than experienced.

Even when we honestly feel love for another we are careful to communicate our feelings in safe and prescribed ways. We say that we admire the person or that we like the person. We have not invented very many good ways of handling the communication of our most wholesome natural feelings.

If we are to have any success in discovering meaning for ourselves we must learn to share love.

Listen to this expression of love in a letter from one of our friends:

> Before I can go, I have some feelings within me that I must express—don't know if they'll be right at my fingertips, but I gotta try. Your letters mean more to me than most of the people I know in the flesh. As I checked the mail this morning, and found your letter, I was joyous. Not even knowing what was inside, I was happy to be in touch with you once again. Happy that you wanted to reach out and touch me. Happy that I was able to let you touch me. As I write this, it occurs to me that the greatest part of our relationship may be the fact that it was unsolicited, unearned, and continues only through our freely giving to one another. We have no obligation, commitment, or responsibility to one another, save that of one human being for another. That is why this seems so beautiful and meaningful to me.
>
> I think a better way to describe my feelings now is to say I feel loved. Wow! Sure makes it all worth it. Wish everyone could feel this way at least once in a while.
>
> DAMN! I just wish I could hug you right now. I'm bursting with joy, and want to share it with you. Don't feel like I've even come close yet.

Another expression of the feeling of love comes from Terry who recently encountered a new friend:

> I love a person. My awareness of my feelings of love is very intense at this moment. The love I have for him makes me feel alive to myself—an aliveness that I seldom feel. There is a tenseness, an excitation, perhaps an expectation of some kind. I feel warm inside as if my soul had been swabbed clean. I do not want to shout or suddenly do some great deed for

the world, or even talk to him right now; I want to sit here in my chair and feel good about feeling good.

Feeling this love for him makes me feel a great deal of love for myself. I am really a lovable and lovely person. I am a good person, and I have some good talents. It feels great to be myself right now and it makes me feel that I will be quite happy being myself for some time to come.

I am within myself touching my being from inside—me touching me—feeling my love for another as a prime force that creates more of me into the kind of person I want to become.

There is a relaxing of self that gives me great strength. My defenses fall and I become stronger. The lines of my face soften, and there is more character in the face to speak to others.

Soothing—exciting; loving him—loving me; a sing-song of different feelings that make up what I am—for I am many things. When loving I am the most of what is best in me.

"When loving I am the most of what is best in me." Each of us would like to function at our best. Each of us *must* function at our best from time to time. Loving and being loved is an experience that offers us a very great opportunity for best functioning. These two written expressions of love show people who are more in tune with themselves because of their loving. They love others and therefore love themselves; they love themselves and therefore love others.

It is easy to *talk about* love; it is most difficult to express the meaning of love. Each man loves in his own way, from his own needs, and in so doing brings his own definition to the experience. Love is only a word—a sieve—that cannot capture the infinite variety of man's experience. It can only focus on the experience and help us talk of it as being different from hate and from other emotions. We can speak of mother love, romantic love, love of one's country, animal love, love of God, self love, sexual love, dependent love, deep love, puppy love, love 'til death, love after death—an infinite array to mirror the magnificence of man and challenge his potential for experiencing that magnificence. We can speak of these ways of loving, but we cannot define one man's loving. I do not know what my loving means, but I know when I'm loving. For those who wish to explore definitions of loving see Fromm's *The Art of Loving* (see Bibliography).

How does the human encounter help?

We have said that all human beings need to share love and that without love we cannot survive. How can we learn to share love? How can we come to listen to the need for love from others and respond with our own needs? How can we risk being ourselves and learn to encounter others in their loneliness, in their need to be loved, in their beginning discovery of their own creativity and beauty?

Man is always searching for new methods and new experiences to find answers to these questions, and there are many answers. One kind of experience that holds promise and meaning has been called the *basic encounter*. In this book we speak of the human encounter. *The human encounter occurs when we meet ourselves or others in the process of our emerging humanity.*

Psychologists and educators have developed numerous approaches to encountering during the past ten years. Such approaches are known by many names: T groups, sensitivity training, group counseling, encounter groups, self-awareness groups, marathons, growth groups, micro-groups, and many others. The most notable developments have occurred at the National Training Laboratories (NTL) in Bethel, Maine, and the Esalen Institute in Big Sur, California. NTL is the oldest and perhaps most widely known organization at the moment. The major emphasis at NTL seems to be on better interpersonal relationships among people who work together. There is a large program for business executives and their staffs as well as for administrative groups in other fields. The focus appears to be on better self-functioning in order to increase company productivity. This may be a harsh criticism of NTL, but it does appear that it considers the organization more important than the individual.

In contrast, Esalen appears to focus on the fuller development of the individual. Esalen experiments with the more exotic aspects of man's being in an attempt to help participants get in touch with all parts of their humanity, often with those completely submerged in everyday life. Some critics would say that Esalen deals in the occult. Some at Esalen probably do, for man encompasses the occult, too, and Esalen expands the parameters in order that participants can experience the farthest limits of being.

Both Esalen and NTL use the group encounter as a method for accomplishing goals. Esalen is oriental; NTL is occidental. Esalen is experimental, curious, risky; NTL is safe, sure. Esalen is hip; NTL is middle class. Esalen is existential; NTL is rational. They represent the contrasts in style of the human encounter. Yet, each does good work, attracts followers, evaluates progress, helps people.

Many other groups also exist to provide opportunities for the human encounter. Most universities have one or two staff members who provide group experiences for students and staff. These group leaders are usually connected with the counseling center, the psychology department, the counseling and guidance department and sometimes with the group of psychiatrists attached to the medical school or the infirmary.

In recent years the group encounter has become widely used in colleges, universities, and junior colleges—sometimes as part of the curriculum. These institutions offer group experiences under such titles as Interpersonal Communications, Applied Psychology, Meaning in Life, Human Potential Seminars, Self and Others, and The Individual in a Changing Environment, to name only a few. The authors feel that more and more institutions of higher education will experiment with encounter groups as a way to make education meaningful for their students and their staffs. Hundreds of institutions are presently experimenting with such methods, and we have included a chapter describing some of their approaches in the manual accompanying this book. We hope this book will provide some stimulus for the programs now experimenting and will encourage other institutions to make the human encounter a college experience.

Regardless of the name, the setting, or the leader, the various approaches to human encounter have a single purpose, a common commitment. Reduced to the simplest explanation—which is really not simple at all—the human encounter is an appointment for the sharing of love. We can use many exotic and scientific terms to describe the encounter, its dynamics, and its outcomes. We can use safe words such as *regard, admiration, interpersonal relationship, respect, acceptance, understanding*; but *love* is what occurs.

Each encounter group is the family of man in miniature—with one purpose, to share in love. Each of us is part of several family groups. We are born by chance into our primary family, but there is no guarantee that love will be shared there. As we grow into adolescence we move through several peer group families as a way of practicing our independence from the primary family. We may then begin our own primary family with great hopes of creating and achieving shared love, a hope often lost in the confusion of the multiple purposes of primary family units. Most of us join a work family or professional family, but achievement, economics, recognition, and production often dim the possibilities for loving. Other social units are formed that have many of the characteristics of family units: bridge clubs, Friday afternoon beer drinking groups, vacation groups, Kiwanis, etc.; but few of these have shared love as a major purpose.

In contrast with these family units the encounter group places shared love as a major and central purpose. The human encounter can help us learn to love ourselves and to love others. If we succeed, the questions regarding the meaning of our existence no longer trouble us. In the following chapters we will describe some of the dimensions of the encountering process, some of the outcomes, some of the experiences of our students. It will be impossible for us to provide you with a guaranteed guide for encountering, for to do so would be to promise you that we can teach you to love. We are not sure we can do that. As individuals we have had some success with our own learning and the learning of our students. In our relationship as discussed in the last Dialogue, we have come to learn that we may never be able to achieve the kind of sharing relationship with each other we have achieved with many. We have come to appreciate instead that we are vastly different people—such appreciation and understanding may be a kind of encounter, certainly out of ours has come a caring for each other that we both value highly.

We hope very much that what we have provided here will help put you in touch with your own capacity for loving. We know that you can share love more than you do; we hope you will.

2

pointing toward human encountering

Robinson Crusoe managed to survive and hew out for himself a good life on his deserted island. But after making a shelter, providing for food supplies, and ordering his working and leisure activities, he finds that life on an island, even in his rough-hewn Garden of Eden, was small compensation for his lack of human companionship. After several years of solitary captivity he makes a desperate escape attempt in a boat of his own making, only to be caught by tides and currents too strong for the small craft. He manages to get back to his island and, exhausted, lies down upon the beach and falls asleep. It is then (in his semi-comatose state) that he hears what seems to him to be a human voice talking to him after his years of loneliness:

> I was so dead asleep, at first, being fatigued with rowing . . . the first part of the day, and walking the latter part, that I did not awake thoroughly; and dozing between sleeping and waking, thought I dreamed that somebody spoke to me; but as the voice continued to repeat "Robin Crusoe, Robin Crusoe," at last I began to awake more and more perfectly, and was at first dreadfully frightened, and started up in the utmost consternation. But no sooner were my eyes open, but I saw my Poll sitting on the top of the hedge, and immediately knew that this was he that spoke to me; for just in such bemoaning language I had used to talk to him, and teach him. And he had learned it so perfectly, that he would sit upon my finger, and lay his bill close to my face, and cry, "Poor Robin Crusoe, where are you?" "Where have you been?" "How came you here?"—and such things as I had taught him.[1]

Even though the voice turns out to be only a poor imitation of human speech in the mouth of a parrot, Robinson Crusoe is grateful. Anything, anything to break his solitude. In order to endure his lonely exile, he makes his pets his dinner companions. He coaxes his two tame cats to sit on either side of him at dinner and feeds them tidbits as he eats. He has not even the companionship of dogs, for his own dog has "now grown old and crazy," and has "found no species to multiply his kind."

It comes as no wonder then that the most awesome and exciting moment of the book, for both Crusoe and the reader, is that moment when Robinson Crusoe comes upon the footprint of another human being.

Such is the experience of human encountering. It is the experience of finding another person in the world to share our sacred inner islands of hopes and fears, joys and delights. The experience happens in many ways and under different circumstances. It is the experience of two people who find themselves in love. It is the experience of a child who runs to his mother with some exciting or tragic event to tell her, and she listens not only with her ears, but with her heart. It is the experience of meeting someone from one's home town in a faraway place. It is the experience of sitting down on a plane next to a stranger and, in the course of a few hours, finding oneself in a deep and intimate conversation, revealing things never before revealed to any other person. It is the experience of two boys who fist-fight until exhaustion, and end up by becoming friends. It is the experience of a father and son who meet as adults and finally talk to each other as two human beings who like and respect each other.

[1] Daniel Defoe, *Robinson Crusoe.*

Human encounter is the sudden recognition that there is *some one* else in this world who is related to us in some fashion, *some one* with whom we can share our private world, *some one* who can share his world with us.

There are some individuals who live alone. One reads occasionally of the recluse found dead in his house, who had lived alone and in apparent poverty, yet who had had a fortune stashed away in the house. Saints and mystics have lived out their lives in isolated desert caves or monastery cells, seeming to need the companionship of no one but God. People like Joshua Slocum have sailed around the world by themselves and for months on end have seen nothing more human than their own faces reflected in the sea.

Most of us, however, need the experience of knowing and being with another human just as we need food and water in order to survive. The human species is a gregarious one: we congregate together; we live together; we survive together.

All our lives we are in contact with other people. From the time we receive our first spank on the behind and begin to breathe, we are in contact with other human beings. Through this contact, we learn to dress, to eat, to talk, to think, and to feel as we do. We even learn how to be human by being with other human creatures. We know this because children brought up in isolation have been found not to display the usual human response to the world around them. When found, the wolf children of India, the gazelle boy of Jordan, the dog child Anna, and the Wild Boy of Aveyron were more animal than human. Children born of deaf-mute parents will not learn to speak unless they are in contact with adults who do speak.

Our contacts with other human beings not only make us human, but also make us the kind of human beings we become. Natives on one South Sea island grow up to be cooperative and peaceful, whereas natives on the next island grow up competitive and warlike. Without getting into the issue of heredity, we can assume that the cultures of these two people are, in large measure, the determining factors of the strikingly different behaviors. (Some of you who have a yen for research may like to investigate the religious-philosophical-psychological question of whether individual behavior is predetermined or the result of free will.)

At any rate, very few people will argue the fact that we are largely molded by the people with whom we have lived. We have been in contact with and molded by other people all our lives. Does this also mean that we have experienced the human encounter all our lives? Not necessarily. The human encounter differs from our day-to-day contacts with people by its special diamond-like quality. Each reader will have to determine for himself which of his experiences, if any, were true human encounters. For the moment, let us say that the human encounter makes one feel uplifted, or wholly and completely understood, or transformed in some way. It *is* a diamond-like experience in its brilliance and in its value. One may "happen" upon it, or be given it, or search for years before finding it. But it is an experience which transcends the ordinary ground of living. It transfigures us and helps us to grow into our infinite possibilities.

Many college students have their first adult human encounters as a part of their college life. As we, your authors, look back upon our college experiences we remember with fondness our favorite teachers, but most of the lecturers have been forgotten with the passage of time. We remember the hundreds of faces that were classmates. But most of all, we remember our human encounters: the first college friends with whom we could bare our souls; those favorite teachers we talked with over coffee outside of class; the night-long discussions in someone's room, too excited by talk of God and philosophy and cabbages and kings to go sensibly to bed. Here was the education that stayed with us. Here was our first initiation into the world of ideas and things through the give and take of human encounter. Here was the beginning of our self-discovery.

So convinced were both your authors of the validity of the human encounter as education that this book was born. Santa Fe Junior College was so convinced of this idea that one whole course was constructed around the human encounter and made one of the six required courses of the school along with English, mathematics, social science, etc. Radical? Perhaps. Valid? Yes. For what is as essential for living together in society as human understanding? So often, college students must rush to class and rush away right afterwards to go to work. They miss the after-class coffee talk. They do not share leisure talking-time with other people like themselves during the small hours of the morning.

What happens to a group of people whose sole purpose is to meet each other in human encounter? Instead of having teachers who are distant and remote, you will encounter human beings and participants in your world; instead of having classmates, you will have friends; instead of passing strangers in the hall, you will pass people you can smile at. A cup of coffee will become an occasion for the interchange of ideas. A fellow student will become a person with whom you share your growing edge. The purpose of the human encounter, the purpose of this book, is to help you discover others who are in the world with you, to help you discover that you are not alone.

What we are calling human encounter is not quite the same as bumping into people and exchanging a few words. You can have hundreds of these bumpings-into-people every day and not experience a really deep human encounter with any one of them. The question then is how do we know when we've had a human encounter? What is it like? That is what we are going to discuss in this section, but in a nutshell (and by way of warning): like falling in love, you are a different person for the experience.

Both of us spent a lot of time trying to define the human encounter.

We couldn't agree on a single definition that pleased both of us so each decided to define it in our own way. In fact, before we started to write this book, we spent hours talking about the possible futility of this whole venture. The idea of trying to teach human encountering via a textbook seemed self-contradictory. Both of us had been fairly successful in helping people to encounter each other and us, and we had introduced this experience in several colleges as a valid educational subject. But we had always been there, in person, using ourselves and our personalities as the instrument in the process. Was it possible, we asked, to teach people to encounter each other long distance, so to speak, through the impersonality of words?

Like the experience of being in love, encounter resists definition— if by definition we mean trying to capture and translate into words an experience which is deeper than words; if we mean freezing into permanence what is mutable and of the moment; if we mean to encompass all its meaning within a small map, thinking that it is this and no more.

We were embarrassed by this difficulty until we remembered that our inadequacy here has been shared by others. Suzuki,[2] the Zen mystic and writer, faced this same problem when he attempted to interpret Zen to Western readers. Westerners have been conditioned by centuries to accept only that which is logical and rational. It is difficult to translate Japanese Zen into our Indo-European language and logic. Zen, he explained, is an inner or "direct" knowledge, one which cannot be externalized into words. As a result, the Zen master taught via the *Koan* (a kind of riddle), the *haiku* (a wisp of a poem), and finally by *silence*. Since it cannot be externalized into words, Zen is rather to be hinted at through simile, gleaned through paradox, and pointed at with nonlogic—all of which can seem absurd to the Westerner who is unable to function in any other frame of reference but that of occidental rationality and logic.

You may have experienced this difficulty, too, if you have ever tried to describe the experience of being in love. Somehow after you relate the fact that you have met the "most wonderful girl in the world" and have described her beauty, you have an uncomfortable feeling that your description sounds as trite as a greeting on a valentine card. At that moment you wish you were a poet. You understand at last why poets must break the boundaries and prosaic rules of language; why they must jumble up and restring the common little words we use in order to describe the uncommon and *this* immense experience. For to love is to be new, to be renewed, to be outside the ordinary, to feel extraordinary, to experience something other than the everyday ways of being-in-the-world. The experience of encountering is the same! But if we couldn't come up with a definition stable enough to satisfy the lexicographers and social scientists, we could at least say what it is *not*; we could describe it phenomenologically; and we could

[2]D. T. Suzuki, *Manual of Zen Buddhism* (New York: Grove Press, 1960).

list some of the conditions under which the human encounter is likely to occur.

WHAT IT IS NOT: IT IS NOT A PASTIME

In a modest but insightful little book entitled *Games People Play*, psychiatrist Eric Berne[3] describes very succinctly the opposite of human encountering. He calls one of these nonencounters *pastimes*, which he says are typically played at parties or social gatherings but actually are re-enacted many times during an individual's day.

> A large cocktail party often functions as a kind of gallery for the exhibition of pastimes. In one corner of the room a few people are playing "PTA," another corner of the room is the forum for "Psychiatry," a third is the theatre for "General Motors," and the buffet is reserved for women who want to play "Kitchen" or "Wardrobe." The proceedings at such a gathering may be almost identical, with a change of names here and there, with the proceedings at a dozen similar parties taking place simultaneously in the area. At another dozen in a different social stratum, a different assortment of pastimes is underway.

We recommend Berne's book to anyone interested in the variations on the human comedy and, in the meantime, let's take note of a few of the identifying marks of Berne's pastimes.

Pastimes are ritualistic and situation-centered rather than person-centered. Like all rituals, they have prescribed verbal and nonverbal rules and behaviors. The extent to which one observes the proper rules and follows the correct progression of behaviors is the extent to which he is judged knowledgeable in social situations—in other words, whether he is couth or uncouth! People who do not follow these rules are considered either eccentric, ill-mannered, or gauche. Berne gives an excellent example:

> A party of women who drop in at each other's houses every morning for coffee to play "Delinquent Husband" are likely to give a cool reception to a new neighbor who wants to play "Sunny Side Up." If they are saying how mean their husbands are, it is too disconcerting to have a newcomer declare that her husband is just marvelous, in fact, perfect, and they will not keep her long.

And as an example of a hostess who knows not only how to follow the rules but how to use them to manipulate the behavior of others:

> "Come now, you girls have been playing Wardrobe long enough. Mr. J. here is a writer/politician/surgeon, and I'm sure he'd like to play Look Ma, No Hands, wouldn't you, Mr. J.?"

[3]Eric Berne, *Games People Play* (New York: Grove Press, 1964), Chapter 4. Reprinted with permission.

Because the aim of the pastime is to re-enact stereotyped behaviors, the pastime avoids anything which is genuinely exploratory, insightful, and growth-producing. In fact, pastimes are a way of preventing a relationship from becoming serious, knowledgeable, or "actual." Berne calls them the prelude to the more serious but deadlier "game."

Third, pastimes are pseudo-communicative; that is, although sentences are being exchanged, there is little or no *actual* verbal communication going on between the speakers (although there may be much nonverbal information being exchanged). In fact, the pastime is a series of exchanged sentences which are not meant to convey information at all, but rather are designed to keep the conversation superficial and inconsequential. As Berne notes, it doesn't matter who says what. All one has to do is change the names and faces; the words remain the same. What is important is that in a pastime certain sentences must be exchanged if the pastime is to be played out correctly and it matters very little who exchanges them. One such pastime, illustrated by Berne, is "Delinquency":

> A: There wouldn't be all this delinquency if it weren't for broken homes.
> B: It's not only that. Even in good homes nowadays the children aren't taught manners the way they used to be.

A pastime, then, is a pseudo-event,[4] in which people are exchanging pseudo-information in pseudo-relationships with each other. It is, in fact, pseudo-communication. This, to be sure, is our definition (not Berne's) of a pastime.

In contrast to the pastime, *the human encounter is a dynamic relationship between the individuals involved (and no others) in an actual one-of-a-kind event, in which what occurs is relevant to the existential moment.*

Unless the reader is a student of philosophy or the social sciences, the last sentence may sound like so much gobbledygook. So let's take the phrases apart and see what they mean in everyday language.

As described by Berne, a pastime is a stereotyped situation. It is the kind of thing we do much of the time and which we call "passing the time of day," "small talk," or "chit-chat."

A: "Hello, how are you?"	(The speaker is not asking to be told the state of the other's health.)
B: "Fine, thanks."	(He may actually have a cold but he knows that he has not been asked that question.)
"Hot enough for you?"	(He is not going to ad-lib an original statement which would involve either one of them in a real encounter; so

---

[4]Daniel Boorstin, *The Image: A Guidance to Pseudo-Events in America* (New York: Harper & Row, Publishers, 1964). (Paperback.)

A: Yep, if it gets any hotter we'll be able to fry eggs on the sidewalk.

What do you hear from Joe Whatchamacallit?

B: You know, that's the funniest thing. I was just saying to the Missus the other day that we haven't seen hide nor hair of him in a dog's age.

he has chosen the topic *weather* which is one of the several "neutral" topics he has in his response kit.)

(Now all the lines have been spoken about the weather. The playlet can end here by going into the ending. goodbyes, or they can start a new playlet as they proceed to do here.)

(The speakers can develop this into a few more sentences or they can go into the ending conversation.)

Notice that the speakers have the same relationship to each other at the end of the playlet(s) that they had in the beginning. They know very little more at the end than they did at the beginning. (They each know that the other hasn't seen Joe Watchamacallit.) Nothing essential has happened; in fact, both persons in this play took care to keep to stereotyped sentence exchanges in order to prevent anything actual from happening. Their relationship remains static, unchanged.

An encounter, by contrast, is not a stereotypic situation; rather it is an idiosyncratic event—which is to say that what has happened to you and the other(s) has never happened before. Furthermore, it can never happen again. Unlike a play (or playlet), an encounter cannot be re-enacted.

An encounter is a first-time experience.

Does this mean that the experience of encounter can never happen with the same person twice? It does not. As a matter of fact, it is easier to seek encounter with a person with whom we have actually experienced encounter than it is to engage in the risk-taking and sometimes painful process of encountering a totally new (and perhaps encounter-naïve) individual. Encounter is a risky business. We sometimes get rebuffed in our efforts to establish contact. And sometimes encounter hurts. It is easier not to take a risk—like returning to a restaurant we know will prove to be a satisfying gustatory experience rather than chance an unknown eating place.

However, when encounter occurs repeatedly between the same persons there is added, each time, a new dimension to the relationship: new areas of being together are being explored, or deeper levels of understanding are being reached.

This definition also includes another pertinent fact: We can never have the same kind of encounter with one person or group of people that we have with another person or another group of people. That is to say, the kind of encounter we can have with a friend is far different from the kind of encounter we can have with a stranger we will see once and probably never see again (although an encounter between strangers can be dynamically intense and rewarding despite its momentary quality).The kind of encounter we share with one friend will be quite different from the kind of encounter we share with another. Think back a moment to your own experiences. Is it not true that you show a different facet of yourself as you relate to different persons in your environment? To your mother, you may be gentler than you are with your father. Or the reverse may be true. By and large, you tend (most of the time) to be more submissive and polite to your teacher than you do to your fellow classmates or even to your friends. Is it not true that some of your friends seem to bring out your serious side, while others stimulate your "comic" sense? If you are of musical bent, for example, you may be able to share the wonderful understanding musicians have with each other; while with another you can share a personal problem with an intimacy you do not share with anyone else. In this latter situation, you know that this friend will react to your personal crises not only with interest, but also with concern and responsiveness to your distress. It follows, then, that your encounter with one particular person will provide you with an opportunity not afforded by anyone else anywhere else in the world.

So too is it with groups.

Each group has its own particular quality that is nonreproducible. Much of this uniqueness is determined by certain demographic factors: the ratio of men and women, the age level and age range of the group, the background and experience of the group members, etc. A group with a wide range of ages may probe the communication difficulties of the generation gap, whereas another which is composed of young married couples may concentrate on renewing the excitement and vigor of marriage. One group of college students may investigate premarital sexual mores which include, in this time and era, such moral concerns as "the pill" and abortion. Also appropriate for a college group is the exploration of new ways to relate to each other in our era of machine and housing development. Each group is its own milieu and, of course, its own happening. Thinking back over various college encounter groups we have facilitated, we remember especially vividly the encounter of three young college freshmen who shared with each other the shame, the discouragement, the degradation of living with an alcoholic parent. Another group of extremely shy, verbally inhibited students spent their encounter course struggling, not only with the problems and causes of their own verbal inhibition, but also trying out with each other new kinds of verbal behavior.

Groups are affected by geographic and temporal factors as well. One group especially memorable for one of the authors was one which met during a presidential election year. Group dynamics became charged with political anger, especially as the pre-election campaigning moved into the home stretch. The success of the group was established when on the eve of the voting the group members could agree that they each had new respect for the others' political party, and that no matter who won, they could retain their feelings of commitment toward the group members of opposite political persuasion.

A group meeting during the day twice or three times a week for an hour will differ considerably from an encounter group which meets one night a week for two to four hours, and both of these will be different from the group encounter in which persons (who can be total strangers) come together for a weekend (or a week) to explore new dimensions of being-in-the-world. The latter event, incidentally, is becoming increasingly more common in our times, and represents some of the ways encounter is being used. It provides married couples with a chance to iron out their everyday difficulties in an atmosphere free from the everyday bogging-down effect of children's needs, incessant interruptions, and the nagging demands of house and yard. It provides a new environment in which the president of a large corporation and his administrative staff can be with each other free from pressures of the workaday world. They can therefore experience each other with the insight and appreciation that encounter can afford and can return to the work world with more creative working relationships. It can provide students and teachers, parents and children, blacks and whites (to list only a few examples), with opportunities for confrontation and meeting. It is one thing to face an opponent across a conference table; it is another thing to sit with him in a circle as you go forward toward encounter with each other. The old animosities are a little diminished when you both sit down together at the dining table, or at the bar, or around the swimming pool. It becomes harder to see the man as an opponent and easier to see him as human like yourself.

But over and above the demographic factors of group membership, there is also the special quality that each individual brings with him to the group. A group which includes several dynamic persons will be different in that the dynamic persons will lend their strength to the whole group, resulting in intense and highly charged encounters, whereas another group with the very same representation of demographic variables may reflect the reserved and subtle quality of most of its members.

Yet, even more specifically, each individual contributes. In an intense group a shy and nonverbal group member may add, through his quiet participation and ability to listen, just enough leavening to keep the group from disintegrating, whereas a diamond-in-the-rough character may provide just the spontaneity needed to spur a reserved group to rise above discussion and journey toward encounter. That totality which is the group includes each person's selfness—his spice, his acidity, his sweetness, his saltiness; all of these from moment to moment are the yeast and reality of the encounter.

How do we know when encounter happens? Perhaps the most sensible answer is the same enigmatic one you heard when you first asked, "How will I know when I'm in love?" The answer came back, "You'll just know, that's all." If you haven't been given an understandable definition of encounter, perhaps it will help to share with you how its characteristics have been described by other students who have experienced human encounter.

Almost always, students describe encounter as characterized by freedom from criticism, ridicule, or judgment. They indicate that encounter is a safe environment in which they can express themselves, and in which they can share their intimate and personal feelings. This type of personal sharing is called *self-revealment* or *self-disclosure*, and is discussed in depth in Chapter 4. Here is how students have expressed this aspect.

> What does human encountering mean to me? It means a chance to express myself and show my true feelings without the fear of being criticized by others.
>
> To me human encountering is something that is between two persons. They can reveal things about themselves that they can't tell anybody else.
>
> A human encounter to me means being able to confide and communicate at any time regardless of the subject or time; someone I can turn to in time of stress and conflict and feel confidence that I will receive the empathy and understanding I am longing for; one in which both persons know the positive and negative traits of each and yet do not condemn or ridicule one another for these traits.

Another thing happens in human encounter: *language becomes actual*. By actual, we mean that the person learns to use language to reveal his mind and heart, instead of concealing his true thoughts and feelings. We mean also that in human encounter, the person ad-libs his lines (he does not re-enact lines from previous playlets), and because he does, he is sometimes surprised to hear himself saying things he may have thought, but never voiced. Or—even more surprising—he may find himself voicing feelings and ideas he had never crystallized before even for himself. Encounter is an astonishing event. It means that clichés or smart-aleck "cracks," the small phrases which are in current fashion, and the noninformative sentences exchanged in pastimes are less evident in the speech patterns of the individual. Such verbal elements are repetitive, and encounter is not repeatable. Instead, the person seeks new ways to express new behaviors, new thoughts, new ideas. He recognizes that clichés and other speech "traps" are similar to the noninventive language of the computer.

Thus the encounter group member learns to talk to others in ways he never dreamt possible. He leaves the familiar and trite home grounds of the pastime and enters the imaginative regions where poets dwell. Emotionally and intellectually, he is in the uncharted, or rather, uncreated waters of his own conscious-unconscious and that of the other(s). And if individuals dare to risk the anxiety of this unknown, then that something "happens" which we call encounter, and becomes known. In coming to know this something, encounter happens to both persons—it is something "in-between" and it is at the same time something in which they are both immersed, in which they are both involved, of which they both partake. Just as food is nourishment for the body, this new experience—if they risk it—becomes nourishment for their "souls," for their "selves."

Ways in which students have expressed this high level of communication and meaning are as follows:

> Human encounter is when you have a discussion with someone that is more than the usual "Hello, how are you?" It is the kind of discussion that reveals the *real* you. It is an intimate conversation with someone.
>
> Encounter is a discussion where honesty, forthrightness, and understanding prevail.
>
> I can talk to people better and especially be able to express my deep thoughts.

Even verbally inhibited students have mentioned the increased use of expressive language.

> You seem to be in a trance because you are able to use words that you don't always use.

Also, students often mention an increased ability to listen; that is, to really open up oneself to another's opinions and feelings. It is the kind of listening which actively seeks the other's feelings.

> A human encounter is when a person has an open mind and has learned how to listen to other opinions.
>
> A human encounter is a special, unique experience that you have with another individual. It is discovering that this person is an individual and that he really exists. *You really begin to understand him as himself. You can see and accept his ideas and encourage them.*

By the same token, a person finds himself with less need to babble, or verbally dominate a conversation.

> I try to understand my grandmother now. When she yells at me, I listen to what's underneath her yelling.
>
> I don't make polite conversation now as much as I used to.
>
> I don't talk as much needlessly. I think about what I'm saying.

This type of active listening consists in listening to more than just the words a person says; at the deepest levels it even overlaps the sense of touch.

> It's reaching out . . . listening to another person—feeling, seeing, touching another.

Participants in an encounter group begin to develop a *group feeling;* they begin to lay aside their rivalries, their one-upmanship, their fight for the limelight, their jockeying for position.

> A human encounter means to me an interpersonal friendliness of a special type: both parties give up and admit their rivalries with each other, and try to help each other be logical and truthful about things.

Instead of competition, there is cooperation. Cooperation becomes the mode, and warmth and caring the mood, of the group.

> Human encounter is the sharing of time with people whom you care about. . . . It's when two (or more) people become closer for having shared that moment.

Some students have described the warmth and closeness as "like having a family that really cares"; others have described the mutuality of humanness—the recognition that the other is related to you and to the whole human species.

> Human encountering means getting totally involved with your fellow man.
> When I think of a human encounter, I think of *human*—a person with a good mind and a beautiful heart.
> Human encountering is sitting down with another human being and realizing that you are human beings. Humans are something wonderful and beautiful and most of us have become machines. . . . Encountering means being able to sit down and realize and be grateful that you are human.

The feeling of *we*-ness (what Martin Buber calls the "united I") begins to develop. The members become a group, not because of fear and threat from the outside, nor for usefulness, but for emotional reciprocity. Yet although a person becomes a member of the group, the group allows him to remain an individuated person—one who has a right "to be himself." There is no coercion to be other than he is; there is no brainwashing.

> It gives me the feeling of being an individual and still have the feeling I am part of the whole group.
> It allows one to experience human "closeness" without becoming overly dependent, maintaining one's independence when the other person is no longer available.

Some of the other dimensions of encountering include change of behavior. Self-reports by students repeatedly note one outstanding effect. The student speaks of himself as more tolerant of other opinions, as less liable to make snap judgments, as more willing to make contact with others. These statements can be categorized under the heading of *more openness to the world*—to the thoughts and opinions of others, to one's own feelings, and to change.

> There has been a great change in the young people of my group [wrote a mother who had gone back to school]. They are more involved in their surroundings and the other students they encounter. The word "aware" might be better to use. . . . They have become better prepared to understand their fellow classmates.
>
> I used to make judgments of people from their masks. I also put on my own mask. Now I can see people as they really are and I let them see more of me also.
>
> I've always felt I have been willing to listen to different opinions—different from my own, that is—but I feel I have become even more tolerant of ideas, opinions of others. I try to look beyond what is apparent on the surface.

They become also more open to their own feelings.

> I am learning much about myself and probably will add much more. I also have learned that emotions are nothing to be ashamed of and I am finding it easier to let down.
>
> I am beginning to find myself, who I am and what I am. It is so interesting to find who and what you are. . . . I feel better inside also, I feel like a person.
>
> Human encountering means . . . attempting to bring out the real me—the innermost me—finding out who I am, and where I'm going. Strengthening— or if need be, changing for the better—my moral codes and beliefs through discussion and questioning—and listening.

There is one more important dimension to encountering. A key word in our definition was *dynamic*. Encounter is a *dynamic relationship* . . . relevant to *the existential moment*. We have talked about the changes of behavior as experienced by students—verbal, physical, emotional— but these are long-range changes. The definition clearly states that the change is immediate—in the lived moment of the encounter. We implied it is this knowledge—immediate and concrete—that lets us know we are encountering the other(s) in the here-and-now. Make no mistake, the change is felt by both. It is, like the experience of love or sadness or anger, self-evident! From that moment, all persons involved are no longer the same; they have shared a part of each other and that can never be reversed. Students find it hard to describe this dimension but they have struggled to do so:

> Most people may think of human encountering as just getting to know someone better. Well, that is part of it. When you encounter someone, they be-

come a part of your life. In some way, they change your life because they become a part of your life and you become a part of them. . . . This will become someone you will never want to forget about, someone you will trust all of your life.

Whoever you are able to encounter, you are related to them.

When I am seriously participating in an encounter I believe I become a very different person than most people see.

At the exact moment when I encounter someone I feel as if I am some place I have never been before. It's hard to describe. Like you and this other person are out in space with each other and looking down on the earth.

Need more be said?

3

on human encountering

A dialogue between Terry O'Banion and April O'Connell, July 13, 1967, in which they attempt to encounter each other as they discuss what human encountering is all about.

APRIL: I guess the best way to start is to decide what we mean by the process of "human encountering."

TERRY: Yes, and for the past several days I have been thinking about a kind of encountering which I think happens all the time in our society. For example, I think people when they stop at red lights look at people in other cars. I do, and I know other people do because they look back at me, and I think often that's a kind of quick encountering.

As in the popular song "Strangers in the Night" exchanging glances, wondering if they'd be taking chances for love, this is a kind of human encountering. I think this is the way people mostly encounter each other in our society; they meet each other at bars and look across tables and they see each other and they send out cues. My only concern is that this is all pretty much sexual encountering and it's the kind of sexual encountering game that people know well, and know how to play—some better than others. Do you feel this is a healthy kind of encountering; does it mean anything at all to you? It may not be the kind we are mainly interested in, but it has stuck in my mind since I started thinking about human encountering.

APRIL: What strikes me immediately as you talk is the fact that we *know how to play this kind of slightly sexual encountering.* It is a game with its own preordained rules. It's a relatively simple game. An attractive person across the way sends out subtle cues and another individual returns some kind of ritualistic response. It has all the earmarks of an established ceremony. If it's preordained, I'm not sure it's even encountering. We know how to go on with this kind of encounter because it leads to a certain . . . goal. *Where we get into real encountering is in the kind of adventure where we can't predict the outcome.* The goal is unknown. But the minute we get into a human encounter that has no definite foreseeable goal, we're in new territory. We don't know the rules, or where we're going, and we become fearful. This is the kind of encountering I'm interested in. It may be a healthier type of encountering just because we don't know the rules.

TERRY: Right. This is rather like what students do when they come to college. They're in a new situation, meeting people in a new way.

APRIL: I read a very interesting editorial once in a science fiction magazine. This was back about ten years ago in the Golden Age of science fiction. The editorial went like this: that all really great men were amateurs—when Galileo and Copernicus were talking about the fact that the earth was not the center of the universe and, in fact, that it was the sun around which our planet revolved, they were amateurs— off by themselves, on the growing edge of the universe and of themselves. Because there was nobody else out there with them; there were no such people as professionals. Professionals have rules on how to play their particular games so they can get along with each other. The amateurs are pioneers. Pioneers have no rules because no one has been there before. When Freud was discovering the as yet undiscovered aspects of the human personality, he was an amateur. In such a sense, we're all amateurs when we don't have rules to go by.

TERRY: Our society has developed so few rules for healthy loving, healthy encountering habits. Parents and children, for example, seldom have very satisfactory ways for encountering.

APRIL: That word "healthy" bothers me, Terry. I'm sure there are some things which are unhealthy. For example, I'm sure that hating is unhealthy, but I'm not sure what other kinds of things are unhealthy or healthy because I can't stand outside of the earth and look down in a godlike manner. Now we know that what may have been "healthy" a century ago is not considered "healthy" now. I'm not always sure I can say "that's healthy" or "that's unhealthy" even for myself.

TERRY: Tell me some of the ways you have encountered people that have been good, April, and let's leave the words "healthy" and "unhealthy" out of it. What have been good experiences, important human encounterings you've had?

APRIL: In terms of people, it's the small encounters. If I go into a grocery store and check out some groceries, I agonize if something human doesn't happen between me and the check-out girl. If I say something, maybe a small joke, and she replies with a smile, we have made a human contact. She is doing her job, and I'm doing mine, and selling has become so impersonal, but just for this moment, we're being ourselves, and in this long day we have a moment to treasure. We're not cashier and customer, just two people somewhere smiling at each other.

Or, the other day, I sat in my car when the train came by, and we had to wait, my son and I. As the engine came by with the engineer sitting next to the window, I did something I haven't had a chance to do for a long time. I waved. And he waved back. And for that moment we recognized each other in our humanity.

These are the things that warm my heart.

TERRY: Are these spontaneous kinds of things, then? Encounters unplanned for? Ones of which we're unaware until they actually happen? Are you prepared in any kind of way for these encounters? Can a person be prepared for human encountering?

APRIL: No, I don't think the encounter can be planned, but you can prepare yourself for the possibility of it happening by taking a chance.

TERRY: A chance to meet another human being face to face.

APRIL: I feel a little badly about this because I argued with Charles Merrill one day on this very point. I said sometimes we pick up cues that say "Don't try an encounter with this person. You may get hurt." He was the one who pointed out that if we are what we are, we can't get hurt by another, and if we are afraid of the outcome, we will close ourselves off from good happenings.

I've got to tell you a story that happened to me once when I was ten. There was a person on our street whose name was Mr. Baer. He was an old German, complete with walrus mustache. You'll recall this was during the beginning of World War II and the Germans were looked upon rather suspiciously. This old man must have been a widower, and like his name, rather an old bear. He had a small, cottage-like house, and he grew plants. He didn't have a wife or children, but he had these plants, which he watered—he loved his plants. Please remember that all we children knew was that we weren't supposed to hop over his plants, his hedge, or his bushes, because Mr. Baer would be there with the water hose and spray us. He was the mean old Mr. Baer!

This meanness of Mr. Baer struck me as I was going to school, and maybe I felt sorry for him. Anyway, I invented a game to play. I said to myself: "I bet if I smile at Mr. Baer every day, someday he'll smile back." So I began. In the beginning, he would be very grumpy and scowl. But I just kept smiling and saying: "Hello, Mr. Baer!" because there wasn't any risk for me. You see, I couldn't lose this game. If he didn't smile, that would just prove what an old bear he really was. So every day I smiled, and pretty soon I saw him softening. It was hardly visible at first. Maybe just the scowl wasn't scowly as much. Then he began to actually look forward to my coming back and forth, because I didn't jump over his hedge, or hurt his plants, and I would just smile and say good morning.

It's funny, but I knew in my heart that he would smile back some day. I knew in some funny way that he couldn't hold out. And pretty soon, he actually began to speak to me. I think he began to wait for me as I went back and forth to school.

I was a little ashamed of myself because I realized that the encounter meant more to him than it did to me. But I had played the game for fun, I think. Or maybe not. I had just lost both my parents, and maybe I felt his loneliness too. But if I had played the game seriously, perhaps I would have been afraid to play. Maybe he would reject my smiles. Maybe we're all this way, we're so afraid of not getting an answer from someone else.

Isn't it Eric Berne who spoke of "stroking" in human encountering in the book *Games People Play*? You walk down the hall and say good morning. And the other person doesn't reply. And you feel hurt. You've given him "strokes" and he hasn't responded, so you won't stroke him again first.

Human encountering, underneath all this, is the recognition that we are related to each other.

TERRY: Every person needs an affirmation of that, a lot of times. It's an affirmation of his humanity, I suppose, which means a recognition of love and the needs of others.

APRIL: Terry, tell me about some of your encounters.

TERRY: Well, I think I probably seek them literally, a great deal. It is hard for me to relate to people on an intellectual level; I relate on a feeling-emotional level about intellectual kinds of things. I sit down and relate on: "Who are you?" "Whom do you talk to?" "What are your ideas?" "What are your thoughts?" "What's important for you?" I used to call it "soul fingering." You have to encounter quickly, for tomorrow you may die. I try to encounter people's souls, you know, because I can't tolerate the shell of a human being; I can't tolerate the daily routine—such as "How do you feel?" "I feel fine." "I feel fine, too." So I would have to physically stick my finger in a person's soul and say "What is love?" Or I would say "Who are you?" to a student and to a stranger.

APRIL: Have you heard the joke of the two Russian women during World War II when they were our allies? Two Russian aviatrixes who had done a lot of heroic deeds were parachuted down in England and were feted by the English. They were given the rounds and wined and dined and were to meet the King and all that. When they were to go to their first English tea, they were instructed on the niceties of English teas. One never discussed politics or war or important subjects like that. One kept to "small talk." We call it "chit-chat." The Russian lady said: "Small talk, oh I understand completely. I will do just that." So she went to the tea, and she was squired around and, finally, sat down next to a very proper lady and asked her: "Tell me, do you believe in God?"

I wonder if it's a Mediterranean-Slavic quality to think that "small talk" is talking about life and death and God, and the shortness of life, and sharing each other's souls. I wonder why the Anglo-Saxon considers this "Just not the thing one does, old chap."

TERRY: Yes, because we can't do it in our culture unless we get half crocked with alcohol. That seems the only time we ever talk about the more essential kinds of things. As counselors, we have come to discuss these things because these are often what students talk to us about.

APRIL: Is this perhaps why we entered this field—because these kinds of questions are so important to us?

TERRY: They were kind of basic-oriental, in terms of myself. I found that to be true for myself.

APRIL: I found I couldn't go to teas, either, and I stay away from clubs, because I'm always putting my foot into it.

TERRY: When I go to teas, I search out a person to encounter. I can go around and be a little charming occasionally, if I'm a bit high, but for the most part, I am just searching out another human being to talk with about "big talk."

APRIL: Terry, what do you mean by "searching out another human being"? Because this is the human encounter. You've mentioned the idea of finding out what his soul's like—what he really believes? What do you search out? Do you search out his feelings, how he *feels* about things?

TERRY: I think mainly that you find out how another person feels. I think all human beings are in the human experience; I think most people are lonely; and I think most people are unhappy. I think a lot of people don't know that about other people, but I think that is true, and human encountering helps you see that. Everyone is in a state of struggle—I truly believe that—and, by encountering, you see this in others and probably that helps you see that you're not in a nonhuman condition; when you see that other humans are in the same condition you are, then you feel more comfortable with it, more comfortable in being lonely.

APRIL: There's a Yiddish phrase that says *Schweltze leben*—"it's hard to live." It's not easy. I once asked a very wise man—(I believe him to be very wise)—what life was all about. Life is hard, it's difficult. The Catholics call it a "vale of tears." I don't think if you do all the right things and if you go to church on Sunday, that you necessarily prosper and become happy. Sometimes you can be a good man and love God and become Job. I think we should strike the word *happiness* from our language. Well, anyway, I asked this wise man, "Why, since it is so hard, are we here?" And I noted his answer; he said: "Yes, life is difficult, but it's a good place to be processed." And I said: "Processed for what?" And he said something to the effect "for your spiritual evolution."

TERRY: April, I don't know that that really means anything to me.

APRIL: Well, let me put it in another way which might have more meaning for you. Supposing we say that even if you don't have any feelings about life beyond death, you are certainly evolving now in that you are not the same person you were five years ago.

TERRY: Yes, it may not be preparation for life later; it may be a continuing preparation of *becoming*, here, now, in life, or preparing for five years from now.

APRIL: Terry, I'll talk to you on that level and agree with you on that basis, but I really hold a more theological point of view, underneath, than you do.

TERRY: Well, before we get into theology, I feel struck by the idea of throwing out the word *happiness*. I think that's a very astute observation. I have talked to a number of student groups lately and have said to them "Do you really know any happy people?" And hardly anyone ever raises his hand. Of course, we didn't immediately get into the discussion of what happiness actually is, and I have been struck by some students' observations that maybe happiness isn't a state for man—maybe there never was such a thing, and it doesn't really have any meaning. Maybe we have to think about another kind of more essential specific criteria to evaluate the effectiveness or good of our lives.

APRIL: Now *joy* - I like the word *joy*.

TERRY: Well, joy has a kind of specific meaning, yes. I think of joy, I see someone bouncing with joy, or exuberating, somehow.

APRIL: I feel joyous many, many times. I think, perhaps, the word as we use it in English has become so equated with a certain number of criteria that we have an image—we have such an image in America, to be happy you have—well, all the things you were saying . . .

TERRY: All the middle-class values, which surround us. I see a giant, happy pig, with a television set plugged in one ear, food from Publix supermarket flowing into the mouth, the body surrounded by the comforts of fairly good, middle-class culture, deep pile carpets, etc.

APRIL: Yes, two children—one girl and one boy—and I always see two mastiffs . . .

TERRY: Poodles—that's what I see.

APRIL: Well, I see two mastiffs, sitting in front of a very nice fire-place. And then, of course, in the television commercials, if we believe them, the wife always looks beautiful, even when she's mopping her floor in high heels!

TERRY: That's the kind of happiness that you talked of once as not being able to get off the elevator from . . .

APRIL: Yes. That's the very elevator I want to get off, because you can't stop—you've got to have *more* of whatever it is that you have. And now, if I can use the word I want to throw out, which is *happiness*, I really think that it applies to *not* wanting more and more, and ac-quiring more and more; just being able to do with less and less.

TERRY: Is this what you would want, April? What are you saying, that you would want to be able to obtain joy by having less and less?

APRIL: Well, yes. It's *freedom* from all these material objects. I believe we become stuck with them. They own us! So, if you don't have to have all these things, you're free of them. I'm a little Hindu here, I think.

TERRY: I think I agree, April. Yes, I do.

APRIL: So, to me, the less that you need something, the more free you are of it. Of course, if you carry this out a little further, ulti-mately we're free of life, and that's the real Hindu point of view.

TERRY: You really do have a deeper theological basis than I realized. Is it a conventional one?

APRIL: I don't know what that means—conventional—when it comes to religion. You'll have to explain a little.

TERRY: Well, I have a feeling that most of the students, especially the younger students, and perhaps the older students are really fo-geyish about religion, and they've really not examined this area. My personal hope would be that one of the most important things they could do would be to examine their whole "idea" about religion; because I think this obviously is the key that is important in their own personal system of values. I think that perhaps many of them have a hang-up in the whole area of religion. They're dealing with the 19th century, or earlier. A hang-up on some religion that has no meaning, in my opinion.

APRIL: I sympathize with them. It's a little like the word *happiness*. I don't understand what it means. I prefer the word *joy*.

TERRY: I like the word *peace* but I think I don't know what it means either, like *happiness*, but at least I know when I feel peaceful.

APRIL: Yes, and by the way, I think the most important encounter I have ever had was with myself. What Maslow might call the *peak experience*. I had one of those almost life-and-death situations, where one asks oneself what is important? What do I want? And what I wanted most was to experience God, to know God. Someone else might put it "to experience the universe" or "to know why."

TERRY: Tell me about it, April.

APRIL: It happened on a sunny afternoon. There was a blue sky, a maple tree on my right, and an old brown house on my left. I was walking down the street to buy groceries. I'd had some of these experiences before in my life and some of them are hard to remember, but this one was so shattering and so overwhelming that the experience was unforgettable. There was a squirrel someplace, the green leaves of the tree made a pattern against the blue sky, very beautiful. I was stepping over a concrete line on the sidewalk. As I did, it happened. I say "it happened" because I don't know any other way to express it. All things became brighter. It was a bright June day, as only a June day in Ohio can be, yet the whole day grew brighter. And time stopped. Or else, if it didn't stop, time stretched out to infinity, and I knew the meaning of so many things, like the old Hebrew phrase "God is one" and I suddenly realized that there was no difference between myself and the house and the trees and the squirrel and the concrete and the sun. It was all one. I felt as though my skin were permeable. It was not happiness, that's the point, it was joy, and it was your word, *peace*, but it was a peace which was wrapped up in an ecstasy, only that word *ecstasy* is so sexual in our society and that was not it.

TERRY: *Gemeinschaftgefühl*—the German word that has the meaning "one with the world."

APRIL: Yes, that fits. I tried to talk about it. To talk about the glow I felt.

TERRY: Did it last long?

APRIL: The moment lasted for a moment. The immediate afterglow lasted for three days, and to this day the glow has never left.

TERRY: This is the kind of thing that you can still feel, then?

APRIL: Yes. Let's say it's given me a direction which I'll never deviate from except in some small ways.

TERRY: How do you mean, it's changed your life? I mean, did you actually choose a different direction, or did it change your life, or what?

APRIL: Actually, it only confirmed something that I had always had in the back of my mind. Our society today, as T. S. Eliot says, thinks that being religious is a bit "kinky." One doesn't feel religious these days. It's considered an act of superstition. I was so astounded by what had happened to me that I didn't tell people for a while and, when

I did, I didn't know how to express it. In the beginning, I would say something like "all my questions had been answered," but later, maybe six months or a year later, I realized that even that didn't express it. The truth was that I just didn't have any more questions!

TERRY: Yes.

APRIL: Everything was one, a kind of unified field theory of understanding. You didn't have to understand, you just knew. That's the kind of thing that the Indians in Taos say, that they *know* that their sun dances cause the sun to come up and the rains to come. They don't *believe* it, they *know* it. I didn't know what to do with my experience. I was young and impressionable then. I talked to ministers, priests, and they kind of looked at me as if "one doesn't have this kind of experience—you're kooky." I wondered whether it had been an hallucination, but I hadn't heard voices. I didn't see anything that wasn't there. It was more, and less, than that. My perception of the world had changed at that moment. It was not the world that had changed. It was my perception, my understanding of it.

TERRY: Yes, I know. I think many people have had these kinds of experiences, some more intensely than others. Research is being done on this. Right here at this college we have been doing research on intensive human experiences—how people describe their most intensive experiences. The other day out at the lake, we were judging some of these, a group of us, and the descriptions of the experiences were so intense that I began to weep as I read about one human being's experience. And, as I began to weep, two other members of the panel began to weep. We sat there and wept about this human experience we'd looked into.

Let me tell you about mine—I was a summer program director for a group of young, oh, 13-, 14-, 15-year-old students, and we were swimming in a lake, and I was their supervisor. Well, we were playing a game of seeing who could dive to the bottom of the lake and stay there the longest. And so it was my turn to go down and hold my breath, and I dived to the bottom of the lake. It was a beautiful, crystal-clear lake, and the sun was slicing through it in all kinds of ways. Well, I dived down and just dug myself into the sand so I could hold on. You know, if you don't let your breath out, you just float back up. I literally, like a crab, got myself burrowed down into the sand, and I held my breath and had my eyes open. In a moment, I just had no questions, I knew the answers. Suddenly, the important thing was that I felt whole; not that I felt self-contained—rather, I felt a part of all beings. I was part of the sand, I was the sun, I was even the water, part of all water. I was part of all living creatures, and all unliving creatures, and everything was a part of me. I was in the world and the world was in me. You know, I *understood*. I don't know what went on except that I knew from that moment and, still to this day feel (and this happened when I was about 20), and have always known it since, that my existence was part of everything—a kind of immortality; I'll never die—because my matter will become parts of other matter. At that time, it was a tremendously intensive kind of knowledge and peace that I existed and was part of all existence. And then, suddenly, I moved—and the children were dragging me out of the water because I'd stayed down so long.

APRIL: Your experience, or rather the effects and understandings of it, sound so very much like mine.

TERRY: Now my cynicism said, "Well, now, you know, your brain—because you held oxygen too long—created the hallucination." This was simply a 'rapture of the deep' experience. And that may be true. Nevertheless, it doesn't take away from the fact that I had an experience. It was a raptured, brief experience. It happened to me. It was a human experience and it was important and meaningful for me in my life.

APRIL: It sounds so much like the understanding that came to me. I've just gotten interested in nothing else. When you were helping to judge these intensive human experiences of other people, were they (as they were with you and me), were they things that happened to the individual? By himself, unto himself?

TERRY: Yes, and for the most part, the one I reacted to most was a negative experience. You and I talked about a positive experience, a good-feeling one. This was a bad-feeling one that I reacted to and it broke me up.

APRIL: Carl Jung in his autobiography says that the important events in his life were not what he did or the great people he met, but the internal understanding of himself. Yet, we are stressing encountering between people. What does this have to do with the fact that the really important encounters are inside oneself?

TERRY: Maybe an encounter doesn't have much reference until we have it confirmed or understood by someone else.

APRIL: That there is something in each of us that relates all of us to all of us . . . it's a very lonely thing, to be way out, by yourself.

TERRY: There may be a great deal of value we derive from *containing* the experience. I'm not saying that people necessarily lose some value—I only say that you would probably gain a great deal by sharing. You gain. It may be that people who contain all their experiences lose a lot by keeping their experiences to themselves. If I kept my little experiences to myself, they might wither and die. I don't know whether that would happen or not. I think my experience will grow if I tell you.

APRIL: Well, sometimes. A writer, by the way, tries not to tell another person what he's writing about before he's written it. Because, in telling it he dissipates it. You see, the author's *experience is in the writing*. The writing is the act of creation. Now, with you and me, the experience happened and then we told about it. The writer's experience happens in the writing and the telling about it is in the reader's reading it. So once we've had an experience, it seems that it only helps us to share. I really believe that art for art's sake is the greatest nonsense! Maybe the artist doesn't think he's speaking to his generation, but he's certainly speaking to someone. Maybe he's speaking to someone 30 years in the future. "You, out there, do you hear what I'm saying, do you see what I'm seeing?" "Do you feel it?"

TERRY: "Hello, people, do you hear me?" Yes, that's it!

APRIL: It's all rather like a little one-act play entitled "Hello, out there!"

TERRY: I think in a way that's what every human being is doing—some of them aren't capable yet of saying it in the "right" kind of way so that they can be heard. People perhaps being willing to say, "Hello, out there!" is a form of health.

APRIL: Yes, and being willing to risk the fact that someone will say, "But I don't know you" or "I don't *want to know* you out there." "I'm scared to know you." Because I think it's fear that keeps people from other people.

TERRY: Sure, because I think it's the natural, human thing, to say, "Hello, out there!" I think as people have spoken to us we have said, "Oh, shut up!" And then they've learned to be quiet.

APRIL: Or, sometimes, the other people say, "What do you want from me?"

TERRY: I've done that. I did that for 12 to 15 years. I would say, "Hello, out there!" and someone would smile and say "Hi!" The answers were saying hello but also they wanted something from me, so I would be afraid and run back in without saying anything much.

APRIL: Once when I was in graduate school, I was sitting in class, and in this class I noticed another graduate student. She struck me as being very beautiful in a very different way, long hair, and she was like her name—Laura. I was very struck by her because when she spoke she said thoughtful things, softly without trying to impress others. Yet she impressed all of us. I remember thinking after a couple of days, "There's a person I would like for a friend." I didn't know how to go about it. Well, I took a chance and I waited for her after class one day and I said, "Laura, you walk in beauty," and I remember her saying, "What do you want—a quarter?" And I thought to myself: "I know that she's a real person, but this kind of sarcastic answer is something that she's picked up because she, too, is afraid I don't mean it." And I remember I made a silent prayer at the time, and at the same time I was thinking (I think all deep thoughts are prayers), "How can I convince this person I really mean what I said; that I don't want anything from her, that I just admire who and what she is." And I said out loud, "It's funny that, in our culture, we can accept hostile statements better than we can a compliment." And, right away, the light broke through, and she recognized that, yes, I was trying to reach her on a real level, and she responded. We became close friends. We're so afraid of this human encounter. We're afraid that it's phony, that we'll be used, that we'll get rejected. We're afraid of someone who approaches us and we're also afraid to go after someone. Terry, I'm sure that the word is not *cowardly*—you must have a better word for it.

TERRY: I don't think *cowardly* has any meaning for me in this respect; I think it's just simply not wanting to be hurt any more; just not allowing yourself to be involved any more than necessary. If you just continue to be hurt all the time, then you'll soon just die. A human being's a pretty good oyster, perhaps for his own sake he has to be.

APRIL: We start out open and spontaneous and free as children.

TERRY: Yes, but people very quickly learn not to be so open. I wrote a poem once that started "Oysters are at least human. They must bare their tenderest parts to eat." Humans really aren't very human; they never bare their tenderest parts, their innermost selves, because, if they did, they'd be hurt. We become very sophisticated, very smooth, and I think college students, particularly, learn to be kind of pseudo-sophisticates. Knowing how to be a college student means to be a certain kind of "cool" character.

APRIL: Right! Don't lose your "cool."

TERRY: Yes. Or someone can "get in" where it's warm and might create heat, and the heat might melt the cool, the ice. Keep it cool, don't let anyone get in. Keep frozen.

APRIL: What if someone loses his "cool?" What happens?

TERRY: Well, sometimes you lose your cool and people accept it. When you have made an ass of yourself, and your real friends don't care. It's not just a matter of being able to have a deep loving encounter! It's also being able to be accepted—just accepted and understood. It's a good comfortable feeling to be able to show a person your stupidity and to have them accept it and you—to be able to show someone that you really don't know, that you really don't understand what's going on.

APRIL: But this problem of not being afraid of knowing each other is complicated. Although we each knew all along, Terry, that we—you and I—could have an encounter with each other, this may be the first time that we have been willing to talk to each other on this level. I wonder if it was because we were afraid of exciting each other too much, that we couldn't handle it?

TERRY: Could be. I don't know. Over a year we've been working together, perhaps we haven't really confronted one another—but yes, we have, too.

APRIL: Yes, but our confrontations were rather negative, perhaps, and happened only when we were at cross-purposes with one another and we had to straighten something out.

TERRY: Okay, but that, too, gives us perhaps the best chance for encounter we had. Any time there's a cross-purpose, or any time there's a negative feeling, or if you feel like someone doesn't like you, or is hurting you, then obviously they are important to you, or you wouldn't give a damn. You just wouldn't care. So already we can make the assumption that *we do care*. Caring is important. It just happens that a fistful of sand got into the works—into the oyster.

APRIL: It may become a pearl soon!

TERRY: That's good! The grain of sand that gets caught in people's cleft gets turned into a pearl when they recognize it or talk about it. I learned that very early. In high school, in the 11th grade, because a girl didn't like me. That hurt! Especially because she was important to me. She was popular and pretty and had a kind of an elite power or something. I didn't understand what it meant to me too well but she was a strong person in the school and I needed her attention for some reason. I wanted her to pay attention to me. She didn't like me, and she was always throwing negative remarks my way.

APRIL: But she must have liked you more than you thought.

TERRY: She must have cared enough to let me know she didn't like me!

APRIL: That's right.

TERRY: So once I wrote her a valentine, and I said: "Gayle, I can't tolerate your attitude toward me. I want you to know that I like you, and that you're important to me, and can you understand what I'm saying?" And this girl just came to me and it's been a long and delightful friendship. She melted and I just recognized this grain of sand and said, "Look, friend, can we do something about it?"

APRIL: I want to go into something that I've always wanted to go into deeply with you, right now, Terry. One of the things about you that in a way upsets me is that I'll never be able to measure up to your kind of brilliance. How's that for bringing up a piece of gritty sand?

TERRY: It's something I don't understand, because I don't feel any brilliance. You see, I don't accept that. I think you're misperceiving something. I feel no brilliance. And I feel the same kind of thing with you sitting here in conversation. Your ability to embroider our conversation with Yiddish sayings, and jokes, and pulling examples from science, makes me feel kind of stupid. I feel—I feel, you see, the kind of thing I think you're feeling. "How could I ever measure up to April's perception of an important and worthy person?" I just feel kind of stupid. I almost feel that you perceive me as stupid!

APRIL: Isn't that awful! Here we are . . . here we sit, and we get to something that's gotten in our way all through the year after working together . . . the fact that you seemed to me so brilliant—what could I possibly contribute to you!

TERRY: So we both kept from each other.

APRIL: Now we are talking to each other about the thing that's kept us further apart than we wanted. That's crazy! Our admiration has kept us away? What were we afraid of?

TERRY: Maybe a little rivalry?

APRIL: Oh no! I've never felt any rivalry with you.

TERRY: And I haven't felt it either. I've always felt that we work well together; I don't think I've ever felt any jealousy. Perhaps kind of inadequate sometimes . . . .

APRIL: That's exactly it!

TERRY: I've always felt that you might be teaching me. That you weren't being level with me; that you were kind of being more mature than I.

APRIL: I suppose this is just an example of how this kind of thing gets entangled all the time with people. If we share this type of thing with them—because I really like to be with people who have something I don't have. I think this is one of the things that pleasures me in the world. To be with a person who is a craftsman—an expert, I mean— an expert in his particular field is a delight to me.

TERRY: Well, we've talked for some time now, and the tape is about to run out. Let's come back to these feelings we have about each other soon. What have we said?

APRIL: May I try to summarize, Terry?

First, that we are continuously learning about ourselves, because this is a very important thing to us. "Know thyself," "To thine own self be true," and all that. And Jesus said, "The kingdom of heaven is within you." But you have to seek it. Learning about ourselves is so very important. It's an adventure and a lifetime.

Then, two, we said that the reason human encountering is important is because others teach us what it is that's going on inside ourselves. By opening up to other people, as we did just now in a small way, we are helped to know ourselves better.

And, three, we've said that here we are, small human beings in this great, big world, so full of so many things, but it's not easy, and some- times it's tragic, and yet at the same time it's beautiful. Or, at least, if we know how to encounter the small and beautiful moments, we can bear the great and tragic ones. I try to teach my students to appreciate this task of living; to live our lives like a painting that is being painted; that we are the painter and we are also the painting!

Fourth, we've said that the human encounter is one method (there are others) by which we can do this: to experience others, to grow in our humanity. But there are little blocks in the way (grains of sand?) and we're afraid of being rejected, of being hurt, of being misunderstood by somebody else. So we cover ourselves with what my husband calls a "body armor"—I think Reik was the first to say this. We desensitize ourselves, we drown it in alcohol, or LSD, or the peyote cult. We even try shortcuts to self-analysis, etc., but you can't go to heaven on roller skates. . . .There are no shortcuts to self-knowledge. What we have to do, then, is get around our fear, and turn our negative pieces of sand that are caught in our oyster into the pearl. If we get hurt, so we get hurt! We try again. And it is difficult because it is the human condition.

II

how do we encounter others?

In Part II we discuss some of the techniques common to human encounter groups. Disclosing oneself to another is a very important part of the human encounter. We have described this process in the chapter on Self-Revealment, in which some of our students speak to you about what this process means to them. In the Dialogue we reveal ourselves; we risk being known to show you an example and, hopefully, to encourage you to risk sharing yourself with others in your group.

In a brief chapter on how to begin we provide some very practical and straightforward methods for entering the human encounter. You may wish to use other techniques described in books in the bibliography, or your facilitator may prefer other approaches he has used in the past. The next chapter is a transcript of a first session of a group class. You will be able to see more clearly some of the characteristics of a beginning group and will come to understand some of the important processes in the human encounter.

In the chapter on Process we illustrate what occurs in the human encounter, relying heavily on comments of participants. There are many ways to describe the process of the human encounter; the dimensions we have described seem to occur often in the groups in which we have participated. The process is probably different for different facilitators and different groups, and you may wish to observe the process that is unique to your group. The purpose of this chapter, however, is to sensitize you to the process so that your experience can be more meaningful; we hope you will save your observation and analysis until you have experienced the process as a full participant.

4

self-
revealment
as a step
toward
encountering

There is already available a wealth of written material on the subject of self-revealment and we refer you to the writings of such persons as Rogers, Jourard, Maslow, Gendlin, and others (see Bibliography). Our purpose here is to describe the difficulties, the purposes, and the outcomes of self-revealment. We hope that you will regard our writing as a preliminary guideline in your beginning attempts to become a more open person.

Some of you can probably discuss yourselves quite freely already; some may even have been doing this for most of your "verbal" life.

Others, however, may recoil from exposing any aspect of yourselves which you feel is too private to share with another. Yet the ability to reveal ourselves, the ability to say, "This is who I am, this is what I am like, this is what concerns me, these are my beliefs," is one aspect of the ability to achieve human encounter.

For the sake of those who may be hesitant to discuss their deepest feelings, let us take a moment to explore some of the reasons for the need to be "on our guard" with other people.

Many of us have been brought up to believe that "wearing one's heart on one's sleeve," showing "weakness" or "one's feelings," is something to be ashamed of, something somehow a little improper—something to be avoided, in other words. In some groups, for example, to show strong emotional feelings is regarded as perhaps even a bit uncivilized. Showing of emotion in public may appear almost as unseemly as the display of other bodily functions.

Some of us have been taught that revealing our true feelings (what we really are, here and now) has no place in a "polite" society; that the considerate person, even in the midst of emotional crises, "keeps things to himself," or "puts on a good front," or "acts as if nothing is the matter." In fact, some societies—particularly the pre-Westernized cultures of the East—followed this behavior pattern to such lengths that Orientals were epitomized as "inscrutable." Actually, the cultured Chinese or Japanese had developed the astonishing skill of smiling under extreme duress (anger, fear, sadness, terror); and on the opposite side of the coin, of maintaining a high degree of solemnity when most elated. Part of this behavior may be attributed to "saving face" or regarded as a protective device against the anger of jealous men or gods; but another aspect of Oriental behavior stemmed from respect for the feelings of others around them. Orientals believed (as many of *us* do) that it is not considerate either to display pride and conceit over one's good fortunes, or to burden others with one's misfortunes.

Those of us who have been brought up in an Anglo-Saxon tradition have been strongly influenced by this same kind of attitude. The English language abounds in expressions for the necessity or the propriety of not exposing our real feelings or inner thoughts. We "guard our tongues," or "keep a stiff upper lip." Small boys are admonished daily to "act like a man," which usually means not to cry in public.

Your authors admire as much as anyone those people who do not waste words, who cannot be accused of "chattering," who "do more than they say," who use their words wisely. We both have a background in English and both have a reverence for the careful use of our language. In no way do we wish to encourage indiscriminate babbling. But although there may be a time and a place to be silent, in the process of self-revealment "guarding one's tongue" can hinder the process of communication with others. It is difficult to get to know someone who maintains a constant reserve, who does not open up to you as a person, or who "plays it cool." We can admire the character of such a person but it may be difficult to feel warmth with and toward him. It is written in Ecclesiastes that there is "a time to be silent and a time to speak." The process of encountering is surely "a time to speak."

While some of us have been steeped in the attitude of keeping a reserve about ourselves since childhood, others of us may have adopted it out of fear of being hurt, or rejected, or ridiculed. When asked to express their feelings of anxiety about revealing themselves to others, students have said:

"I am afraid I'll be laughed at. I was always a fat girl and people never took me seriously."

"I'm afraid if I really open up to someone, and show them what I am really like, they'll be shocked."

"I don't trust people. When people get to know a lot about you, they have power over you."

"I've been hurt by people I thought were my best friends. I don't intend to get hurt any more."

In a beginning encountering group, therefore, it is necessary to share anxieties and fears that the participants may have about self-revealment. Sometimes by merely bringing these anxieties out in the open the person finds the imaginary indictments of others are groundless and the ghosts of previous hurts are laid to rest.

Another facet of human encounter groups that must be discussed is *the principle of confidentiality*. Each member makes a pledge that what goes on in the group remains there—is not talked about to outsiders. It is a sacred trust. Any encounter group must begin with the primary rule that what goes on in the group, what is said by members of that group, is held to be as sacred as the confessional or the revelations of client to lawyer. For there is nothing of the quality of being on trial in an encounter group, nor of having to confess things to others. Each one has a right at all times to maintain privacy—there is no obligation to reveal anything. Indeed, it is difficult to imagine anyone being able to coerce such things out of group members. Nevertheless, it does become easier for people to become self-revealing, in spite of anxiety, when the participants of the group have committed themselves to confidentiality. By the way, this pledging of confidentiality seems necessary in encounter groups *only* at the beginning of the meetings; as the group continues to meet, an attitude of mutual trust and responsibility to that trust seems to develop quite naturally. The people in the group come to take the attitude of confidentiality quite as a matter of course, as if there had never been any other attitude to begin with.

We can now turn our attention to the outcomes of self-revealment.

First, there is the obvious therapeutic release which comes of being able to speak of some of the things we have been afraid to discuss with others. Sometimes, merely getting these worries out in the open is enough to dissolve them (just the sympathetic listening of someone else is enough to lighten a burden). For example, one young man wrote:

> I have realized that people have taken time to talk about my problem. Two people especially have given their time to me. These two helped me to understand myself and others. For years I have been looking for something, but did not realize what it was. They helped me as I found a place and purpose in our meetings.

Another group member, remarking on the growing bond between the members of this group, wrote:

> We feel that the other person is at least listening (whether he agrees or not) and we will listen to him. So we are discussing, not arguing, with each other.

But at a "deeper" level, self-revealment does something more than provide therapeutic release. In 1956, a writer named Colin Wilson published a book called *The Outsider*, in which he attempted to characterize the present age as one of existential meaninglessness; he wrote that the reaction to this meaninglessness resulted in a "sick" society, and that the symptoms are revealed in our era as boredom, alienation, and the inability to "lay hold of experience." Although his theme was not new,* Wilson did focus, by way of his title, on the loneliness modern man feels—that he is perhaps looking *at* life and other men, but is not involved *with* them. He experiences himself as separate, and phenomenologically speaking, as an outsider.

We are not prepared to debate the existential meaning or meaninglessness of life at this moment. Our own reaction is rather personal: When we are involved with and committed to mankind, even in that small aspect of it that we touch as wife, husband, mother, father, teacher, and friend, we find meaning. When *I* and *Thou* (to use Buber's phrase) reveal ourselves to each other and recognize each other as inhabitants of the same phenomenological world, I and Thou are inside the circle of human relation.

To the extent, then, that we can open ourselves to another human being, to that extent do we feel ourselves as part of the society of men—related to them and they to us. We are no longer *outside*, but *within* a circle of human belongingness.

As we reveal ourselves, as we permit others to reveal themselves, we are able to take off the masks, the armor, that we use to keep people from knowing us. Eliot said succinctly that we "put on a face

---

*Among some of the writers who have been concerned with man's alienation are: Fromm, Sartre, Camus, Samuel Beckett, Ionesco, Heidegger . . . the list is long.

to meet the faces that we meet." For as we become less hidden, and more open with each other, we realize that *we are capable of reaching toward each other* across our physical separateness. And, ultimately, there occurs the phenomenon, the diamond-like moment of emotional and spiritual communion, of human encountering. Let us quote, though, from the writings of the students who have experienced this quality of belonging—this feeling of being an *insider*.

> I feel great at times and at other times I have a feeling I can't explain as yet but it is one I am aware of, I know is there but I don't know what to do with it yet. Somehow, I don't feel alone anymore. I feel that I am a part of people.
>
> I feel much freer, a feeling of not being so alone since we started this term. I feel now there is some hope, a hope for the future which was lacking at the beginning of the term. I feel a comradeship for the first time in my life with one or two other people in this class and that helps immensely.
> . . .
>
> I guess the purpose of this course is to encounter other people. . . . This course gives you the wonderful feeling of being wanted and also that there are people who care about you and this is very important in life, what keeps you going. To feel not wanted, out of place, or left out is terrible, is miserable.

If we have helped students to feel related to others around them, if we have done nothing more than help them to feel like insiders, then this kind of a course has been justified. We believe that helping people to achieve human encounter should be one of the main concerns of educational institutions, and, for that matter, of all institutions.

Up to now, we have spoken of two outcomes of self-revealment: the therapeutic release of one's inner concerns and the experience of involvement and belonging. A third outcome of self-revealment entails the affirmation of oneself while in communication (that is to say, in communion with others). As we give voice to that which we are, to that which is central to our being, we *affirm ourselves;* even as we become involved in the community of man, our existence as separate and unique entities is clarified and affirmed. This affirmation is something more than merely not conforming to some outside societal pressure; it is something deeper than a mere inflated ego; it is something more positive than the confirmation of your existence or your right to be. It is the exciting discovery of *your* awareness of *your* uniqueness from all others at the deepest level of your being. This third outcome was the one most frequently alluded to by the members of one class committed to the goal of human encountering. Here are some of the various ways they expressed it:

> In the sharing of experiences in this class, the student has the opportunity of evaluating himself and his needs. By encountering the other members of the class, whether meaningfully or superficially, he enlarges himself and begins to look within himself.

In this course, the student should learn about others and through transposition, himself. I know I have. It is through others that one sees himself. The class members should feel free to reveal themselves when they feel it is the time.

. . . I somehow started thinking deeper about things, to care more about myself and other people.

This class has given me a chance to stop and try to see who I am and where I am going.

This course is for the enlarging of the minds of everyone who is introduced to, or given the chance to participate in, this type of class. . . . Participation will advance as the students' minds and hearts open up and advance.

I am a better person because of this course for now I think more deeply about such topics as love, death, and life.

The purpose of this study is to "open the door" to the student, to open his mind, his heart, and his mouth. By seeing himself, something in common with others, and differences in others, he may encounter himself and recognize others as persons, not people.

5

the authors reveal themselves

APRIL: Terry, we've said that the reader in this book is going to encounter a lot of people: he'll encounter himself, other people, other students in the class, teachers, and, we hope, he'll encounter his parents and friends, children, husbands and wives. We've also said that he's going to encounter us—you and me. We are committed to taking off our academic robes and being not just two names on the cover of this book, but real people.

TERRY: We're not really even going to try to *talk* our roles; we're just going to try "to be"—rather more as if we were, in fact, in the classroom ourselves.

APRIL: Well, then, why don't we introduce ourselves? Why don't you tell the reader a bit about yourself, Terry, and I'll talk a little about me.

TERRY: It's difficult to *talk* to a person in written form. If I were in the class with him, it would be easier to be personal. How much can we afford to tell them? What are the kinds of things we want to tell them?

APRIL: I know. What always bothers me when I want to get to know my students is when I say to them: "Tell me about yourself." And what I often get back from them is the usual sort of autobiography that they had to write in high school. It usually starts: "I was born in Wakaloosa, Iowa, on January 10th, 1940." Or, if they're a little more sophisticated, they say: "On January 10th, 1940, a really important event occurred. It was on that day that I was born." Really kind of factual, and I don't know any more about him than if he'd said "I'm 18."

TERRY: In other words, you think there are other things about people that are more important—like, what do you answer when someone says, "Who are you?" And I guess when I say this, I mean, "Come on out of hiding! Let's really get to know you." Only people are afraid to reveal themselves, so I think if we could do it, they might be able to, too!

APRIL: Right! More like that! Here we are, both authors of this book. We've got Ph.D.s at the ends of our names but this doesn't have much to do with us really.

TERRY: Let's tell them what we are like *now*, rather than how we came to be what we are. What are you now, April? Or what am I?

APRIL: You begin, Terry, even though I suggested it. I'm a little nervous about all this. It hasn't been done very often—mostly in autobiographies. Carl Rogers did something like this once.

TERRY: Well, I'm a person who is searching for some kind of way of having more meaning in my life. And education has been the vehicle that I have used for this because of the lower class that I came from. Education is the only channel I had. So I have embraced education and have now earned, through a bachelor's and master's to a Ph.D., some success. At the time of this conversation, I'm Dean of Students in a junior college. I've done this for three or four years and will now move on to teaching in a university situation, training other deans of students for junior colleges. I feel I can do this pretty well. I'm fairly successful, and its important to me to do my job well. This is a major key to knowing me.

APRIL: I see you as very successful in the field of human relationships. A lot more successful, by the way, Terry, than I. I see a look of puzzlement on your face, but you're expert at walking into a committee and getting people to work together. I've seen you help people pull out their ideas. I've seen you walk into a high school and talk to them in a way that they respond to you, not as an administrator, but as a human being. I've seen you walk into a room as a newcomer, and make people feel like they've known you all their lives.

TERRY: I don't feel that kind of confidence that you are talking about at all, April. I think I have a quality; I think there's something a little special about me in that respect—I think I do believe that. People have said this to me. I have had enough human encounters to feel quite assured that there is that special quality about me. I don't understand it very well. Maybe the special quality that is most important to me is being human. Being a human being, regardless of whether one is an administrator or whatever, is the important thing for me. To know some people and to know them very personally and very intensely. For me to be known, too. And that, to me, is about the most important thing there is. If I don't have that, well, hell, I could care less about whether I am a successful administrator or teacher. It would have no meaning at all if I didn't feel that I had a few close friends.

APRIL: Yes, it's this special quality about you which is outstanding to me. Someone we both know said to me the other day: "What do you think of Terry O'Banion?" And because of my feeling toward you, I was very close-mouthed. I don't know why. So I didn't answer, and she answered her own question. She said that no matter when she sees you, you always look very immaculate. You look as if you'd just come out of the shower. And I remember thinking at the time that that was such a superficial thing to say about you. My answer should have been that you have a tremendous ability to work with people— an openness—an ability to recognize each personality where he is, and the ability to meet him where he is. I admire people who have this ability. You and my husband share this, by the way.

TERRY: I suppose that telling people who I am would have to be really what I've said: yes, I'm a successful person in terms of our society (how society judges us), but for myself, I have also used other criteria—I'm still kind of an awful cynic and a great pessimist really at heart. I may never be able to feel a great confidence in myself and will always be struggling with this thing—I probably will never achieve a sense of great peacefulness. But then I've come to feel that perhaps no one ever achieves this, and perhaps it's not even a very important goal to achieve peacefulness or happiness, or something. But the important thing is that I've experienced *human joy;* that I try to plan for it, and on occasion have been willing to take risks so that I may have it. I've learned to plan a way of life of encountering people, of making big talk.

APRIL: By the way, I admire the way you do take risks. I think you open up and say things to people that I would be scared to tell myself, right away, until I knew them better. Yet your openness doesn't alienate them—it only draws people closer to you.

TERRY: I think any time you're open, you beget openness in others.

I think I've learned that. I think I've learned that very, very well. And I think that works for anybody. Any time you are willing to disclose yourself, any time you're willing to pull off the mask and say, "Hey, look me over!" other people are going to respond to you.

Well, how would you like to talk about yourself? I feel kind of blah!

APRIL: I was hoping maybe you'd say something like you came from a poor white southern family.

TERRY: I think I've done this several times when I had the encounter classes. And I think I've worn it out. I tried to do it last night and flopped. The only thing that was successful was that I recognized the flopping. I said this out loud, and the students helped me.

APRIL: Still, it's that part of *you* that I find miraculous. Try once more.

TERRY: Well, it sounds constructed in this day and time but I came from a really poverty-stricken background, of the lower social classes. I was literally born in a log cabin that my parents had built with their own hands. Even though I'm only 30 years old, I wasn't born in a hospital, I was born in this log cabin that had no inner paneling; it had rafters overhead. For a year, I actually lived in a little, one-room shack in the Everglades, where my father was working. We had a dirt floor. My mother cooked on an open fire.

APRIL: I've never known these special things about you.

TERRY: Well, I can recall very vividly that we had to dry our own meat in the sun—jerked venison, just like the Indians did, and that there were cypress poles outside of our little hut on which the venison was hanging. And the panthers sometimes would come and steal this. . . .

APRIL: Panthers!

TERRY: Yes, there were panthers.

APRIL: I didn't know there were panthers in Florida. How did they get there?

TERRY: I don't know, but they were there.

My father would have to shoot them. So, you see, that kind of background, pretty poverty-stricken really. We had a very unstable family situation. My father left home when I was six and never really lived at home very much. He likes other women, and has been married six times at last count and that was several years ago, so it could be seven or eight by now. My mother's been married three times. Both my grandparents—each has been married twice. So I come from a long line of unstable homes. I lived in a kind of environment that could only mean unsuccess; that really led to poor mental health, and I was very mentally unhealthy all the way through childhood. Through pre-adolescence and adolescence I was a very despairing, a very lonely child who created worlds of his own; who did not ever communicate with people because people always hurt. There was no family there. My mother worked constantly to keep the family together. My mother worked seven days a week; walked three miles to town where she worked in a restaurant; left home before daylight and came home about midnight. There were three sisters. And so there was never any affirmation of my worthiness. There was never anyone to say, "Terry, I love you." There was never a father to say, "Son, you did that well." There was never a father to put his arms around my shoulder. So I never had any physical or verbal communication that I was worth anything. I never felt very worthy. Maybe this has been my hang-up—to appreciate myself. And my achievements have been to show myself that I *am* worth something. My whole life has been one need for achievement to climb, to build, to do things well, to do things right, to convince myself that I *do* have worth.

APRIL: That's interesting! You know the first run-in you and I had was because I expressed *my* feelings of *your* worthiness. In that moment you got very upset at me, and that was our first real rift, do you recall?

TERRY: Yes.

APRIL: So much so, that I was astounded—it was the first time you'd rejected me, and you rejected me out of the fact that I had recognized your worth verbally.

TERRY: Yes, it's hard for me. I have to have people recognize my worth. I constantly need feedback. . . .

APRIL: Only they shouldn't say so out loud!

TERRY: Somehow, to be as direct and honest as you were that day—it was upsetting, because the moment it's direct and honest, I feel . . .

APRIL: You felt it wasn't direct and honest?

TERRY: I don't know. Maybe so. If it were direct and honest it may be that I wouldn't perceive it as that. But I apparently didn't. Maybe I felt you were playing up to me, or something.

APRIL: I wasn't. It is a joyous thing for me to admire something expert in somebody. The consequence of your reaction was very fine, though. You helped me again grow a little. I had looked at you as at a great white father. You made me an individual working on my own.

TERRY: Oh God, how could a 30-year-old punk from a small town in South Florida be a great white father! I walked out of the Everglades barefoot at 15!

APRIL: Yes, I admire you for this, not because you have become something else, but because you've had experiences I've never had— you've jerked venison, you've lived in the wilds. You could survive.

TERRY: Oh, yes, I could survive barefooted in the Everglades very well.

APRIL: You've done a very wonderful thing.

TERRY: Not at all. And you know, a part of this helped me (part of not having people) in that I grew close to nature, and became a kind of nature lover. I used to run wild with a couple of dogs I had. I'd just run through the woods with them like a free animal. And I used to embrace trees—literally.

APRIL: Wordsworth talked about that—

TERRY: Yes, Wordsworth is my favorite poet. Because he understands that. He understands what I feel. I used to get out and just yell— y-e-l-l! to the world and to nature, you know. And look at the sun until it just glinted me to death.

APRIL: Something out of the *Yearling*, really. . . .

TERRY: Yes. I walked into a little forest once, it was a cypress hammock in South Florida, and there was a little island of greenery, and I sat down and snuggled up like a squirrel under a tree, and knew at that moment that I was one with nature. That was another intensive moment, snuggling up to nature—because I felt very comfortable there. That gave me some comfort. You see, there were no people. So, sometimes, people can *encounter nature*. This is the thing for me that has meaning. And I think that probably today in our society, we've all moved to the cities; we've all lost something there. I think man has probably lost a confrontation with nature. Not that nature is some god or something, but that nature is *touch greenery*—if you crush it in your hands, this is an encounter, too.

I used to eat flowers. I would smell gardenias and have no control, and just eat them. I encountered nature, because there were no people. But nature can't give you feedback like people can.

APRIL: Let me go back, now, to something you said. You asked what is important to tell people about yourself. I think a lot of people have experienced unhappy childhoods, perhaps not like yours. The important thing is that you came out of it. We can never change our childhoods. We have all had these kinds of negative and positive experiences. Even in your poverty and in your sadness, there were beautiful things that happened to you. They didn't happen to other people—they are yours! Even the negative things, because they are the things that are going to make you climb and struggle and challenge; and the positive things of course you'll maintain. Both will be your unique individuality. We don't have to change our childhood. You don't have to change the fact that you had an unhappy childhood. It made you what you are now.

TERRY: Yes, that's right. We capitalize on the uniqueness that is ourselves. We can't be different from what we are. We have to develop those kinds of things we have, and we've got some special qualities. We've got to develop those. That's all we have!

APRIL: I once asked you if you could love that little boy that you once were, remember?

TERRY: Yes, I think so. I love some of him, but I still wish he hadn't had to be so hurt.

APRIL: If he hadn't hurt, do you think you now would be so understanding of other people's hurts?

TERRY: I don't know, maybe not.

APRIL: I'm a little at variance with people who say that people who've never had painful experiences—who've had mostly happy experiences—in their lives, that these become the really tremendous people in the world. I think that a person who's never been hurt, who never had to roll a little (my husband calls it the growing edge of the personality), has been understanding of the hurts of others. But if you know how to make this hurt work, this becomes your greatness. Our greatness actually lies in our weakness, and how we make use of our "soft spot." Because we're all so different in our weaknesses. These soft spots are our salvation if we can work them through. Does that seem right to you?

TERRY: Yes, I think that makes sense to me. Because I don't think there are any other kinds of people; I think there are very few people who have stable, good, happy lives. I don't know any of these people. I've read enough autobiographies to believe that couldn't possibly be true.

APRIL: So many young people say: "The reason I'm so miserable or mean or neurotic is because I've had a terribly unhappy childhood. My parents gave me a car, and sent me to the best colleges but they didn't give me love." That may be sad, but when I hear someone say it I want to giggle. They can hang on to their silliness and be miserable, or forgive and grow.

TERRY: Yes, some people do this. If we didn't want to pick ourselves up by our bootstraps, we could hang on and become very nicely schizophrenic, and withdraw from it all. What makes a person not do that—so many people do?

APRIL: There's a human choice factor. I do not believe that everything is predetermined. I think there's some free choice involved.

TERRY: You have that choice, yes, to say, "This way, I'm *not* going to be."

APRIL: "I'm not going to weep the rest of my life about the fact that my childhood was so unhappy. All right, it *was* pretty bad, but I can't keep nursing that hurt. I'm going to give up my resentment, give up my hatred, give up my shame, give up my guilt—and grow!"

TERRY: "As much as I can—not let them be the controlling factor. . . ."

APRIL: Right. Rather, "I'll make those painful and suffering experiences useful to me so that I can become a better person for someone else who may have also experienced this."

TERRY: You know, I didn't give them up until I started thinking about other people. I hugged that hurt, the despondency, for so long, until I was about 20 or so. I kept hugging the hurt—and still do it occasionally, go back into the depression, for about a week, say, with the teddy bear of my despondent youth, but I find that this doesn't lead anywhere, you know.

APRIL: A friend of mine, I won't mention his name, but he's written a couple of books and he's a psychologist, once said to us at a meeting, "My trouble is that I didn't have a happy childhood, and I wish I could change it now." And my retort was, you know, well, "What the hell, none of us did!" I mean, who *did* have a happy childhood? Now there are some people, I suppose, Montaigne was one of them, who said he had a beautiful, happy childhood. Well, that's what he said. I don't know if he really did. I think we've all had experiences of hurt, and what are we going to do about it? We've got to make it work for us. Through our sufferings we have become human beings, and being human means understanding the hurt and suffering of others. Well, for instance, psychology calls it *sublimation* or *transcendence*. The person who was once a skinny runt becomes an athlete. What's wrong with that? Not what's wrong, but how beautiful that is! I don't think I could tell all the things that happened to me, because the things that happened to me were—well, I just don't think I'd want to reveal them at this point.

TERRY: Well, what *can* you tell? I don't think people ever reveal themselves completely to any other living human being.

APRIL: Well, my story is a kind of case history, you know. It could be very well written up. If I were a social worker, I'd recognize it— like Marilyn Monroe should have been a social case history. It was pretty bad. My mother died when I was eight, and my father when I was ten. My mother was Jewish, my father was Protestant. I had sisters who died. By the time I was 15, I'd had a religious training in three different religions.

TERRY: What, Catholic, Jewish, and Protestant? I thought you'd had a little Oriental thrown in somewhere, too?

APRIL: Well, that came later! During the winter months, I had to live with my Protestant relatives who were quite prejudiced about Jews and quite prejudiced about me, for a number of reasons I won't go into. I lived in a cellar—I starved at times—I used to steal peanut butter. I was a pretty terrible little girl; I mean, I was kind of bewildered on the inside and I didn't know how to relate to people, not at all. I was moody, and sad, and confused. And I didn't dare let anyone know what I was feeling inside. I wore one of those masks we talk about somewhere in this book. There were some very kind people on the outside. I didn't have nice clothes, and only one pair of shoes and I didn't dare come home with good marks from school.

By the time I was 17, I had lived with so many families, and so many types of families, I'd acquired an insight into many different ways of living. That is, I understood them but I didn't understand how to live with them. For a long time, I longed to have not had this unhappy childhood, to the point that I was ashamed that I had it; that I'd had these things happen to me, these very terrible things. It was the shame I had to live with. One of the ways I had to survive was to hate—I hated people. Because, you see, I had my own little private concentration camp, right over here in America, which nobody knew about. If I told people, they didn't believe me—it was too incredible. I tried so hard to get out. I faked lots of things to call somebody's attention to it . . . like phoney amnesia and a death in the family. But of course, they only backfired and I was caught in my own fibs. And nobody then would believe anything I was trying to tell them.

Then, I went to a girls' school and all these girls had had relatively more normal backgrounds, and I'd come from all these experiences and I wanted to talk about God, and life, and death, and love, and they wanted to talk about boyfriends and clothes, and so forth, and it was just terrible! You know, I was pretty neurotic and confused, and I didn't know *what* to talk about, and my thoughts and comments were quite different as a result of my background. So my real purpose was to become as much like everybody else so people couldn't tell that I was that different. For a long time, I worked at this—not to be visibly different from others.

TERRY: You wanted this.

APRIL: Yes, oh very much! And so I knew that if I worked at it long enough I could do it. My husband says I don't really get away with it. And the fact that I've had all these experiences has resulted in the fact that I can talk to all kinds of people everywhere. But, you know, I'm kind of proud of the fact that I'm a middle-aged, middle-class, American woman, with five children and married to a very delightful Irishman, born there, and who happens also to be a psychologist. I can pass sometimes. Of course, I really can't pass, but at least I know how to play the game—I know enough of the small rules that people will accept to consider me as being *just enough* different and kooky, so that they accept me. I had to learn these games. Someone had to teach me, so I'm kind of interested in teaching somebody else—how to do these things. You learn the rules, and you learn them just so that you don't have to play the game any more—you can walk away from it.

TERRY: You learn the rules—not to let them become the way of life but so you can be free of them?

APRIL: Yes. And so you can ignore the little stupid rules.

These things are all there in my background but *what I really want to say is:* All of this isn't me. What I would really want to say about me is: "Yes, these things happened to me, and I'm telling you this for the readers, because I want to let them know that these things happened to us, and we weren't born with silver spoons in our mouths, and we weren't always healthy people. I think we're healthy now at least in our willingness to take a chance, and we're fairly successful in our professions, depending upon what need achievements we have."

But the most important thing that happened to me was the fact that after I became about 21, I realized that my method of living—hatred—was inappropriate. It wasn't just inappropriate, *it was destructive.* I didn't have to hate any more to survive. Hatred kills the person who hates.

TERRY: How did you learn that?

APRIL: Oh, I'd known it a long time ago, because my parents were pretty loving people—kooky, but you know, loving—and I knew all the time I was in this dreadful home that *there was another way to live.* And *that was love.* Families could experience love and be together, and people could be loving to each other. I was always very religious, oddly enough, so that I knew there was a thing called love.

I knew a man once who had absolutely never experienced love when he was a child, and still doesn't believe there's such a thing as love. Like a Hawaiian who doesn't understand what snow is. But, fortunately, I kept within me this memory of love. And then my Jewish relatives were loving in their funny way—so I could experience that—and I could see love between other families, and I could see them experiencing love with each other. So it existed. And some people loved me to the extent that they could, so I knew it was there, and I had to work at it. Then, I spent some hours in therapy, to get the wound cleaned out, and I married quite an unusual man, but most of all I reaffirmed the fact that love is the way to exist, and this is what I would say as to where I am. The most important thing to me is to love people. To teach my children to love. To love as many people as possible. To tell people to give up the resentment and the hate, because resentment poisons and hatred can kill us. I'm not always very successful at this—sometimes people can just rile me. A Catholic sister I once knew said to my children—"You don't have to like people, you just have to love them." And that helped me. I know that I have a long way to go in being a loving person. This is *my* path, *my* journey. Does that say who I think I am?

TERRY: Very good. I'm glad!

EPILOGUE

APRIL: Why did we tell our story to the reader, Terry?

TERRY: Well, I think that we both feel that knowing people is very important, and that that, itself, is the process of human encountering, and I think we've both just given an example of it, *although we have told only a very small part of who we are.*

We're not talking about abstracts now; we just did it. We tried to tell the reader about ourselves.

APRIL: That's right, because as I was talking about myself, I felt my own affirmation; as I listened to you, I felt I knew you better, admired you more.

TERRY: I think we were demonstrating the process—but not just to teach students, but because we are honestly attempting here to communicate with what—right now to us—is an invisible audience.

APRIL: Can we bring them closer, do you think?

TERRY: Here we are—we're just two human beings, we're not two distant authors—that's right—we're not just going to tell you about human behavior, we have been behaving. We're not just going to *write about* behavior: we have attempted here *to behave*. Even though briefly we have been behaving in terms of what we're trying to talk about— human encountering. We believe human encountering involves letting you know about us.

APRIL: Now, we're not just saying that they should go out and do this thing with someone else—in fact—it would be unwise, I think.

TERRY: It might be. I think they'll have to learn their own way of communication; for some of them, it might just be a question of walking up to a stranger and revealing themselves. It may, indeed, be that way. And it may be that they'll have to try out some styles, take some risks, try on some ways, until they learn *for themselves* what's meaningful here. I don't think they can just do as we did, necessarily.

APRIL: Maybe they'll just discover which way is right for them.

TERRY: Right. They might very well begin by answering the question, "Who are you?" from their teachers or friends. It might be a very good way to begin, and it might be a brand-new experience for them.

6

the human encountering experience: how do we begin?

Well, let us begin by making two assumptions.

The first is that you either have had the experience of human encountering and would like to have another opportunity to have the experience again, or you are at least willing to entertain the idea that the experience actually exists, and is not a figment of your authors' imaginations. If you have never had the experience of human encountering you may have the feeling that the whole idea sounds, if not exactly like hogwash, at least a little bit like fantasy-land. And that's all right, too. We don't expect anyone to imagine what a cake will taste like until they've actually eaten it.

The second assumption is that you actually want to try to experience human encountering. Now you may want to try it but have certain reservations about it, or are a little afraid of what it entails, or feel that you don't know how to go about it. Don't get discouraged by your reservations and doubts because this is as good a way as any to begin; that is, by getting all your worries and doubts out in the open and sharing them with the other members of the group. They, too, will have their reservations and theirs may overlap with yours. Well, let's get down to the mechanics of it.

Here we are in a group of between eight and fifteen people, each of us perhaps a little shy, each of us not knowing quite how to begin, or what to say. So far, so good. We have never yet walked into a strange group without wondering what will develop out of it, and what place we will find in it. It takes time for a human encounter group to develop and the whole process is not without its difficulties.

The best way to begin, then, is to get to know each other a little bit—at least by name, if nothing else. This can be done in several ways which are listed below in order of ease of getting to know each other. We might mention here that the more difficult the technique the group chooses to take the more immediate and deep is their beginning experience in the process of human encountering. With any technique listed, you can probably come up with an idea that will be equally good or even better than ours.

1. You can pair off with each other and retire, either to an isolated part of the room, or to an adjoining area, and interview each other for about ten minutes with the purpose of getting to know your partner in such a way that you can introduce him to the others in the group. People who have not had a whole lot of experience introducing themselves sometimes can barely manage to croak out their own names, let alone add some interesting facts about themselves. This method of introducing each other minimizes the possibility of this kind of stage fright.

OR

2. The group can decide to plunge right into the process of self-revealment by introducing themselves and again by adding something about themselves that will help the other members to remember them. Incidentally, human encountering groups generally do better by operating on a first-name basis, since the title Miss, Mrs., or Mr. is just one more obstacle to developing an intimate feeling between group members. So, if you have a nickname you like to be called, be sure to mention it; the use of nicknames is a good way to help others get a feeling that they are beginning to know you.

OR

3. The group can plunge even deeper into human encountering ex-

perience by the most difficult technique of all. We can sit with each other in our anxiety and silence (sometimes a human encounter group reminds us in some ways of a Quaker meeting) until someone breaks the silence. Let us call this person "the opener." He is at this point the first person to "come forward." He may do so by introducing himself and giving a little background on himself.

Or, he may do so by approaching another member of the group who has caught his interest and try to get to know him right in the group situation. If the person being approached by the opener responds openly and gratefully we are off to a good start. Sometimes, the person being approached will "negate" the opener and answer in monosyllables as if giving the impression he doesn't want to be "picked on" or that he wants to be "coaxed" into revealing himself, for whatever private reasons. The opener can convey exactly his impression of the negating person, for example:

"I get the impression you are feeling uneasy. Would you rather I didn't get to know you in the group?"

and this alone sometimes helps the negater to overcome his private obstacle and meet the opener with sincerity and trust. If the person continues to negate, then our suggestion is to leave the negater alone and go on to someone else in the group who is more open and indicates a desire for human encounter.

Or, the opener can talk about his own nervousness and anxiety about human encountering and encourage the others to share theirs. Actually, the opener may do all three and become a coleader of the group by encouraging the others to do the same.

Don't be afraid to voice the negative feelings you have about this beginning situation. The sooner the negative aspects come out, the sooner they can be dealt with and in most instances overcome.

Now that we have gotten to know each other by whatever method the group has chosen—and it must be their choice—what comes next? Well, almost anything. And all we can do now is to provide some general guidelines for you to keep in mind as your particular group begins its journey. For it is axiomatic that no two groups are alike and each functions according to the unique make up of the group itself. Each individual in the world has his own journey to travel; the same holds true for each group. In only one way are all human encounter groups similar: Their destination is always unknown.

The following chapter is a transcription of the way one class started out after they had read an early draft of this book.

7

encounter
in the
classroom

GROUP I—MEETING I (April O'Connell, facilitator)
HOW WE BEGAN ONE GROUP

Just as the group is about to begin, it is interrupted by a very disturbing incident. The tape picks up after we settle down after the crisis.

APRIL O'CONNELL: How do you feel about the course?
DAVID: It's a required course.

ALEC: I don't know how much good it's going to do me but I'm sure it's going to do me some good. It lets you be able to meet people. I haven't had too much trouble with them. People that have had trouble meeting people or people that have trouble in expressing themselves will benefit a lot from this class. Since I've had no trouble . . . I know I'm going to learn something. It won't be as much as someone who is highly withdrawn.

A.O'C.: I don't think a person who doesn't want to participate in these groups should be forced into them.

STEFAN: I tell everything in my heart because I like to know people.

A.O'C.: Stefan, maybe it's because you live how many thousand miles away from your home?

ALEC: Well I live in Centerville, true . . . but if the students don't participate, if they don't say anything, if they just sit in class, they listen . . . a third of our grade is class participation . . . right? Supposedly!

A.O'C.: Hmmm.

(There is a digression here as the students refer to the incident noted above.)

A.O'C.: How do you feel? Do you feel that this course is going to invade your privacy?

ALEC: No.

A.O'C.: Why? Why do you feel so secure?

ALEC: That's the way I am. I'm free and loose.

A.O'C.: Let's see if I've got all your names straight. (Identifies each member of the group.)

A.O'C.: Brownie, what do you think about this? We've had kind of a small crisis to begin with.

BROWNIE: I missed it all. (General laughter)

NICK: I don't know what this course is. I'm looking forward to it. In one all Negro college, we had small groups like this in a psychology class. It's unlimited, I think. For those who have not had a great deal of experience, it's great. For those who have, it's still great and it's an opportunity to meet yourself, more or less. For those who feel like they know themselves, there's just no end to it. You aren't going to learn how Einstein developed his theories or anything like that; but you're going to learn things about yourself . . . things that are invaluable in other courses from now on. I'm really looking forward to it. I have high hopes for it.

A.O'C.: Thanks. I hope we meet those high hopes.

A.O'C.: Ella, how do you feel about this course?

ELLA: I think I'll like this course. . . . I think I'll be able to express myself better after this course.

A.O'C.: Ella, your voice is so quiet, would you change places with that fellow so we can hear you on the tape recorder? (An exchange of seats) Thank you.

A.O'C.: I hope we can live up to the expectations. Let's first define what each of you would like to do. Each of us has some kind of idea about what's going to happen. And you must have something you particularly would like to do in terms of "I."

ALEC: Ah . . .

A.O'C.: (Teasing) Alec, you're one of our "starters," why don't we begin with you.

ALEC: (Teasing back) Gee, thanks! What I'm expecting out of the course!

A.O'C.: What would *you* like to get out of the course?

ALEC: Well, a good grade to begin with. I need that. But mainly, in my opinion, the best thing for me would be to learn something about myself. Nobody can honestly say, well, draw a diagram and say this is me. I mean, no one person can do it. In high school they have a book called *Mirrors*.

A.O'C.: What high school was that?

ALEC: Centerville High School. And you read these things. And all it is is a story about a boy who's withdrawn. Almost every story has some particular characteristic this boy has that *you* have. They've designed it this way. And you can honestly see yourself in place of this boy. And in group discussion the students get to express their problems and how they came out of it and how they're trying to solve it. I mean, maybe the stories don't have their exact problem, but something similar to it. In groups like this, you can try to figure yourself out and remedy your own problems.

A.O'C.: Can you say an "I?"

ALEC: I said "I."

A.O'C.: Using "I," what would you particularly like from the course? Let's use "I" rather than "You."

ALEC: All right. I rather would like to find myself as I truly am, or something of this sort.

A.O'C.: This is, to me,—I don't know how the rest of you feel—the purpose of education.

ALEC: Well, no, you couldn't honestly say that . . . in this day and age you're demanded to have an education. You can't just say "I'm a great worker and everything." The guy says, "Well, what degree do you hold? You don't hold one. Well, I'm sorry, here's a guy with a degree." He might not be better than you, but he's got a degree and he gets the job.

A.O'C.: Okay. That's a very concrete reason for going to college but you're saying that over and above this . . .

ALEC: This is a place where you don't learn academic facts. I mean, this wouldn't be an academic course. It would be something here that you could treasure yourself.

A.O'C.: Okay, so at least beside the requirement, you can get something out of it.

ALEC: Right.

A.O'C.: Thanks, Alec.

Who else would like to try? Dexter?

DEXTER: Like I said a while ago, it's not going to get you a job but it's going to enlarge your mind. You got to find yourself. What it's supposed to do: I don't think it's going to build your knowledge like in other studies. It's going to build your person. Some people, they make straight A's; they come out; they can study but all they know is a book. In their spare time, they read and read. They don't go out and socialize or go hunting.

A.O'C.: Can you say "I" now?

DEXTER: I don't know. (Alex laughs.)

A.O'C.: You're saying you want to grow as a person—

DEXTER: I need to understand things. More self-control . . .

A.O'C.: Good, good.

DEXTER: More determination . . . I can't put it into words.

A.O'C.: For hunting. I bet you do.

DEXTER: I know I can study . . . and it won't take but a few minutes to do it but I can't get down to reading and I can't adjust inside myself to doing that. Like "working out." I'm supposed to "work out" this quarter and all it takes is a schedule inside myself. . . . And making time for everything.

A.O'C.: I think I hear what you say. You want more discipline. You want to be able to concentrate your efforts at school.

Someone else? Brownie? Do you want to try?

BROWNIE: I'll go ahead.

A.O'C.: If it's painful, don't.

BROWNIE: It isn't! Ah . . . I love to do this. It's just kind of strange. Ah, what I want out of this is ah . . . is mental maturity.

A.O'C.: Mental maturity . . .

BROWNIE: Ah . . . I want to know why people think the way they do. And to have the ability to express yourself to other people.

A.O'C.: So you're saying, "I would like to be able to express myself." We're practicing "I." Could you rephrase it with "I"?

BROWNIE: Ah . . . let's see . . .

A.O'C.: It's hard, isn't it?

BROWNIE: No. *I* . . . need the ability to express myself better. That's it.

A.O'C.: Good! I *know* we'll be able to help you. I know this because it's one of the things that students say when they finish the course. "I can express myself better than I've ever been able to." "I'm not so shy." "I'll talk with a group." I don't know how many people have been able to say, "Well, it's taught me to study." I'm not so sure of that.

ALEC: It could teach him how to set up his determination, though!

DEXTER: I can do this outwardly, but inwardly, I can't. . . . Like last quarter, I set my pattern down. I knew what I wanted inside and

I studied for your first two tests and I passed them good. But for the other two I played cards, I couldn't set a pattern inside. I think I'll be able to set up a pattern, I think. I know what I want; I just can't get it.

(Two new girls walk in.)

A.O'C.: Come on in, Maria, Myrna; I'm glad to have you. Have a seat.

(We all laugh because we are all crowded together in a small office.)

We're very together! This is the best we could do.

DAVID: Yeah! We're real together here.

A.O'C.: A little crowdedness. . . . We're talking about what each of us (using the word *I*) wants to get out of this course. So far, there has been expressed: One said he wants to find himself. One said he would like to be able to express himself better, and of course, "mental maturity" was one of the phrases he used. One said he would like to learn how to discipline himself *inside* for book learning, for what it takes to go to school. . . . Am I expressing you right?

DEXTER: Yeah, and but also like "working out." I don't "work out" like I should.

A.O'C.: . . . Over any kind of activity . . .

DEXTER: Yeah, get things done.

A.O'C.: Do you want to take a crack, Stefan?

STEFAN: Well, I want to know how I'm doing. . . . I want to know people and me too. What are *they*, too!

A.O'C.: When you say you want to know how to deal with people . . .

STEFAN: No! I don't know whether the way I am dealing with people now is right or wrong!

A.O'C.: Stefan, I have a very personal reaction to you. People like you right away. You're very open and I get the impression that you know this, too.

STEFAN: But I want to find out *what* I do . . . for people to like me.

(General laughter)

DAVID: He says, "Hi!"

A.O'C.: He says, "Hi!" He goes forward to meet people, doesn't he?

DAVID: Well, he doesn't go backward, that's for sure!

(General laughter)

A.O'C.: Isn't it amazing for a person who hasn't lived in the U.S. . . . (actually, he's lived all over the world.)

DAVID: Stefan, you're a man of the world.

STEFAN: I have lived in different countries but not all around the world. I can't talk about people; I talk about myself. I want to see if I do something wrong with some people.

A.O'C.: He's already an open personality; he wants to become more open. Isn't that right?

STEFAN: That's right.

A.O'C.: Nick?

NICK: I want something like he said. I don't think I have any trouble meeting people. I know when I was a freshman and first started to school, I could study and make good grades and all, but during class discussion if someone said something I didn't agree with, if it wasn't the same point I was on, I felt not insulted but "run over" a little bit. I never could understand why other people didn't think like I did. . . . Like what I was saying wasn't important and it was . . . one of the most important things going on at the time. It was meeting other people and understanding other people and talking to other people. It kind of develops your attitude and you can understand not *why* people say things, but that people have a *right* to say other things and you begin to listen to what other people are saying. And you try to work it out. . . . What you're saying and what they're saying and how it all fits together so if you put the puzzle together it all makes one big picture.

A.O'C.: Can you make a very clear statement with "I"? If you can't don't worry.

NICK: I'm not holding back; I just don't know what to say. I want to meet other people. I want to be able . . .

A.O'C.: To understand others better?

NICK: To be able to *accept* others better. To be able *to recognize* other people.

A.O'C.: To *accept, to recognize* . . .

NICK: To recognize them, I think! . . . I feel I recognize myself. I know what I am and I know basically where I'm trying to go but on the way, I understand now that I can't get there without other people. It's no longer me alone. But I know that other people are going to be there waiting for me and along the side of the road I should greet people I know, and know people and know why they're standing there . . . .

A.O'C.: *Experience* other human beings?

NICK: That's the only way we can be a *real, real, real* person.

A.O'C.: A real, real person . . . (April and Nick both laugh.)

Maria, I've never seen such a natural introduction, using your phrase. I guess it wasn't really your phrase. Would you like to follow? Or shall we go to Ella?

(Maria nods.)

ELLA: Well, first I'd like to be able to express myself in the group and class discussions and to sometimes understand myself. I do things, and I don't understand myself sometimes. And maybe in this course I can learn why other people do different things.

A.O'C.: So what you're looking for is to express yourself, understand yourself. I know we'll be able to help you. As I said before, this is the one thing that students have said.

Myrna?

MYRNA: This may seem crazy but she was talking about doing things and you don't know why you do them. I do a lot of things—mostly on impulses—and most of them turn out right. This may seem very crazy . . . like ESP. Most people would think I am crazy for believing that.

A.O'C.: Myrna, are you saying that when you follow your impulses you act correctly?

MYRNA: Ah . . . usually.

A.O'C.: Then what is it you want from the course?

MYRNA: Well, mostly I wanted to know my inner self. And maybe to know the reasons for what I do. I really think nobody knows what they are doing, that what I do is jump into things without really looking.

A.O'C.: Do you like that method of behaving?

MYRNA: Well. . . . (Everybody laughs.)

A.O'C.: Does it ever go wrong when you follow your impulses?

MYRNA: Sometimes.

A.O'C.: Sometimes . . .

Maria, by the way, do we all understand that we can always pass? (All nod.) Do you understand that, Maria?

MARIA: Oh, yes, I know that. (She smiles.)

A.O'C.: You know that's the first time I've seen you smile. You look beautiful. (Some laughing in agreement.)

MARIA: This reminds me of something. We've been doing this for about a year now—it's group therapy, with young people my age. They call it "Young Adults." We just sit around for an hour or two and talk and smoke and get put on tapes and television.

A.O'C.: Maria, where is that?

MARIA: This is at Centerville Health Center. I'm really not afraid of it. I've been doing it for so long now.

A.O'C.: Maybe this (course) will be a drag and a bore.

MARIA: No. I enjoy it. But when I talk out . . . (rest is inaudible).

A.O'C.: I'll never make you talk unless you want to talk. *I* won't. Maybe somebody else will challenge you. Maybe someone else will say, "Maria, I think you really want to talk," and encourage you. I don't know.

NICK: You know, one time in the service I was a chaplain's assistant and we had seven or eight chaplains' assistants—a Jewish boy, two or three Catholic boys, and some Protestant fellows. We had quite a few arguments. We didn't argue religion but we just argued about who was going to do this work and who was going to do that work because it all had to be done. But one day, we got into a latrine—all of us, all seven or eight of us—and we said now let's get this over with, let's stop this arguing . . . and one brilliant guy thought up this idea . . . let's all get together and chew each other out. Take turns and say what you wanted to say about everybody else and see if that doesn't clear the air, and we'd start all over again. We just started and we'd take turns, "Well, I'm going to start with you."

A.O'C.: A truth session? They can be painful.

(General laughter in agreement)

NICK: We were going to go around in a circle. Here we were, all sitting on the concrete floor, in the middle of the latrine. (Laughter)

A.O'C.: May I just interpose something? I understand sometimes they do this in a girls' dormitory—they call it "lemon sessions." And they tell terrible things to each other in order to straighten them out in some way. I think . . . that's awful.

(Laughter)

Alec seems to demur.

All right, I'll debate that with you. No, I won't debate that— ah, no! I'll discuss it with you. You have a right to your opinion. Well, let's finish this first.

NICK: Well, first of all, a little boy started. He was a real short kid and he was from Providence, Rhode Island. He said, "I'm going to start over here and he went all the way around the circle saying everything bad he could about us that he felt. And we just stood there like this, you know. He went all the way around this way and it got back to Ernie and he said, "Wait a minute, I'm not finished." He started again and, before he got through with the first fellow, he was talking about himself. He began to cut himself down . . . talking about himself, saying things he knew were wrong with him. And when he was finished, the next guy started, and we went all the way around like that. And by the time we got through we were so . . . there was nothing left. There was no animosity . . . we all ratted on ourselves to each other and when we went back to work, it was fabulous.

A.O'C.: You mean you all got out into the open the things that had been bothering you?

NICK: Yeah! We started off in a real good way. We cut each other down. We all could do that . . . we were good at it because for about three weeks we'd been batting back and forth, you know, cursing each other . . . and we'd fight every minute.

ALEC: Chaplain's assistants . . . (Laughter)

A.O'C.: This way, you got out into the open all your irritations?

NICK: Yeah, and when we started next time there weren't any real irritations left.

A.O'C.: You continued this?

NICK: Every day, for a year!

A.O'C.: You mean you had an encounter group going all by yourselves?

NICK: For 20 minutes, every afternoon, before we'd leave work. Every day.

A.O'C.:   That's extraordinary!

NICK: Every day. It was fabulous! I still hate one of the guys. (Laughter)

A.O'C.:   Go ahead, Alec. I'd like to know what you have to say about lemon sessions.

ALEC: I can't talk about the girls' dormitory lemon sessions but I started one of our own at Centerville High School. I was President at the time, or let's say Coordinator, because I wanted to get the work done. And there were some guys and they were going to have a cut session.

A.O'C.:   You called it a "cut session . . ."

ALEC: I called it a cut session because . . .

A.O'C.:   You were going to "cut" each other . . .

ALEC: Well, we were going to rat on somebody . . . it's true it's going to hurt somebody. It turned out that everybody found themselves. This was mainly with the officers—they weren't doing their work and everything and I was doing half their work. I mean, no club could work that way, so I had to do something. So I figured this would work and it did. We got in there and we dressed the officers down and we started going; and after I finished, they did the same thing to me.

DAVID: They cut *you* down.

ALEC: Yeah, they cut me down. And they said I pushed too hard and stuff like that. It was true. I was. I knew I was. It was a fact that I was doing their work. At least that's the excuse I used. You know, everybody tried to defend themselves later . . . but . . .

A.O'C.:   May I make a point? That you, Alec and Nick, experienced a situation where you all lived together and that in some small ways you bothered each other. Your group was a kind of release of hostility which made your conditions easier to be with each other and to be better friends afterward. But we meet as relative strangers. . . . So I'm going to establish one of the small ground rules. We have a few already. One is a kind of confidentiality. We don't gossip. I'm not worried about this because this automatically comes as we meet together. I mention it at the beginning but it comes of itself. Just automatically, the group assumes that nobody gossips; because nobody is interested in it.

The second ground rule is the use of *I*—that's very hard.

ALEC: You got that on me the first day!

A.O'C.:   I know I did. (Both laugh.)

It's hard to use the word *I*—we tend to use the word *they* or *you*— that puts it away from us.

The third rule is courtesy to each other. Not a courtesy in terms of *please* and *thank you*—not a social courtesy, but a courtesy that comes from being considerate of the other person. Every person here is right about what he thinks. His acts may be wrong, and his conclusions may not agree with yours, but he has a right to his opinions; they are valid.

So we listen to a person, really listen, and try to understand how he is right to himself.

DEXTER: It would be nice if everyone felt that in the world.

A.O'C.:   If we attack his opinions . . . let us suppose he has some outrageous idea . . . let's say that he thinks that the President is a communist. I don't think there are many people in their right minds who would say that he is a communist (laughter), but supposing he did . . . but if we shut him up and attacked him, he would not be able to express *why* he thought so, and . . .

DAVID: He'd resent it, too.

A.O'C.:   He'd resent it and he'd only become more convinced that we were all communists. . . .(General laughter)

And that it's a kind of conspiracy and that we don't give him a chance to think his way through and to reveal his reasons. Now this doesn't mean we can't ask, we can't challenge, but we don't attack. . . . Is this anything like you've experienced? Or is it a little more "wild" in your group?

MARIA: We have three psychiatrists and a psychologist and two or three students and they're always constantly attacking. It seems like every move you make . . . every flick of your eyelash . . .

A.O'C.:   You're "interpreted." They make an interpretation. . . .

STEFAN: *Make* her *talk*. They give her a line to start talking, you know. I saw this some place on TV. They make the patient talk.

A.O'C.:   (To Maria) Do you sometimes have the feeling that everything you say is going to be held against you?

MARIA: No . . . it's just that they *watch* you and you'll be talking about something and they watch you do this and they watch you do that.

A.O'C.:   I've been told by students that I have a bad habit and I wish you'd help me get over this by calling it to my attention so I can do something about it. I tend to interrupt people and don't give them a chance to think. This is one thing I can get out of our meetings this term.

ALEC: Do you promise not to get mad? (General laughter)

A.O'C.:   No, I don't promise not to get mad but I promise not to hold it against you.

(General laughter)

I can't control my feelings. . . . I may take umbrage and feel riled and . . .

(More laughter)

DAVID: Yeah . . . oh, what were your reactions?

ALEC: Oh, I reacted on just a few subjects . . . and, let's see . . . I . . . I *disagree*. I mean, I know Terry and you . . . but, I'm like him.

When you said "really like" . . . you said nobody can understand what you're *really* like. And the main thing that started getting me was . . . back here on page seven . . . was your word, "so many young people say the reason is their unhappy childhood." *So many.* All right, I go along with . . . there's *quite a few*, but what we consider a small hurt as a boy . . . big deal! It's part of growing up, but that doesn't necessarily mean you've had an unhappy childhood. But the way Terry puts it is . . . let's see. . . . *"Very few* people have a stable, good, happy life" as a child . . . . He says your father gives you a car, my father's given me two cars and I'm on my third . . . actually, he's paying for the school, I'm paying for the car, or vice versa . . . and, ah . . .

A.O'C.: Is what you're saying, that *you* didn't have an unhappy childhood?

ALEC: Well . . . everybody has some hurts. I mean, I spent two years off and on in the hospital because I got shot in the eye. But, I mean, if someone wants to say, "Golly, you had an unhappy childhood, I mean it wasn't really unhappy. I was eight years old, and I probably don't remember it.

A.O'C.: You got shot in the eye and it wasn't unhappy!

(General laughter)

ALEC: That's the way I am!

A.O'C.: Can you see out of the eye?

ALEC: Well, I've got light perception—dark and light.

A.O'C.: Which eye is the one you can't see out of?

ALEC: This one. The one that's got this funny-looking pupil. But, I mean, just because some guy . . .

(Laughter)

But that doesn't mean you've got an unhappy childhood necessarily . . .

DEXTER: Being in a hospital for two years?

ALEC: Off and on.

A.O'C.: I think what you are saying is that . . .

DEXTER: That being in a hospital off and on could have been worse than two years straight.

A.O'C.: Well, that growing up is painful and things that mean so much to us as children . . .

ALEC: It's part of growing up!

A.O'C.: They don't mean so much to us as adults but as children they could frighten us to death.

ALEC: Like you wanted a bicycle. Santa Claus didn't bring you a bicycle. So what! You didn't get your bike!

A.O'C.: I can agree with you that *you* did have a happy childhood in spite of a trial . . . good Lord, a physical trial of being off and on in a hospital for two years. . . .

DAVID: I had to go into the army and I didn't very much want to go!

A.O'C.:   Yeah! I can very well contemplate that people can look back and say they had a happy childhood.

ALEC: True! But the way Terry gave his life—well, it sounds like Abe Lincoln! You know, living in a log cabin and being illegitimate. I don't know that Abe Lincoln was illegitimate. . . .

A.O'C.:   Are you thinking Terry was?

ALEC: That's what it said! (Look again.) Excuse me, I must have misread it.

(General laughter)

I thought I read it; excuse me, I didn't mean to say that if it wasn't true. I *thought* I read it. I'm sorry.

(General laughter)

But anyway, his life with nature. Gosh! So many people give their lives for it.

A.O'C.:   He *did* say he got that much. That was something special.

ALEC: Like I like hunting. This is the greatest! Like I go and freeze in the morning just to go out and go hunting. Like last night . . .

(A discussion of Alec's hunting bobcats the preceding night ensues.)

A.O'C.:   Does anyone want to respond to Alec's refusal to take Terry's statement that everybody has an unhappy childhood?

You, Stefan?

STEFAN: I had an unhappy life when I grew up.

A.O'C.:   You mean it is unhappier now than it was then?

NICK: I did! I had an unhappy childhood.

A.O'C.:   Did you?

NICK: Yeah!

ALEC: You didn't get your tricycle!

NICK: I never got a tricycle in my life!

STEFAN: That doesn't mean you had an unhappy childhood!

A.O'C.:   Nick is saying that he knows what unhappiness is.

ALEC: Well, you've got to have a ground rule. What is happiness? What is unhappy to me is different than to Terry.

A.O'C.:   Yeah. What was it to Terry?

ALEC: What is it to Terry and what is it to me? That's where the conflict comes in. To define happiness.

A.O'C.:   What was it to Terry as you read it?

ALEC: Well, he didn't really have a father.

A.O'C.:   Right! That's one essence of his unhappiness.

NICK: Mine was just the same as yours, I suppose.

A.O'C.:   The same as *mine*?

NICK: My mother died when I was seven. There were 11 kids. My father left, and my two brothers and I went to an orphanage home and stayed for a year; then we got out and stayed with some more people, and then we came back to our own home town and stayed with our family. Then my father came back and I stayed with him for another year, and then I went back to my home town and stayed with my aunt about three or four years, and it went on like this for 18 years. I never got a new pair of shoes. I bought them [my first pair of shoes] myself when I got in the service. And, it's unhappy! The question I had was when *you* were talking about being ashamed and Terry was too—at what point do you become *unashamed*? There's a thing here . . .

A.O'C.:   Did this speak to you, Nick? This shame of having had an unhappy childhood?

NICK: Yes, very much. Very much! My wife had no conception of what an unhappy childhood meant! Her father was an ex-serviceman and they weren't rich, but they had enough money to give her anything she wanted and she didn't have the problems I had and it was hard for me to open up—to my *wife*, even! And to let her know what my life was like before I met her. Because by the time I met her, by the time I started college, I had made my own stake in life, so to speak . . . and I knew where I was going and where I wanted to go. It curved four or five times (it's curving now) but . . .

A.O'C.:   I'm not completely sure that *I'm* over all my shame.

NICK: I know I'm not in as secure a position to be unashamed— where I'm able to say, "Ha! Ha! Ha! It happened to me." Maybe when I get a Ph.D. I can say to myself, "Well, you got the Ph.D. in spite of. . . ." Then I'll be able to say "Ha! Ha! Ha!"

A.O'C.:   Do you think that *my* getting a Ph.D. (you may be right) —helped me?

NICK: It has to be!

A.O'C.:   That it was a mark for me that I'd overcome this background—and the same for Terry?

NICK: I feel I've got to reach some peak! Some recognition somewhere, where I can say, "Ha! Ha! Ha!"

A.O'C.:   "I overcame it!"

NICK: Yeah! True! If I go back to my home town. . . . Everyone in Franklin, Kentucky, knows me because of what I was in high school, my social position, I was a football player. . . . I knew everybody in town; I dated one of the richest girls in town, and stuff like that. But everybody knows that, behind me is all that trash in the garbage can, and to open up the lid and say, "Ha! Ha! Ha!" to the trash inside the garbage can, I've got to get out of the garbage can and be able to leave it alone, and say I'm beyond it! And to go back to it, and walk the streets. . . . But I'm no longer stuck there. And I think one of these days when I reach a peak, I can do that, I hope! But I do feel there has to be a peak! Something for me to reach to—some goal.

A.O'C.:   Thank you. I think we've come to a natural close. We've had a good beginning.

(General laughter)

End of Session

8

the process of the human encounter group

The first meeting of a human encounter group is full of questions, concerns, fears, and hopes:

BEN: One, two, three, four, five, six, and *he* makes seven—counting me makes eight. Eight of us sitting here like a bunch of loons wondering what to do. Why doesn't *he* say something? Isn't *he* the teacher, the leader, the great group facilitator, whatever they are called? The handout indicated he had three degrees; he oughta know something for God's sake. There, he crossed his arms, maybe that's a signal we are about to begin. What the hell? He just keeps sitting there and looking at us, probably sizing us up one by one.

JOAN: I must get a new pair of shoes—these are scuffed so badly. There's a store by Brocks that is having a sale—$8.98 a pair, I may buy two pairs if mother will give me the money. Those are pretty shoes she has on—wish I could wear that style, but . . . I wonder what she's *really* like inside. I won't look at her, I'm not going to look up at all—the way *he* looked at me, when I came in, as if he knew me! I won't look at anyone. I'll just sit here and answer their questions—if they ask me any.

PEGGY: What would they say if they knew what I was thinking and feeling? I know they are impressed with how I look—people always are. The little, mousy one keeps sneaking looks at me and I can see her eyes turning green with envy. Poor soul, if she only knew. What if they all knew! Is that what we are supposed to do here—tell each other about how we think and feel? Wouldn't they be shocked to know that Miss Beautiful doesn't feel so beautiful after all. God, how many times have I been over and over this story with myself! On the outside I'm as cool as they come, poised, always the right clothes, and I know exactly what to say about nothing at exactly the right time. And people keep flocking to me as if I really had something to give. But I don't let them fool me. I know the hurt in me, the well of tears that is just underneath, the feeling that it's all a game, with me in charge. Would anyone love me if I weren't pretty—hey, that's enough for now—don't lose your cool right at the start—they might throw you out or you might throw yourself out! I wonder if that's what we are supposed to do in this group—learn to lose our cool?

ALBERT: Let's go, man. We've fooled around enough and that Gloria, or whatever her name is, is going to talk our heads off if we don't get started. I know where I want to begin—with this weird dream I had last night. I've read some Freud, and I want to see if they see the same thing I see in the dream. Maybe they can psychoanalyze me—that would be great, man! And I can help the Doc there, too, with all the names. I'm pretty good at analyzing my friends: George has an Oedipus complex, Sally is bordering on schizophrenia, when Charles drinks too much at the Friday night parties he becomes a manic depressive, and Lou is just plain screwy. Let's get the show on the road, Doc; this is going to be a blast.

GLORIA: (Aloud) I asked Miss Jessup about this group and she told me it was a big waste of time, and I would be better off to do individual research, and besides a lot of kids didn't like it. They said all you do is sit around and talk. I'm sure that's not true of course; that it's really to help people who have serious emotional problems. Like this roommate of mine. She is really nuts and ought to take a course like this. She's all the time talking about her parents and the Establishment.

She's really messed up. I suppose a course like this would be good for a person like her. Of course, it probably can't do us any harm either. It'll give us a chance to get to know people. I suppose the best way to start is to introduce ourselves and tell where we came from and what we're going into and. . . . (Why don't I keep my big mouth shut? Why do I always think I have to keep things going?)

DAN: I wish I felt better about being here. I've wanted to have this kind of experience for a long time—there are so many things I want to explore. Lately it seems I'm not making much headway on my own no matter how much time I spend reading and working on myself. I've talked with me so long now I know all the questions and answers I will give to me; they don't satisfy anymore. If I only knew what I really wanted—peace, happiness, joy—these must be the right words, but I don't think I have any real idea of what they mean. I've known a little of each or I wouldn't make such intense demands on myself for more. Will I ever really know how to live my life? Will I just get better at asking that question or will I begin to accept some understanding of the answer? I'm worn out with this struggle; I hope this group will help. I will work hard in here, but I'm concerned that others will only play at working. I wish I had a little more confidence in them, but they seem so distant: something must really be bugging the girl who is talking so much, but the beautiful girl seems to know who she really is and seems to enjoy it. I wish I were that cool.

BARBARA: I wonder if I should say something. I'm tired of listening to that girl chatter on and on about herself. Are we supposed to say things right out when we feel them in a group? What if someone says something to me I don't like? Will I leave, get angry, or cry? I probably will blast right back for I can give it as good as it comes. If someone doesn't say something pretty soon I'm going to ask why. Maybe when I ask that, someone will say something. The leader should cut that girl off and get us started; if he doesn't do something in a minute then I'm going to. I don't like this one damn bit. What are we supposed to do!

STAN (The Group Facilitator):   I suppose I oughta stop that girl and get us started. She's shaking up the troops and shaking me up a little, too. Wish getting started were a little easier for me. I'm never sure what my first words are going to be, and I'm always afraid they are going to catch in my throat. Well, might as well jump in and see how it goes.

These are contrived descriptions of the thinking and feeling of a new group about to begin the human encounter—contrived so they do not appear to be quite real. But they illustrate part of the flavor of a new group—the questions, doubts, fears, hopes—and perhaps most important of all, they show that each participant is already beginning to be in touch—tentatively and uneasily—with parts of his human beingness; each one knows that this is not a cocktail party or a discussion of Saturday's football game.

The human encounter is serious business. Most of our communication with others is at a level distinctly less intense, less direct, and less open than that of the human encounter. Also, we have become so conditioned to social interactions (to the casual, flip, verbal exchanges which pass for communication) that we find ourselves in a state of discomfort when we approach the situation of the human encounter. First, it is an experience which is out of the ordinary and anything new and extraordinary tends to cause us anxiety. We dread the unknown. Second, we have lived so long in a world described as "cold," "hostile," "a vale of tears," etc., that we are suspicious of the emotions of love, tenderness, honesty.

The authors are convinced that a few people experience the human encounter (are *real* in their relationships with others) as a way of life. Some people have probably had from birth the kind of living environment that affirms honesty, openness, trust, caring, relating (dimensions of the human encounter), and this allows them to relate in these ways with themselves and others. Still others may have achieved a style of human encountering by choosing to invent their own lives. Through reading, introspection, individual counseling, human encounter groups, and various other means a few others have developed life patterns that allow them to experience the human encounter as *weltanschauung* —a way of life. Most of us have met such people and recognize them as extraordinary human beings; that is, they differ markedly from the ordinary way most of us relate to one another.

As we have said, the human encounter is serious business: the purpose is to put us in touch with the deeper aspects of ourselves and to help us be in touch with others at that level. Since this is not our usual way of relating we are uneasy, out of our element; our comfort is disoriented. Such feelings, if they are recognized, help the group go beyond their first feelings of uneasiness, suspicion, fear.

First meetings of human encounter groups are similar. The following elements are most likely present in all first meetings:

THE PRELIMINARIES

Selecting Territorial Space. "I'm sorry, you have my chair." We know from the study of certain animals the importance of territory for living creatures. Lions, for example, stake out a certain area of the plains and invaders of the territory are attacked. Birds select a certain spot for a nest and sing to warn trespassers away from their area. Many of us have experienced the sharp rebuttal that comes when we have unknowingly placed our hand too close to a family of wasps.

Man also demands respect for his territory—the physical space in which he lives. He builds his nest in the middle of a plot of ground, and around his "castle" he often builds hedges not unlike the moats protecting ancient fortresses. Man locks his door and protects his family from the outside world. He gladly participates in a Halloween ritual, in which he bribes youngsters for their pledge not to act destructively on his territory.

Inside man's house the importance of territorial rights becomes even more apparent. Each family member has a special place to sleep —many have their own rooms—and a special chair to sit in at meal time. The "Father's Chair" commands respect and distance, at the dinner table and in the TV room.

The importance of territory is always with us, and the need for territorial space is probably one of the earliest dynamics in a newly formed group. Some members will immediately reach for the more comfortable chairs; others will take the most uncomfortable chairs as a matter of choice. Some will sit with their backs to the windows to avoid the glare of light; others will manipulate space and people to be near or far from the source of heat and coolness. Some group members will carefully arrange their space (fluff their nests) for more comfort by rearranging a pillow or pulling up another chair for a foot rest. Others will choose territories that border other special territories: next to the group facilitator, far away from the group facilitator, next to a pretty girl, next to a man who smells of shaving lotion, or next to their best friend. Sometimes the group selects a spot for the group facilitator and jealously guards the territory from any who would dare invade it.

We don't know much about the meaning of territory in man's life and very little about its importance in the human encounter group. We do know, however, that it is a dynamic in the group process and that each group member needs time to settle down in his own territory before he can orient himself to the group situation. Environment, we believe, is of such importance to the group encounter that we have included one whole chapter on that aspect alone. At any rate, each member needs a few minutes to find his territory by whatever personal processes he uses and a few minutes to fuss about arranging it for his occupancy. Once the territory has been staked out each member will usually return to the same territory following coffee breaks or in subsequent group sessions. For this reason, it is probably a good idea to continue meetings of the groups in the same environment. New environments mean new tasks of staking out territory which may interfere with some developing processes if repeated each time the group meets.

On the other hand, a change of environment with its consequent change in group dynamics is first aid for an apathetic or tied-in-knots group. It has implications also for the group that has grown so comfortable in their staked out nooks and crannies that nothing dynamic is happening. This area is an exciting one for research and should suggest some interesting experiments.

Introductions. "My name is Alice Jones. What is your name?" A name is our entrance to a person. Naming is the process by which a person is lifted out of the background of our unawareness to the foreground of our attention. It is by the process of calling someone by his name that we address him in the I-Thou relationship. By his name a man becomes not a thing, but a person to whom we can relate. By giving his name to us he invites us to know him; we give him our name and issue the same invitation.

Our need for knowing names is so important that despite the fact that we can't remember all the names much of the structure of a group's first communication has to do with introducing names. Some groups go around the circle asking each member to tell his name; others ask for some background or for a statement of what each hopes to get from the group, thus making it easier to relate the name to the person. Still other groups use name cards to pin on their clothing or to stand in front of them.

There is an obvious need to know names in a group—no one wishes to be addressed as "Hey, you." Some unobtrusive method could be introduced to accomplish this purpose or names could be learned as each person focuses attention on each other person during the course of group meetings. If the group is small names will be learned very readily, of course. The group facilitator should probably learn all names as quickly as possible and address members by their first names when he speaks to them. This example will help other members become comfortable with names and their comfort is probably important in building a framework for later group cohesion.

Getting a Set. "What are we supposed to be doing here?" Once members have been introduced to each other there are several approaches to moving into the process of the encounter. Often group facilitators will orient members to the process by telling them about some of the purposes of the encounter and by discussing some of the things they can expect to happen. Facilitators will usually indicate the kind of role they will be playing in the group and will often set up ground rules for the guidance of the group. Some typical ground rules are: (1) All members should attempt to listen to the person speaking and try to understand what is being said. (2) Members may talk about anything they wish. (3) Members must hold in strictest confidence all that is revealed in the group. (4) The group will always begin at a certain time and end at a certain time. Ground rules differ according to the facilitator, and some facilitators urge group members to set up their own ground rules.

A brief orientation in the beginning helps provide needed information so that group members can begin from some point of understanding. It also provides an opportunity for members to ask questions which may be bothering them about the purpose of the group and their involvement in the process.

Some group facilitators approach the encounter by asking all members to share in some activity. One popular method has been developed by Herbert Otto called the Depth Unfoldment Experience. In this approach each member communicates to the group in a brief period of a few minutes the incidents in his life that have been most important in forming his personality. This method and many others by Otto are described in greater detail in the book *Group Methods Designed to Actualize Human Potential* noted in the Bibliography.

Still other facilitators believe that groups should struggle with their own direction. In this kind of group the facilitator will listen carefully and reflect the mounting uneasiness and eventual frustration and even hostility. Such group facilitators believe that group members will define their own directions and will assume more responsibility for the group if they have to do so from the very beginning. Group members will hold "conversations" and will experience frustration but eventually they will move into the process in which interpersonal relationships are established. In this kind of group, members will ask for structure and guidance.

The Need for Structure and Authority. "I wish we would vote on an agenda. Why doesn't he tell us what to do?" Out of the frustration of not knowing what to do, group members will often revert to a call for orderly procedure. Someone will suggest an outline to follow; another will suggest a list of questions that each is to answer in turn. Some members who have read about the techniques used in groups will recommend that the members play roles or stand back to back for five minutes without talking.

Although most members feel the need for structure few of the suggestions find ready acceptance. Something in the group process must keep the group from boxing itself in with too much structure at this point. It is possible for skillful group leaders to use structured techniques to help the group develop cohesion, but group members may miss something in the experience of struggling to develop their own structure. The authors believe that each group is unique and has its own problems, its own patterns of relating, its own goals; techniques that structure group activity too early may tend to diminish the potential for idiosyncracy that resides in each group.

Because of the discomfort of the new opportunity for relating and the need for structure, group members in most groups will ask, and even demand, that the group facilitator assume an authoritarian position from time to time. Early in group sessions the demand is in terms of direction: "Why doesn't he just tell us how?" "Aren't there some guidelines to follow?" "What do you want us to do?" "Do you really know what you are doing?"

If the group facilitator does not respond to the group requests for structure and direction there is likely to be anger and open hostility. Group facilitators must be prepared to accept such anger and hostility and to help group members see the value in assuming responsibility for their own growth and direction.

The Silence. "Why doesn't someone say something?" Silences are likely to occur numerous times throughout the group process. Sometimes they will mean that a great deal of suffering is present; at other times the silence will be a recognition that a group member is struggling intensively with a concept or a feeling about himself. Embarrassing circumstances may cause silence. Exhaustion may bring a peaceful kind of silence. A period of silence may be a prelude to another stage of activity in the group process.

In the early phases of group process, silences are probably indications that the group is groping for direction and cohesion. Group members are silent because they do not know which way to go. Often in these early stages a quality of gamesmanship will develop in which group members spar silently to see who can hold out longest without making sounds. The focus shifts from any context of feeling that has gone on before and is concentrated on the "silent game." "I won't speak first." "What would happen if I suddenly blurted out with something?" "Why doesn't the leader say something?" Such silence becomes a deafening roar until someone breaks in and provides the relief that each wants.

The authors believe that such silences do not contribute to the development of the group; they may actually hinder the group process. Why should group members have to be deterred in their mission by the "silent game"? Is any good accomplished by allowing such silence to continue? The human encounter is serious business; person-to-person communication is the essence of that encounter. The "silent game" only blocks the channels of communication that must be open if encounter is to occur.

We know one reason why the devotion to silence is so prevalent among groups, and we feel that the group facilitator must assume responsibility for such silences. In the early interpretations of Rogers' *Client-Centered Therapy*, many counselors, counselor educators, and psychotherapists assumed that the facilitator should be "nondirective" in his approach to communication with others. "Nondirective" is usually interpreted to mean that the facilitator assumes no responsibility for the direction of the group process. The nondirective theory has been promulgated in graduate schools that prepare counselors, and one still hears the term pronounced with dignity as if it had real meaning. Practitioners of this approach feel that silences have major import in the group process. They will sit silently for hours waiting for the group to become self-directing. Some groups have been known to meet for only one hour with such "leadership."

The authors believe that there is little meaning in the nondirective approach. We have seen a number of counselors skillfully *directing* a group in their nondirectiveness. There are many positive factors associated with nondirectiveness that more properly should be associated with the more meaningful term *client-centered*, and these factors are discussed elsewhere in this book. When nondirective means not being involved, not going out—which is what encounter means—then we cannot accept it as having much use in facilitating human communication. When nondirective means allowing prolonged silence that is full of noise then it is absurd.

That is not to say, however, that all silences should be broken and interfered with. Silences that are not facilitating should be called to the attention of the group so that the group can get about its mission. Silences that are facilitating—ones alive with the sounds of a person growing—are immensely important and must be carefully nurtured to allow the growth processes to come to fruition. The group facilitator must have a keenly tuned self to hear the differences in the silent human sounds that group members make.

THE BEGINNING OF COMMITMENT

The Risk Taker. "I would like to share something with this group." Once the preliminaries are settled the group members become a little more comfortable with each other. The preliminaries have been a time of testing to see if the group facilitator will allow openness, honesty, and responsibility to emerge. Individual members have been testing each other, sometimes with direct questions, sometimes by listening to and observing their responses to others. At the point of tentative trust one person is usually brave enough to put the group to a major test by sharing an important part of his life.

This person can be called the *risk taker* or the *sharer* or the *starter*; he is usually present in all groups. It is not particularly important to describe here his personality characteristics—even if we knew how—for we are primarily interested in how his sharing affects the group process. In some cases the group facilitator may be the risk taker.

As authors we have not enjoyed naming things in this book because we are afraid readers will assume that there is some special magic in the naming. The authors named it that; therefore, it must be that thing. Naming, that is, categorizing events under selected titles, is important only for the sake of communication; our names only reflect our approach and our style—name your own things from your own experience. Thus with *risk taker*; we are concerned that you do *not* see the risk taker as a thing, an entity to be dissected, or most importantly as a *role* to be played. We are only saying that in our experience it appears to us that someone in a group takes a risk by sharing part of himself. It appears to be a natural development in the process of the human encounter; *it is not a role to be played.*

The risk taker probably senses some degree of trust in the group and probably has some need to share his self with others at the moment. The group facilitator will often be aware of the dynamic at work in the person and may facilitate his sharing by recognizing him: "What does that quizzical look on your face mean, John?" "Mary, would you like to tell us something?" "How does that make you feel, Bruce?"

The risk taker is that because he risks part of himself—he places part of himself on the table to see what the group will do with him. It is a most courageous act and one that leads to healthy consequences. In one sense the risk taker says to himself, "What the hell, what do I have to lose? I'll share this much. If they reject me for that it will be no worse than all the times I've been rejected in the past. If they accept me then I'll share more and more." Such sharing becomes the ground for the human encounter.

The risk taker may share himself through describing his feelings or by indicating that he has problems to work on. He has many beginnings: "I feel lost." "I'm not sure what we are supposed to be doing here, but I would like to tell you something that happened to me recently." "This is a new experience for me and I'm nervous about it." "I've never had a chance to be in a group like this and I'm very glad that I'm here."

In many instances the risk taker shares himself by telling his "story." Our story is not something we have made up in the sense of a fairy tale. *Our story is the way we talk to ourselves about how we came to be the way we are.* We have repeated it to ourselves many times. We keep our story close to us because it explains us to ourselves; it would help explain us to others if only we could share it.

Our stories are major events in our lives, the incidents that have played important roles in shaping our personalities. In a group it is very important that we be able to share these major events with others. When we have been able to reveal a hidden and troublesome aspect of our behavior to others we ease the burden of guilt that is usually associated with it. When others do not respond with reprimand and shock but with understanding and tenderness we are uplifted, we grow in trust, we begin to look at the incidents of our lives with new perceptions. The first time a group member shares his story with others can be one of the most rewarding experiences of his life.

Stories are often very long and elaborate, extending over a person's lifetime. In some cases they can reflect the activities of a single year or a single incident that was of great import in a person's life. They are usually quite real in the sense that they probably actually happened to the person, but the stories probably leave out important related events—the *whole* story is not told. The person telling the story probably cannot tell the whole story because he is not aware of it. The following accounts are abbreviated stories that illustrate the concept:

My mother died when I was seven. There were 11 kids. My father left, and my two brothers and I went to an orphanage home and stayed for a year; then we got out and stayed with some more people, and then we came back to our home town and stayed with our family. Then my father came back and I stayed with him for another year, and then I went back to my home town and stayed with my aunt about three or four years, and it went on like this for 18 years. I never had a bicycle in my life. I never got a new pair of shoes. I bought my first pair of shoes myself when I got in the service.

At this point in his story the teller brings it to the present and asks a very important question:

And it's unhappy! The question I had was when you were talking about being ashamed—at what point do you become *unashamed*?

He is asking: How can I come to accept my story?, or How can I discard it? That it is a story is clearly seen when he tells us that his wife doesn't understand it:

My wife had no conception of what an unhappy childhood meant! Her father was an ex-serviceman and they weren't rich, but they had enough money to give her anything she wanted and she didn't have the problems I had and it was hard for me to open up—to my wife, even! And to let her know what my life was like before I met her.

Another story of an unhappy childhood is described as follows:

I was always a dumb, dirty, pimpledy-faced kid. There was another kid like me in grade school, and we had a fight every day because one of us needed to win at something. My father drank too much, and we had to keep moving to new jobs—there was never any communication between us. We lived in a big old dirty-yellow house on a hill, and I used to pretend that it was the big house on the hill, but it was only a big old dirty-yellow house where a dumb, dirty, pimpledy-faced kid lived.

This was a very painful story to tell and some deep, bitter tears came with it. It touched others who had experienced much the same and there were many shared tears during the telling. Following the session the teller told how he had felt during the telling as if he were that little boy again. He was struck by the feeling that as he sat there in the group his feet could not touch the floor; he was fully experiencing his story in the moment of its telling.

There are other stories illustrated in this book. The authors tell theirs in the chapter The Authors Reveal Themselves. Others describe their stories in the chapter on Human Experiencing and in the chapter of a transcript of the group process. The concept of the story may be useful to group process as a way of asking others to share parts of themselves. It may be helpful for group members to write down their stories so they can be examined more closely.

The Sharing of Selves. "Thank you for sharing that with us—may I tell you my story?" Once the risk taker has broken the ice by revealing himself to the group, others are encouraged to share themselves as well. One group participant writes:

> You have made life more meaningful for me by letting me identify with you in your feelings of emptiness and indecision, by letting me tell you my story, and by pointing out directions which I might consider going from here on out.

Self-revealment begets self-revealment—this is a basic principle underlying the group process. Jourard in *The Transparent Self* and again in *Disclosing Man to Himself* (see Bibliography) provides a great deal of research evidence to support this principle. The act of revealing one's self to others assumes a measure of trust and confidence on the part of the one revealing. The person revealing himself says, "I have trust in you as human beings that you will not hurt me, and I am confident that if I tell you this you will know me better and, therefore, like me better—no matter what I tell you." Because he risks himself and is not cut down, we are willing to risk ourselves.

Openness, honesty, trust, and confidence begin to develop as group standards when others begin to reveal themselves. "It is now *safe* to tell my story. He told his and they listened and they seemed to care. Several people cried and one girl went over to him and put her arm around his shoulder. I feel they will accept me in the same way." The sharing of stories helps to build relationships.

THE BUILDING OF RELATIONSHIPS

Responses to the Stories. "I feel your pain. I am beginning to understand." Self-revealment requires response. If we share parts of ourselves that we don't usually share, we must have feedback. We must know how what we have revealed is received and how it affects others. If there is no feedback we are not likely to reveal ourselves again, for we most often interpret the lack of feedback as disapproval. It is difficult to conceive of a group in which there is no feedback.

Feedback usually comes to us as sympathy or empathy. There may be little difference in these terms, but *sympathy* has come to be identified by many as a kind of pity and smothering consolation. One group identified several of its members as "glad girls," who always responded to a person in terms of "Oh, you poor little thing. You have had such a difficult life. I feel so much for you." The classic statement typifying this kind of sympathy is "I know exactly how you feel."

Sympathy that smothers us with caring diminishes us as human beings. It communicates that we are weak and incapable and in need of mothering. Often such sympathy denies our very person. When someone reveals some negative feeling about himself and the sympathizer responds, "Oh, that isn't you at all. That couldn't be true about you. You are too good a person," then the person revealing not only has not been helped, he has actually been rejected. His honesty and his courage have been rejected as well as the fact of his feeling. Sympathy negates, denies, smothers, hides; sympathy offers false sweetness and light in the face of the reality of loneliness.

Sympathy is the conditioned response pattern of society. We receive sympathy from parents, peers, Boy Scout leaders, ministers, teachers, spouses, and even our children. At its best, sympathy is a kind of guarded caring for others, a willingness to become involved with their lives. It usually comes from good motives, and can develop into the more mature kind of caring known as *empathy*.

Empathy is the experience of *feeling with* another person, rather than smothering his feelings as sympathy does. Empathy is the struggle to understand how another person is feeling at the moment. The listener opens himself to the experiences of another person and *feels his feeling*. When people listen to (understand) another with mind and heart), then caring and accepting (loving) usually occur. "You cared enough to hear."

Empathy is communicated through such verbalizations as "I feel your pain." "I can see how much you are hurting." "I am beginning to understand." "I accept you as you are." It is also communicated through nonverbal cues: a touch of the hand, a big hug, shared tears, eye-to-eye contact, a nod of the head, the quieting of other persons who are not listening. Through such communication caring begins to be shared among group members, primarily between individuals and clusters of people in the group.

Mask Removing. "Won't you tell us who you really are?" When an underlying caring is evident in a group and when affection forms the base for further exploration, group members then become more able to remove their masks—that is, to examine the social roles and pretenses which pass for involvement with others. In mask removal there is an attempt to go beyond the façade, beyond the story that is told and shared. When mask removal occurs, group members are beginning to feel safe within the group, safe "to be really oneself." Hence the question, "Won't you tell us who you really are?"

When this question is first asked, it may be because the group has reached a moment of crisis and growth, a moment in which the call for intimacy and involvement with each other is needed. One group participant expressed this moment in these terms:

> The personal benefits (growth, liberation, well-being) occurring from encounter will increase or diminish with variations in honesty and openness. To me, only when we have the courage to accept the risks of pain, and even of damage, will we realize the value of encounter to its fullest. If we choose a route of avoidance, we are simply robbing ourselves of *becoming*, diminishing the experience of life—in a sense choosing *death*.

Each one, when it is time, struggles to remove the mask he has carefully built up over the years. We will need to *destroy* this mask, to take away its structure, for it binds us to our shell, and blinds us to the possibilities in ourselves.

Removing the mask sometimes can be painful and agonizing for those who participate with the person in his crisis. The pain comes from the situation itself, the experience of being without defenses. With *no* defenses—which is a *verbal concept* since even the person undergoing a psychotic episode has still *some* defenses even while his primary defenses are dissolved—the person is in a severe crisis situation. The unfamiliar experience of being *ultimately vulnerable to the world* can be shattering. Both danger and hope for growth arise from this situation.

If the group has a foundation of shared experiences, out of which comes the affection and understanding which provides safety for the members, this moment of crisis may be safely bridged. Without such a foundation, the person runs a greater risk that the crisis will become, with this brief moment of pain, an overwhelming experience of failure, of "being damaged essentially in oneself." Moments of crisis demand a kind of fundamental caring and affection for the person if he is to be helped through the pain until he completes his moment of growth and understanding. Without that caring he risks himself, and he often fails because he is met with yet another "mask."

It seems to us, however, that growth does not necessarily entail severe pain. We prefer an approach that is more gentle, less traumatic to the members. A bud of a flower opens in its own time and according to its own rhythm if we can be patient with it. If the bud of the flower is pried open too quickly the blossom may be destroyed. Each group member thus unfolds himself according to his own pattern and his own pacing if we support him in his coming-forward.

This is not to say that growth is a "piece of cake," a process in which one does not get his hair mussed up, or his self-esteem damaged now and then. For the old patterns of behavior will need to be destructured, and that always, in some measure, is painful for the person. In order that the old ways can be seen by others and by oneself, we must go "below" the upper edges of our accustomed behaviors; we must become intimate with our own central being. (Berne says games, roles, and masks are used so that a person can avoid the anxiety that comes with intimacy.)

This process of moving closer to our essential selves can be a frightening and painful experience, at least in the beginning. When we make the transition and remake ourselves in this moment of crisis, the experience then will have been successful; and it will be cherished. Before the moment of success, however, we experience anxiety, discomfort, and confusion; we are unsure of ourselves because our mask is for the moment gone. As one group participant described this experience:

> What has happened to me? It depends on which "me"—for I can shift into a sort of overdrive and take the hills and curves with hardly any effort. To this "me" nothing has happened—for there is no real life there. Things can happen only when there is life. But when the "me" whom I know as alive is continually unseen and/or deliberately blacked out, it is simply a matter of survival to shift into the overdrive. This is my deep terror—that one day the gear shift will get stuck in overdrive.
>
> To the "me" which I hope is the real me—something has happened. An infusion of oxygen, sort of—and the beginning of a greater unwillingness to be unseen and blacked out just in order to be alive. I say *beginning* for there is still no real staunch decision. It hurts too much—has hurt too much. And I am still not entirely convinced that any real purpose will be served. For the real me is a threat and an accusation against those elements where the power lies, and those elements will not accept this threat with equanimity. Yet, the most immoral thing one can do is to refuse to be who one really is.
>
> These encounter groups have made me more and more uncomfortable in my "overdrive"—and I feel I will eventually be able to really make the moral decision. The difficult thing is that *other* people are more comfortable with me in my overdrive gear shift—that is, *most* people. Some in this group have refused to let me stay there—God bless them!
>
> How do I feel now? I'm afraid—not a nameless fear but a fear based on a real grasp of the pain to come. A fear of running back like a coward—a feeling that it is better not to start at all than to start and then quit. Confused—I am still not sure of all boundaries. Very much alone, but not lonely—surrounded and supported, but without real contact.

This person expresses very clearly the existential vacuum of recognizing her aloneness in coming to terms with herself—in moving from one level of "me" to another level of "me." The mask is off; she has recognized what must be done in her life, but it is deeply painful for her to recognize it and to move forward in her growing. This is the human encounter with self brought about because others have shared in the human encounter with her—and she thanks them by saying "God bless them!"

Another group participant removes her mask piece by piece and exposes how she truly feels about herself:

> The first ugly is my fakery. I'm a phony! I'm not intelligent—I'm glib and well read. I'm not compassionate—I'm a lonely coward. I'm not a force—I'm a balloon, blown up by what people expect of me. I'm "socially ept" and lucky enough to look it—oh, God, what would I do if all the things I'm not showed on the surface?
>
> I'm a snob. Not a name-dropper perhaps—as much as a name-collector. There are tricks to attracting the name-people; I know them—the tricks, I mean—how have I managed to fool them so?

I'm greedy and self-centered. I want some of this for me. This what? The acceptance? The popularity? The sharingness?

She risked much by sharing these feelings about herself, and much more, in the group, but her courage served to encourage others. Mask removing is much like "story" telling except that the "story" is familiar behavior retold. Mask removing becomes a new experience for the remover and reveals new parts for his consideration. Story telling can remain a peripheral experience; mask removing goes straight to one's central being.

The knowledge that there is a deeper aspect of being in each of us is expressed by another group participant:

One of the outstanding changes that has taken place in me during this encounter is the decrease in my apprehension and fear of becoming a more open person to and in the group as well as to myself. I suppose that various events in my life in the past two years had enabled me to lose sight of the me who was an open, loving person as contrasted with the "me" now who is *devoid* of almost any feeling—positive (love) or negative (hate). I can only say that as I saw me in the last meeting I was and *am* at a good, happy time and place in my life as opposed to the hell which I had been growing out of but which evidently left me without feeling—registering only what others wanted to see.

When I met one of our group facilitators who was so obviously (to me) full of warm and open love, I saw a reminder of what I had once been. I did much thinking after the last meeting and must admit I was anxious and fearful. But I came to realize that to avoid further exploration would only result in a sameness of emotion. I feel (perhaps wrongly) that I am a strong individual and perhaps a "loner" who has never fully trusted too many (only one) other people with the real me. This week I began to *love* as well as *hate*—a luxury which I have not embraced for some time. I am still probing myself and realize that I have much growing to do, but I also know that I am on the *brink* of awareness. I only hope that I can share this with my friends, students, and loved ones for their enrichment also.

This person says "I used to be the real me, but something terrible happened so I put on a mask to be devoid of any feeling." This is a common experience for many of us, perhaps the reason we put on masks—to keep from feeling because life hurts so much. But a person in the group reminds her of how she used to be—of her real "me"— and she begins to move forward to being herself again. She could stay where she is; after all, compared to a former hell, she is now in a "good, happy" time and place—that is, it hurts to feel so not-feeling is now a good place to be. But the sameness of not-feeling (existential death) is no longer an alternative because she has been encountered in a group—she has gone out to the group facilitator and has felt love—given and received—and now she can even feel the goodness of hate again. She will continue to encounter others and herself and hopefully will learn to wear her own face with all the beauty that can be transmitted through it to others.

Group Recognition of Closeness. "Do you feel this good thing that is happening to us?" From time to time group members will gauge the group feeling and point out the feeling of closeness that exists. Such feelings of group cohesion and caring often follow intense sessions of mask removing or story telling and are very important for the development of a "we" feeling in the group. It is this feeling of solidarity, a mutual bond of trust and caring, that allows individuals to explore and experiment with their own growth and development. It is the same primitive feeling that exists in primary family groups that allows members of the family to go out and confront the world because they know they can come back to the security of the basic family group. In one sense the human encounter group becomes a family unit, the primary purpose of which is to share love.

Only *most* members need feel this closeness for it to provide the security needed for further progress. Some members will not feel the closeness even though they recognize the feeling in others and wish to share in it. Still others will remain highly skeptical and will feel that the closeness is artificial and contrived. Some group members may never feel the group warmth and still may benefit from being in the group. There is a peacefulness, however, that does come from experiencing shared love with other human beings, a peacefulness well worth being open to.

The kind of group recognition of closeness, the recognition of a common bond and a common purpose, being discussed here is not particularly intense and spectacular. It is rather as if there were some degree of understanding regarding unity—it tends to lessen when attention is called to it. We are sometimes embarrassed to recognize that we have been drawn close together or we are mildly skeptical, feeling that it's too good to be true. These experiences of closeness have been described by a number of group participants:

> Today was good. I felt near and dear to several persons. Their expressions of themselves helped me; they reached out to me and I to them. Across a room I felt a kinship—a love. There was giving and receiving. It was good, disturbing, too, but good.
>
> I came to this conference expectantly since I know what can happen when individuals become interrelated parts of a "unified I." But even though I *know*, the glory of it is new each time, and each time I grow a little. This group has been an ever-increasing joy.

Some group members experience the unity of a group in a religious sense. For them there is a communion of spirit, a communication among the beings that moves beyond beings and becomes *being*. Expressions of such experiencing seem to indicate that such persons gain a great deal from the human encounter for through their experience they are in touch with the ground of being, the common human element that binds men together and perhaps, in a religious sense, transcends human individuality.

> It's 2:00 A.M. and I'm still thinking about what the hell is going on within me. I keep thinking about what went on today—I'm excited! Maybe this was group catharsis, but there was more. So I have uncertain and unspecified feelings. Spontaneity, expression of feeling, love, and anger are some of the elements.
>
> I don't think I could have felt so deeply about others—in a caring way—if it had not been for this experience. . . . I'm so eager to see the others next time!

Sometimes the closeness is in terms of *we*, but it is quite often in terms of expressions of caring for individuals. The group becomes the place we can care for another in an open, safe way. When a number of people care for several people, caring is compounded and helps to create a climate of closeness in the group. In one group of faculty members following the second meeting (each meeting was for two days) of their encounter the following expressions of caring for individuals indicate the closeness in the group:

> I was most surprised to learn that I liked and respected Ruth—she is a deep, sincere, and highly intelligent woman.
>
> My feelings for Tom have opened up! My first feelings were anger—he was opposing and lacked an understanding of Ruth. This was really difficult to tolerate. Then Tom became a real, genuine person that I had compassion for. I really like Tom now and I am so glad.
>
> I was truly touched by Tom, Ruth, Bert, George, and Joe.
>
> John became, or is becoming for me, a friend. Maybe that word best describes what I feel toward members of the group. I feel like now they are becoming friends. The process of friendship has begun.
>
> It made me feel very sad and love her a great deal more than I thought I could, to learn that she too had suffered so much.
>
> He is really a great kid, and I love him like I do my own boy.
>
> I could not be truthful if I said I learned to love *all* the members of the group. Some I loved and do love very deeply now.
>
> When Mark expressed his love for Bert by word, look, and act I sobbed because he expressed my own love for my own loved ones and, in a sense, in the only way that is open for me.

THE SHAKEDOWN

Confrontation. "Get off my back; this is none of your damn business." Confrontations can be positive, but frequently they are decidedly negative. A confrontation is less an encounter than it is a collision of people. The collision can be a blood and guts battle between individuals or among a small group within the group. Often it will occur because two people have been skirting around the edges of each other in a game of tag, playing at touching each other, and suddenly the game becomes a deadly serious confrontation—a butting of heads in an attempt to barrel into the being center of the other or to avoid being barreled into. Such a confrontation may begin as a confrontation of ideas or positions on religion, government, sex, or basic philosophy. Although the battle may rage in terms of the *content* of ideas it is usually waged in terms of *persons*.

The confrontation is often a battle with self, a struggle with the projection of ourselves onto the other person. The one battled represents that in ourselves which we hate and despise, and we can vent all our hate on it when we see it in another without, we think, doing damage to ourselves. If we can defeat the despicable in them perhaps we can subdue it and be finished with it in our own lives. Thus the one confronted may represent (re-present) that very aspect of ourselves with which we struggle!

If confrontation is just those hate-full moments of perceiving the world in this enemy who confronts one in the here and now, it is at the same time (and this is paradoxical to those who perceive the world as good *or* ill, instead of good *and* ill) just at that moment also that one calls to the other for aid and assistance. For the moment of confrontation is also the moment of caring—no matter how crippled this caring may be, nor how distorted the reaching out to the other. We *are* involved with those we hate and with those we resent just as we are involved with those we love and with those we appreciate. No less!! We do not confront those toward whom we feel indifference. Confrontation, even in its rage and defeat, is a call to the other. Even in its distorted form as projection, it is a way of saying, "Encounter me so I do not drown, die, cease to be!" It is a call toward life and hope; a call for assistance.

Confrontation occurs in the *here and now*. Much of the story telling and mask removing deals with past events and feelings about self. Confrontation is behavior that develops out of the interaction of the present group members—it is living and experiencing life *here and now*. Most of the behavior is available for all to see and react to and participate in.

Rogers describes such confrontation: "In one of the last sessions of a group, Alice had made some quite vulgar and contemptuous remarks to John, who was entering religious work. The next morning, Norma, who had been a very quiet person in the group, took the floor:

NORMA: (Loud sigh) Well, I don't have *any* respect for you, Alice. *None!* (Pause) There's about a hundred things going through my mind I want to say to you, and by God I hope I get through 'em all! First of all, if you wanted us to respect you, then why couldn't you respect

John's feelings last night? Why have you been on him today? Hmm? Last night—couldn't you—couldn't you accept—*couldn't you* comprehend in any way at all that—that *he felt* his unworthiness in the service of God? Couldn't you accept this, or did you have to dig into it today to find something *else there*? And his respect for womanhood—he *loves* women—yes, he does, because he's a real person, but you—you're not a real woman—to me—and thank God, you're not my mother!!!! I want to come over and beat the hell out of you!!! I want to slap you across the mouth so hard and—oh, and you're so, you're many years above me—and I respect age, and I respect people who are older than me, *but I don't respect you, Alice. At all!* And I was so *hurt* and *confused* because you were making someone else feel *hurt* and *confused....*[1]

Such confrontations may frighten group members but they also serve to move the group beyond the "nicey-nice" response patterns that are usual and at the same time unreal. One member of a group described the value of a confrontation in which he had participated:

The confrontation was the most *instructive* of all the experiences of the group, in a nondidactic way. Its instructiveness seems to me to have been in proportion to its *intensity*. And I think that its intensity was a product of two things. First, we are all conditioned (unfortunately) to avoid raw emotions, and there was a lot of primitive fear percolating through the group, stimulated by the spectacle of raw emotion. Humans evidently firmly believe that there is a lot of predatory viciousness in humans, to be so afraid of unleashing true emotion. Second, the confrontation of Bob with himself had a more deeply real quality (at least for me) than anything the group had experienced before.

Working Through the Rift.   "How do we pick up the pieces?" Working through the tangle of shredded emotions may be the most constructive activity of all processes in the human encounter. When everything is out in the open, when honesty and attempts at honesty have torn the group apart, healing must occur. Human beings cannot exist torn apart. Just as the human body has a built-in mechanism to heal itself when wounded, so does the wounded human spirit (mind, soul, heart) attend to its own healing. To be otherwise is to be *inhuman.* Groups will heal the rifts; they cannot do otherwise. Highly skilled group facilitators can probably help the healing to be more efficient and effective—they can certainly help the healing to come about more rapidly—but leaderless groups will also attend to their own healing.

Torn groups, in their exhaustion, may have to call a truce for a time and agree to table conflict, if this is possible. Whatever keeps people apart, however, must be bridged. Tabled conflict will hang

[1] Carl Rogers, "The Process of the Basic Encounter Group," in *Challenges of Humanistic Psychology*, ed. James Bugental (New York: McGraw-Hill Book Company, 1967), p. 270.

heavy in the air until resolved. Once the confrontantion has been experienced, there is no hiding from working it through. (There is a difference in recognizing that a group is approaching a confrontation and choosing to avoid it; once the group is *in* the confrontation there is probably no way to turn back.) Each member has now invested part of himself in the confrontation, in the here and now of the experience. Each member is now hooked into the group dynamic, and each member's growth—each member's moving on—is inextricably woven into the situation. Each one has responsibility for himself and for each other person. "How can we help ourselves?" becomes the focus for concern. "How can we *reinvent* our lives to move beyond this tangle?"

The authors have no ready answers for these complex questions. It is difficult to work through a rift; there are no easy and simple guidelines. If a degree of caring, a climate of closeness, has developed earlier then this foundation of caring can be relied upon to sustain the group during the working-through phase. Someone will likely point out, "What happened to us? We were doing so well. There was a great deal of communication and feeling for one another three weeks ago until we started on this horrible thing. Don't we have any of those earlier feelings left?" The statement, "Don't you two love each other anymore?" can be a powerful stimulant to help clear the air and begin the healing process. If there was caring present earlier it will now come forth to bind the group together again so that the rift can be mended.

One member describes his feeling when a rift was worked through.

As the group conflict subsided my own conflicts began to melt—not disappear. I could come to rest at peace with my fellow human beings. They seemed at peace with me. I felt we had won a small victory together and could face the future with more confidence in ourselves and others and with assurance of love and support from the group.

THE UPLIFTING

If the human encounter has been experienced by most members in the group; if trust, openness, honesty have been obviously evident; if there has been caring, the group is more likely to share in a transcending experience. In such an experience members transcend their normal modes of functioning and reach degrees of intensity they never thought possible. It is an experience in which spirits are uplifted in a sharing and caring that is astonishing to observe.

Such moments are characterized by great displays of *joy*. There can even be yelling and dancing as group members express how they feel. There is usually a great deal of touching and hugging in these moments.

It is difficult to explain such feelings to those who have not experienced this kind of group joy. We are quick to be suspicious of such activity; it sounds mysterious and occult, and our Western minds do not trust mystery because mystery is not rational. Even those who experience it often doubt their senses and question the validity of their objectivity. When others remind us that such an experience is "unreal" we are often quick to agree and hurriedly make the internal adjustments for our participation in the "real" world—where such "unreal" joy is not allowed for human beings.

One group in which one of the authors was a co-facilitator experienced the uplifting in a very dramatic way. The group had grown together over a summer, had experienced confrontation, and had worked through that confrontation. This session was the last afternoon of a two-day marathon toward the end of the summer. One group member suggested that the group form a circle with arms around each other and that each member stand in the middle in turn with eyes closed. The one in the middle was turned around several times and other members were then allowed to express, nonverbally, any warmth or caring they wished to express to him. Immediately one person reached out and hugged the person in the middle—others joined in and the person in the middle was surrounded on all sides by people hugging him, squeezing, putting their cheeks against his cheek, rubbing their heads against his, clutching his hands and his arms in theirs. It was electric. The tears of happiness and the tears of pain that come when we understand the love we have missed gushed in great torrents. There were human sounds of tenderness, guttural (caring from the guts) and grunting and soothing. Perspiration flowed and intense human contact continued for an hour.

Each member took his turn in the center. Some were afraid; some were overwhelmed with how others cared for them; some did not want to quit when they had been around the circle. Each time a new person came to the center there was an upsurge of feeling; no one was left out—all gave and all received.

There was a special kind of tenderness when members would wipe away the tears of another and place the wetness of those tears on their own faces. The symbolism in that act of sharing pain, happiness, and love is obvious.

At times there was a playfulness characteristic of elementary school children at recess. One member put all his weight on another member and made him drop to the floor, both laughing. There was a play at tripping between two men—much as fifth-grade boys do to show their caring for each other. Many people delighted in ruffling the hair of the one in the center after which they often held that person very closely and patted them tenderly. Several members were lifted physically in a horizontal position to the ceiling of the room by the group. Some were bounced in the air. Those bounced and lifted were always relaxed and with their eyes closed appeared to be at great peace with themselves—their trust of the group was evident.

There was also a great yelling—the human cry of pain we know well, the human cry of joy is startling and splendid. Several joined in chanting—there was *cheer*leading. There was the crackling sound of human beings bursting from their shells, spreading their joy, and yelling their wholeness into the emptiness of the universe.

The authors realize that this experience sounds terribly dramatic. It was.

In a group that is just beginning to achieve cohesion—a bond of caring—one member has already experienced the uplift for himself. He had been talking about levels of his experiencing.

> You know, when I write about this third level, though, I feel quite uncomfortable using the personal pronoun *I*. This level can be described as reconciliation or rapport or reconstruction. My identity, somehow, has come to belong to the group. Wait a minute. That's not right. Until Friday afternoon it would be correct to say, only, part of the group. During our first meeting my experience at this level was primarily reconciliation. After Friday night it became reconstruction and even rejuvenation. So many anxieties had accumulated previous to that. I still felt left out of the group. Maybe this was because deep down inside I am afraid of being left out and alone. Maybe this was because before we worked through the hang-up the group was not together. Probably both. Anyhow, in a rush, my attacks brought counter-attacks of unexpected acumen. But I was outplayed by someone else who was a Devil's Advocate, not the Devil.
>
> Suddenly I sensed this. Suddenly I perceived. I perceived that my feelings were connected with the feelings of the individuals in the group. And then came "flight." My "trip" was glorious. The Jefferson Airplane song "Don't You Want Somebody To Love?" registered in me as applying to the people in the group. Joe was somehow me, Tom was somehow me, Sally was too, and Peggy and everybody else. I guess that this is what people have described as euphoria. I have had "highs" as high before, but this was a unique kind of high.

Another person in the group wrote later of the experience described above, "Steve was like handing out lollipops to everyone. I do not understand much of that, but it was fun. This was a shared experience."

A person sitting next to Steve experienced the euphoria also:

> I was hoping that session would never end because I, along wtih Steve, must have been flying. While having been emotionally touched by single events and general feelings within the group before, I had not experienced such sustained emotional feeling over so long a period.

Other groups will experience the uplifting in a less vocal, less vibrant kind of way. A peacefulness, a knowing that there is love in a group that needs no outward expression, will often be present. The Christian religion has called this experience "The peace that passeth understanding." Human beings know such peace. It is often accompanied by a feeling of identification with the unity of mankind, a feeling of oneness with the world, *gemeinschaftgefühl*. Man in the company of others has come home to himself to rest, and peace follows.

CHANGES IN BEHAVIOR

We do not have a great deal of information regarding behavioral changes of group participants. That change occurs seems to be quite evident to those who have experienced the human encounter. Most speak of being more open, more congruent, more spontaneous, more alive; such outcomes are difficult to measure. "I understand myself better" has little meaning except for the person saying it. Changed behavior that is evident outside the group is probably a major test of the effectiveness of groups, but it is quite difficult to gather much evidence. The authors are interested in the research aspects of these questions and are involved in several major research projects to evaluate outcome. Since this book is not being written from a research standpoint, however, we only point out the importance of research on outcomes and move on to those who report behavior changes.

The human encounter group is often the very first opportunity an individual has to examine himself and explore the facets of his behavior that make him unique. Many are amazed and pleased with what happens to them because of their experience.

I am gaining new insights into other people and into myself. My experience with people of religious and cultural backgrounds other than my own has been very limited. I grew up and have continued to live with Catholic middle-class people. To know intellectually that there are wide differences among people as well as great similarities is not the same as to know it experientially. I find that though the basic similarities are more impressive than the differences, I would have been put off quite easily by the differences had not the encounter experience forced me to delve below the seemingly different exteriors. This is not to say that there are no differences below the surface. Ways of thinking and feeling are *very* different. The attempt to understand people of such varying life styles is a rewarding and broadening experience. I feel that I am now more open to others because of these encounter experiences than I have been in the past.

The new insights into myself that I am gaining are extremely valuable to me. Without self-knowledge, it is impossible to know others and to live a rich, full life. I want very much to be the most human, loving person I am capable of becoming.

During the past week-end it became apparent to me that I overreact to other people's hurt and that I am overprotective toward them. No one was so upset as I at the prospect of further confrontation, nor did they believe that real damage could be done to an individual in these encounter sessions. Since my concern was comparatively much greater than anyone else's, it seems reasonable to conclude that it arose not out of love and sympathy for others but out of some need of my own. I have the beginning of several answers right now, but I will have to think about them much more.

I am delighted at the great benefits I have received from these encounter experiences. I want nothing more than to become a free, congruent person who loves fully according to her capacity. The encounter experiences seem designed to do just that. I have experienced more benefits already. I look forward to even greater ones.

One man indicates that his behavior has meaning outside the group:

How do I feel about this experience? Right now I need to express my love for life in a concrete way. My wife is waiting.

Another person describes his change in this way:

To sum up, I feel I am further along the road to understanding myself than perhaps I have ever been, certainly more so than in a long time. I was out of touch with myself when this group started, and now, not always, not completely, but occasionally, I see myself a little better and sometimes like what I see a little better.

For another person the feeling is one of aliveness—liveliness:

Truly, I believe I've become more compassionate and caring about others— *I feel more alive!* But—it's rather embarrassing to reveal this.

I do feel happier within myself now—I feel like bubbles are coming out when I open my mouth. And I sit and stare, thinking how could this happen? and did it really happen??? Was it possible???

The experience for another group member is similar:

This experience has broken down a wall that has been inside me. I felt so good to get it out of the way for a while that I really want to keep it down. It would help me to be more sympathetic toward other people and to reach out when they are trying to call to me.

Some people get feedback from friends outside the group that indicates others are aware of the change as well:

Things that have happened in this group have made me change from a scattered person to a well-balanced human being. A lot of my friends have told me I don't act like the same person, and am I ever glad. They say I've become a more outgoing person. I've had a complete change in personality.

This same student describes other changes that occur following subsequent meetings of the group:

I feel as though this group we have formed has brought us closer together. I can proudly walk by one of the five persons in the hall and they greet me with a warm hello and smile. I've become very close to all of them, including the teacher.

Some of the reasons I don't talk unless I'm asked is simply I'm afraid I'll be wrong, but from now on I'm going to talk in our small groups. I'm going to start here in the small group and talk and then on Monday, when our large group meets, I'm going to build up my confidence so I can talk in front of the large group.

These excerpts are only a sample of the ways in which human beings describe changes that occur in them because of the human encounter. Though brief, the descriptions do convey some of the flavor of excitement, hope, struggle, and pain that accompany change in behavior. Each participant in the human encounter—whether it occurs in a group, with one other person, through individual introspection, or even through reading this book—should note carefully his changes and his changing so that he can direct more precisely the invention of his developing life style.

WHERE TO NEXT?

When has a group completed its work? Is there an *end* to the group process, to the human encounter? The ending of a group is sometimes determined by outside factors such as time commitments of the members or of the facilitator or costs involved. If the encounter group is scheduled in a collegiate setting the end of the course or the school year will bring closure. Sometimes members move away or get involved in many other activities that make it difficult for the group to continue.

Group members may decide to quit because individuals have achieved goals or feel that any further effort would be useless for them at this time. Some sense that *this* group has accomplished its mission for now may lead to consensus to stop.

It would be interesting to speculate what would happen if a group continued for weekly sessions over a period of many years. At first, many group processes similar to those described in this chapter would probably occur. Individuals would work through encounters and confrontations that they had not had an opportunity to work through before. Each member would probably have *his time* in the group. Group members would have an opportunity to experience the entire gamut of human emotions. Greater unity might develop—wider rifts might occur.

It is likely that members would begin practicing their group learning outside the group to a greater extent. Buttressed by the group, they would feel encouraged to "be themselves" with their bosses, their spouses, their friends. On the other hand, if the group became a security blanket, members might be more hesitant to confront the outside world. The weekly group meeting could become a narcotic, a trip, an excuse. Drug addicts might be more prone to use groups in this way, but the accounts of group experiences in Synanon point to the use of groups as anything but a narcotic. Some group members would probably tend to use the group as a way of avoiding the world, but it is not likely that other group members would allow such surrogation.

A sustained group might break through barriers into realms of human experience relatively unknown to man. We know that man's capacity is much greater than the use he makes of it. We know that in special moments he can transcend his normal functioning. We have some evidence from Rogers that man can be a more fully functioning being and from Maslow that man can be self-actualizing. What heights and depths can man reach in himself and in relationship with others? Man is rapidly conquering the universe. Twenty years ago speculation about landing on the moon was regarded as poppycock and dangerous interfering with the unknown. It was a mystery to be left untouched. What of the cosmos *within* man and *between* man and man? We have only touched the edge of the frontier in the exploration of ourselves and our fellows. Our instruments of exploration have been a few crude sticks and a string or two. The human encounter, as a process in a group, and as a goal for the uplifting of man, seems to hold promise as a base for the full exploration of our human beingness.

What is the human encounter? It is man loving. It is man sharing his pain, sharing his joy. It is the celebration of man growing. It is the recognition that man is totally alone in the universe—and ultimately together. *The human encounter occurs when we meet ourselves or others in the process of our emerging humanity*. What we can become through the human encounter, what we can make of our humanity, holds great promise for each of us.

III

some
dimensions
of
encountering

The encountering process is a way of becoming more aware of our human qualities. In Part III we have included examples of some of the various dimensions of what it means to be human.

Since most people have had experience in discussion groups, we contrast these with the encounter group. In this way we hope to help you understand still further what it means to participate in an encounter group.

In the chapter on Human Experiencing college students describe their most intensive experiences and the effects these experiences have had on their lives. They have experienced many of the same joys and pains that you have.

In the chapter Yes, but Have We Really Achieved Encounter? we suggest guidelines that will help you measure your progress. We use Martin Buber's description of the I-Thou relationship as a frame of reference for this discussion and encourage you to read his original statement.

In the chapter on Leadership Style we become individual authors and speak openly and frankly about how we behave in a group. We have a marked contrast in styles, and we hope that you will understand our central message here: *Every person is a facilitator with a unique style.* We reveal ours and we hope it will help you experience your own more intensively.

In the final chapter we talk about life and death, the basic concerns of all men, in much the same way that college students discuss them in their residence halls until four in the morning. In this brief way we attempt to reveal ourselves to you even more as real persons.

This section is included for reaction or as stimulus material. It has been our experience that when *others* talk about the more important things in life or attempt to reveal themselves openly, then it becomes easier for *us* to do so. If your group does not seem to be interacting well enough, if the group interaction has been sustained at a superficial level, then this material may stimulate group members to become more open, more trusting, more intensive, more prepared for the human encounter. Further, this material may encourage some students to consider their own intensive experiences, their own ideas concerning life and death, or the possibility of revealing themselves to another person through the process of writing. The class may wish to write about some of their experiences and share these with the teacher and with each other.

9

"is an encounter group something like a discussion group?"

Well, something like.

But we never want you to confuse the two. We have, in fact, seen beginning encounter groups (with all the earnestness that typifies the American get-it-done-and-get-it-done-well attitude) begin to define goals, set target dates for their accomplishment, assemble guidelines for orderly procedure, describe (and thereby limit) topics that will be discussed, etc., etc., etc. Of course, an encounter group may easily begin to sound and act very much like the familiar everyday committee meeting or group discussion we experience in school, or like the staff meeting where we work, or like the clubs and organizations we belong to. Although task forces and committees can be very useful for their purpose, encounter groups that are run like committees are simply not encounter groups.

To help you avoid some of the pitfalls of beginning groups, we'd like to devote some attention to the differences between task forces, committees, and discussion groups on the one hand and encounter groups on the other. We should caution the reader to remember that the differences we mention are at times arbitrary. An effective committee for example, may sometimes incorporate some of the features we characterize as distinctive of encounter groups.

1.   ENDS VS. MEANS

A group discussion (particularly in its committee form) generally has definable goals: to investigate a subject; to brainstorm new ideas; to draw conclusions; to suggest committee actions; to make recommendations. The group discussion is a means toward those goals. The extent to which the discussion group (or committee or task force) achieves its goals, is the extent to which it is adjudged "successful." Now anyone who has been involved in committees or other types of discussion groups knows that some committees are enjoyable, and these are usually the more successful committees. The "enjoyableness" indicates that the committee is relatively free of the bitter tensions, angers, resentments, and conflicts that drain the strength of any group, and that what disagreements and differences do exist actually contribute to creative problem solving. The enjoyableness of the discussion group has, however, little to do with its central purpose, since the goal is to make a recommendation, pass on a resolution, etc.

A human encounter group ordinarily entails the achievements of "self-growth," "increased self-awareness," "more full expression of one's potential," etc., and these can be considered by-products, not ends in themselves. It is the act of being with each other, the relating, the interacting among other group members in the here-and-now moment, the *means*, in other words, which is central to the encounter process. Human encountering is *a way of relating with other human beings*, and in this sense, the process (the means) is its own primary end.

What we are saying is that there are no formal resolutions, no summary, no conclusions necessary in a human encounter group. The verbal interaction doesn't have to "go" anywhere. There is no time schedule or deadline to meet; and no *foreseeable* purpose to be achieved.

In this respect, then, an encounter group has much the same characteristics as the primary group as defined by Kingsley Davis.

A primary relationship, ideally considered, is not regarded by the parties as simply a means to an end but rather as a value or end in itself . . . . The relationship . . . is intrinsically enjoyable.[1]

Our first primary group is our family, particularly our parents or parent substitutes, and any siblings we have. It is a group from which we derive (hopefully) emotional support. Later on in life, we look for friends with whom we can form a primary relationship. An encounter group, when it is successful, encompasses much of the same characteristics of closeness, feelings of ease, comfortableness, and mutuality. These characteristics are discussed in more detail in Chapter 11 in which they are correlated with Martin Buber's I-Thou framework. And, in fact, members of a good encounter group often refer to their encounter group as a new kind of family.

2. POLARIZATION VS. UNIFICATION

A group discussion (no matter how noble the intent) often can end up having "sides," usually two (pro and con), but sometimes several factions. The existence of a goal necessitates a common group decision; and the latter is not an easy achievement, for even seemingly similar people may hold widely differing beliefs. Someone often has to give-in somewhere along in the discussion—an uncomfortable event for a person convinced of the rightness of his position. Moreover (as the so-called "rules" of the "discussion game" go), each person on a committee tends to "sell" the validity of his point of view. The ultimate example of this is the debate method with its either-or dualism, and its emphasis that one side or the other is the "winning" side, without benefit of either compromise or the construction of another large frame-of-reference, which can incorporate the polarity of opinion. In real life, however, an argument is rarely "won"; instead, someone "loses face." Public defeat tends not only to cause a person to retreat publicly, but also causes him to tighten his defenses. He becomes even less open to the opposite point of view. Of course, debate rests on either-or propositions: win or lose; right or wrong; innocent or guilty (as in law courts). Yet we know that in the realm of truth, innocence, beauty, etc., either-or is a logical absurdity; that is, such propositions exist only in the abstract, and have little counterpart in the real world of living, breathing humanity.

Since there is no apparent goal in a human encounter group except that of being with each other, there is no contest, and thus no one has to compromise on a position for the sake of common decision. There are no sides because no one is wrong. Rather, each encounter-group member is inviolably right in so far as he speaks *from himself*,

[1] Kingsley Davis, "Primary Groups" in *Life in Society*, eds., Thomas E. Lasswell, John H. Burma, and Sidney H. Aronson (Chicago: Scott, Foresman & Company, 1965), pp. 171–78.

of himself, and *for himself.* He does not have to defend himself, or to retract his opinions when he talks of *his* feelings, *his* experiences, *his* perceptions. In these he cannot be wrong. Encounter members do not have to choose sides or vote. They learn through a successful encounter that what may be "truly right and just" for one person may not be so for another. There can be as many right sides in the encounter group as there are members. And most conflicts occur when one member denies the validity of another's being-in-the-world. This usually occurs between two persons, and these two persons have the right to forge out for themselves, if they will, a world in which both can live with respect for differences. This is authentic conflict. When an entire encounter group explodes into sides, something is wrong. Such conflict is not authentic; it is coercion, censure, or brain-washing, rather than two persons trying to establish a common realm.

But, by and large, encounter helps people toward a world view that allows for diversity of thinking and being-in-the-world. No person has to retreat from his position because he is never put in the position of being wrong. And when an encounter group is characterized by lack of fear, when there exists an openness to variety of being and expression, when each is accorded the right of his individuality, the group members tend to reach a commonality of free choice and free expression. Because they are challenged but not attacked, because the environment is safe and change of opinion does not mean "losing," encounter group members are more able to change their public and private behaviors easily and naturally.

3. FORMALITY VS. SPONTANEITY

Group discussion, even when not rigidly adhering to rules of order, does tend toward formality. There is a reason for this; namely that opposing points of view sometimes elicit emotional reactions in the group members and a certain amount of formality helps to keep these emotions from erupting and thereby disrupting the business at hand. In the great houses of representation (the United States Congress and the British Parliament) members of bitterly opposing sides maintain a certain formality of speech. Although every gesture, every facial expression and nuance of voice reveal thinly-covered hostility and anger, the debators will still address, or allude to, each other with the most polite of titles: "The esteemed opposition says . . ." or "Our respected colleague. . . ." This kind of formality serves to prevent complete disintegration of group cohesion when all other connections have become unglued . . . an essential consideration in diplomacy and in some committee situations when real encounter could be disastrous.

Since there is little need for common assent, and since no one has to win an argument, there is little need for formality in a well-run encounter group. Formality is designed to hold spontaneous emotions in check.

Spontaneity is not an accidental by-product of human encountering;

it is rather, a fundamental aspect of encountering. What distinguishes human encountering from pastimes and games (described earlier) is the stereotyped language and behavior of the latter two. The human encounter, however, is aimed at exploring new ways of behaving, new approaches to relating, and thus must necessarily involve the untried, the unknown, the unpremeditated, the unplanned. But that requires letting go of the internal censor of our actions and thoughts. It demands permitting oneself the luxury and the wisdom of the child's spontaneous reactions to the wonder and glory of the world around and within him.

4. OBJECTIVITY VS. SUBJECTIVITY (Facts vs. Feelings)

In group discussions, as we have come to understand them, the *personal* has little place. Theoretically a group discussion deals with "facts" (that is, the individual's perception of truth backed up by what seems to him to be convincing evidence). Ostensibly, *issues*, not *personalities*, are the concern of the group. Revealing one's feeling is considered "bad form," and personal reference is kept to a minimum. All of this, of course, is aimed at keeping the discussion "objective" and "factual."

A skillful committee member can, of course, manipulate his words in such a way that he seems to be objective regarding the matter at hand. By quoting authorities (which at the moment can't be checked); or by the use of certain one-upmanship phrases such as "I'm sure that you will agree with me when I say . . . ," or "Tom here can verify the fact that . . ." (Tom is not asked to); or by the ploy that has popular appeal today—"I think we only have a semantic difference," he steers the direction of the discussion toward his viewpoint, obtaining assent by leaving the less skillful members helplessly silent.

This example aside, however, and assuming good will on the part of all members, it still remains that the group discussion, committee, or task force attempts to reduce subjectivity, personal reference, and preference to a minimum. Incidentally, there are times when a free give-and-take of personal feelings would do much to relieve some of the boredom and deadness one often experiences in a committee. And, to be sure, your authors have been involved in some experimental approaches to committee work in which some of the more formal aspects of procedure have been discarded and encounter-type expression adopted with some interesting and positive results. But that is another story. In its present typical form, at any rate, a discussion group tries to avoid the elements of personal prejudice, personality conflict, and personal idiosyncrasy.

Perhaps it is this aspect more than any other which distinguishes a human encounter group from a group discussion. The encounter group begins with the subjective, focuses on the subjective, and proceeds by means of the subjective. The encounter group does not ignore the subjective; rather it takes pride in it! The members learn that the word *I* is the highest authority there is. They learn to express just those aspects of themselves which are repressed in a group discussion, namely, their feelings. They learn that the personal and the subjective are not only valued, but are actually sought. Emotional experiences can be shared. The sight of someone weeping would embarrass members of a discussion group; in the human encounter group the experience of weeping may actually indicate that an event of heroic nature has taken place.

The human encounter group, then, is committed to the subjective: It starts in the belief that the best way to achieve objectivity is to focus on the subjective. We believe that by enlarging the subjective, we clarify and thereby separate our own prejudices (prejudgments) from "what is."

5.   RESTRICTEDNESS VS. OPENNESS

We have already implied that in a discussion group the members are necessarily more restricted in their external movement (interaction) with each other, and in their internal movement (insight and growth) within themselves. Because of the discussion group's need for a purposeful goal (be it a decision, an action, a recommendation, etc.), the behavior of the group members must be directed toward that goal.*

An encounter, on the other hand, is dedicated to the possibilities of change. No disapproval is leveled at inconsistency; rather, the group member can begin to discover (with amusement and pleasure) the underlying inconsistencies and prejudices (prejudgments) within himself. Moreover, he is in no way expected to resolve these inconsistencies until he can or wants to. Since he cannot be wrong he is not judged for taking various positions which are inconsistent. Even when these inconsistencies are pointed out to him, he does not have to find excuses, or rationalize his behavior. For example, he does not have to be wary about revealing aspects of himself which seem inappropriate to his outer image.

Because he is never wrong, the individual finds it easier to be open and undefensive about what he says. Because stereotyped behavior and language are not expected of him, he finds it easier to explore new kinds of behaviors for himself. He can behave in ways that correspond more to the moment-to-moment changes within him than to any kind of stereotyped role in which he has been placed. He finds it easier to change his position, his beliefs, his values, his actions from one moment to the next (if need be) in order to increase his self-understanding and his understanding of others. Because of the acceptance he experiences, he does not have to rigidify his thinking and feeling; he is more open to change within himself and in his relationship with others.

---

*Members of a discussion group, in order to achieve the goals of the group, assume the roles they have played in similar situations; often there is little opportunity to practice new behavioral patterns.

10

human experiencing

How do I *experience* myself? Inside of me feeling me? Outside of me feeling the inside and the outside? How do I know when I am in touch with me? I put my arms around myself—have I got hold of me? I dig deep, deep down into the black boxes of my being and discover a tender stub of fungus—feeling under a heavy, damp stone—have I got hold of me? I take flight of my touching-doing-seeing-acting-being and watch me in myself, curious and enchanted with these strange human powers to observe myself—have I got hold of me? I take another step, simple as shifting to a new position, and I watch me watching me, me now with a smile at the marvel of it all—have I got hold of me? *How do I experience myself?*

How do I *experience* others? Inside of me feeling them? Outside of me feeling the inside of me feeling them? Inside them feeling them? Inside them feeling me outside feeling them? How do I know when I am in touch with another? I put my arms around another—have I got hold of him? I dig deep, deep down into the labyrinths of his being and discover black mushrooms growing in a gray field—have I got hold of him? I step back from the other and watch me touching-doing-acting-seeing-being with him, delighted with the secret me out there watching me and him—have I got hold of him? I close my eyes and see clearly me watching me and him—have I got hold of him? *How do I experience others?*

Is my way of experiencing mine alone? Must I bear it all alone? Can others feel as I do? I need to know. It's scary sitting here in the middle of me— good, too, damn good—but sometimes scary. I need someone else to sit here in the middle of me with me, to hold my hand in the dark, to share my roars of joy. And I want to sit in the middle of others to see if what they are saying about how things are is true—and to share in their joy and in their pain.

That's most of me—wanting to *experience* others and wanting to *experience* myself. I can talk about it better than I can do it. How is it for you?

Here is a human being asking about human experiencing: How do I experience myself and others? How do I come to know myself and others? How can I share myself with others? How can others share themselves with me? Part of the human purpose is to know and to be known. It is a purpose only partially fulfilled in the world in which we live.

Many of us harbor experiences which we feel make us less than human. We may have had very painful and frightening experiences in our lives, or we may doubt our abilities so deeply that we feel we must be the most inadequate of creatures on earth. We may have experienced that which is ugly, sordid, perverse, degrading—and we may be certain inside ourselves that no other person could have experienced such pain.

The authors believe that it is particularly helpful if we have opportunities to hear about these experiences of other people and to share our own experiences with others. In the human encounter such sharing often occurs. We come to trust others in the group and to feel that they want to know us, so we are willing to share ourselves with them. We begin to allow others to visit our cocoon, and we don't care if they see what is not beautiful. In fact, we want them to see what is not beautiful because if they accept us after they see us at our worst then they must truly care.

When others have accepted us under such circumstances we are more likely to accept ourselves and others under similar circumstances. We come to accept and care for people regardless of the experiences we or they may consider ugly or evil. Such acceptance allows us to know and care for a large variety of people in the world. We come out of our cocoons and discover others who have come out of theirs. We find, too, that many people still choose to live in their carefully constructed cages, and it becomes one of our purposes in living to release others from the loneliness of their retreat and to enrich ourselves as we encounter them in the process.

We grow in trust and confidence when others accept that which we perceive to be the worst in us. But such acceptance may not be sufficient to maintain a continuing human relationship; we also need to have that which is beautiful in us accepted and understood by others. The sharing of our beauty may lead to more meaningful encounters than the sharing of what we regard as ugly.

The idea of beauty is one of man's greatest conceptions, and he is capable of experiencing an infinite variety of beautiful things, acts, and wishes. Most of us have experienced the beauty of nature (sunsets, flowers, mountains, beaches, waterfalls, stars) and the beauty of objects (art forms, music, movie stars, velvet, gem stones); but how many of us have experienced the beauty of man alone and man relating? What is more beautiful than:

A man weeping?
A young girl on her first date?
A family welcoming home a soldier son?
A grandmother rocking a grandchild?
The eyes of a four-year old?
First love?
An old man welcoming death?
First birth?
A man weeping?

There is much that is beautiful in the lives of all of us. To share such beauty with another person is to add to our own growth and to aid in the growth of another.

In the paragraphs below a young man compresses ten years of struggle for meaning into a brief account. He shares his experiencing, which is a special kind of beauty—the beauty of searching, struggling, integrating, understanding, accepting, growing.

At the age of sixteen I discovered that I existed. Previously I had not posed any serious questions regarding the grounds for my being. In other words, my being had never been called into question. Therefore, my being had never been verified.

Thus I began the long process of introspection, of self-examination, which I still continue (ten years later). I discovered two basic facts:

(1) that the morality I had inherited/assimilated from my parents was not my own and was therefore false, and I set out to fashion my own interpersonal ethic;

(2) that the universe did not seem to validate my existence and that the protests of religion to the contrary were empty protests, holding no meaning for me. Thus I set out to examine my place in the universe.

For five or six years I went through a process of data gathering and reality testing. It was during my first year in graduate school that I came to the end of the loose threads I had been inspecting and following. I was able to take the ends and tie them together, thus ending, in a sense, one phase of my "search for meaning."

I had always been interested in the physical universe beyond our planet. And it seemed that meaning for me would have to account for my relationship to that universe. I saw what Camus called an "absurd" relationship. I saw myself as one person in one family, one community, one state, nation, continent, hemisphere, and finally, one planet. As if this were not enough, "my planet" is only one of several, circling one star out of hundreds of thousands of stars in our one galaxy, the Milky Way. (We are located somewhere on the outskirts of our galaxy.) This galaxy is one of millions of galaxies, each with hundreds of thousands of stars like our sun. There are even *clusters* of galaxies, clusters of clusters, and so on.

Obviously the relationship between one person and a universe of this magnitude is so disproportionate (in human terms) as to be . . . absurd. With this and other similar thought-feelings I experienced a deep confrontation with "existential absurdity." I understood that the universe was utterly devoid of meaning (that I could *comprehend*), in the sense of "possessing" something which simply awaits "discovery." I understood also that my existence was utterly devoid of meaning . . . EXCEPT INSOFAR AS *I* COULD GIVE IT MEANING! *I*—not the universe—became the SOURCE of meaning for my existence, and I would live immersed in meaninglessness unless I *chose* to live *meaningfully*. In existentialist terms, *I* was assuming the responsibility for meaning (not the church, the state, the parent, etc.), and such meaning would be determined by the *choices I would make*.

What a liberation from dependence on and subordination to Empty Outside Authority!!!

What a sense of strength I could enjoy from having mutinied and taken over control of the ship . . . having assumed responsibility for my life!

A scary and lonely position to take, but ultimately exhilarating.

I understand now that there will be no such thing, no *entity* with the title of "Meaning." Meaning is not a thing, it is a PROCESS, which continues so long as I am psychologically living and growing. If I stop growing, if I stop evolving and testing, if I stop looking for alternatives, I will have died psychologically (that's the worst kind; it's Living Death). My life would then "grow" meaningless again. However, I intend to die physically first, before MY Meaningfulness inevitably expires, which it will when the *people* I have touched no longer exist. I will then be Officially Dead, and my "immortality" will have expended itself.

. . . and the indifferent universe will continue. . . .

It is usually quite startling to learn about the many dimensions of human experiencing. Why don't you suggest that a group of people try to share experience and talk about how it feels? If you are using this book in a course it would be relatively easy to ask each class member to respond. If you have developed some trust and confidence in your group, then each one could respond openly to the class. Such openness will certainly build trust and confidence even if it is difficult to do and proves to be embarrassing for some. Class members may feel safer, if this is early in the term, by writing down their responses anonymously and letting each class member draw a response to read aloud and perhaps react to aloud. Develop some technique for sharing responses that will lead to more understanding, trust, and encountering in the group.

You may wish to have group members respond to one or several of the following questions:

What is the most beautiful thing you have ever done?

What makes you feel ugly?

How do you feel when you think about the worst thing you ever did in your life?

What is the most intense experience you ever had?

What makes you cry?

How do you feel when you are functioning at your very best?

What would you like to experience that our society says is bad?

It might be a good exercise to have each member of the group make a list of similar questions and have the group choose the ones they would prefer to answer. For such questions each of us has an answer and each of us is an expert. Our answers can form the content of a course in which our experience is the textbook. The final test will be self-administered in terms of how much we have learned to trust and accept others, in terms of how much we have shared love.

In the rest of this chapter we are sharing with you some responses of college students who have described their most intense experience. The narratives were gathered by Dr. Stanley Lynch as part of his research.[1] After a brief presentation concerning the humanistic movement in the behavioral sciences and the need to better understand human experience, Dr. Lynch requested each student to respond in writing to the following:

All of us have experienced feelings of intense personal pleasure and intense personal suffering. Take a few moments to think of your *most intense*

[1] Stanley Lynch, *Intense Human Experience: Its Relationship to Openness and Self-Concept.* Dissertation, University of Florida, 1968.

experience, the one which had the greatest personal impact. Describe your feelings as completely as you can. You may include any details, however intimate or personal they may be. You do not have to sign your name or otherwise identify yourself.

When the student had completed his response he was asked to reply to the following question:

How has this experience made you feel?

Read the following responses carefully and listen to them speaking to you. These are college freshmen, an evening class of a junior college, which probably accounts for the large proportion of older students. But all of them are human beings—human beings who have experienced intense pleasure and intense suffering. What are they saying to you? How do you feel about yourself when you experience these others? Listen to these human experiences and listen to yourself as you do.

A 20-year-old woman reports an experience which occurred when she was 18 and 19:

> I love a boy who doesn't come from a very wealthy family, and he doesn't have a high school education. My mother has tried for two years to keep us from seeing each other because she loves me and wants me to have better things in life. The boy went to night school for a while just to date me. Mother has been completely fair about this whole thing and I still am treating her badly. After he quit night school she made me stop dating him, which was fair. I am still seeing the boy, but my mother doesn't know it. If she finds out I am sure she would mentally break down under all the stress and strains of life. The boy realizes now the importance of school and has a day job and is planning to go back to school at night. If I marry this boy I know we will not be rolling in money but we will be together. I know my mother is only thinking of me and she has always done everything for me that is possible. I also know the boy loves me and I love him.
>
> This experience has made me feel bad. I am happy all the time when I am with the boy and when I am around my mother I feel guilty for seeing him because I know my mother disapproves. There is always a wall between me and my mother about some things and when the boy starts talking about her I feel bad. He can't understand her and I can see the way he feels and the way my mother feels. It's very confusing and complicated as you can see by the way I wrote this.

A 24-year-old woman reports an experience which occurred when she was 23:

> My most intense personal experience was a quiet, satisfied, very sweet moment while lying in bed with a man I love very much. We had just finished making love (sexual intercourse) and all desire was well spent. I don't know why that particular moment meant so much to me but I was very content just to lie close to him—not touching. The moment had meaning

for me that has been very sweet and meaningful to remember. I think I have never felt so close to or so much a part of another human being.

This experience has helped me to feel that there is more to life than the constant day-to-day struggle of trying to find a purpose to life in the social-business world.

I feel very humble to have had such a meaningful moment with another; although I have had many satisfying sexual experiences, this moment means very much to me.

When I think of this experience I feel very close to the earth and much a part of all living things . . . and I have more patience with other people because I feel a *part* of all mankind.

A 21-year-old woman reports an experience which occurred when she was 15:

On my 15th birthday I was raped, while on a date with a boy whom I considered almost a brother to me, he was the boy next door. We went out to go to the show, at which we never arrived, but instead went south of the county line for liquor—which at the age of 15 made me feel very grown-up, drinking and dating! I was so shocked! *And horrified!* And there was nothing I could do—he was twice my size, to fight would have been to no avail—so I submitted—too drunk and groggy to really know what was going on—but to know that I knew it was *"wrong"*! I had been told and taught that this part of life was wonderful and beautiful to be shared between husband and wife and NOT BEFORE MARRIAGE.

At first [I felt] horrible, like a nasty little tramp. For three weeks every time I looked at any boy I got *sick*! But then the "next-door boy" came again and we started going together—having relations for ten months—until I was sent to live out of the U.S. for 18 months! I felt no "love" for this boy—only the satisfaction that I got out of "going" with him.

Now I am not sorry I did not save my virginity until marriage—for I really think I'll never be married—I love and enjoy the single life too much. I have received too much pleasure and utopia from single life—and I know that I have brought pleasure and happiness to many others.

This may not be important, but I want to tell you how my past experiences have made me feel about marriage. For many people I know it must be wonderful and they are satisfied. But for me I look at it with much doubt. I do not want to get married because I don't think or feel that I could live with the same man for 5-10-15-25 years! It's bound to get old—and I hate boredom. I'm sure to meet someone whom I want to live with while I'm married (if I am). I think that companionship and affairs are wonderful—and can be resolved without any hard feeling—if both parties have the understanding when they first go into this relationship knowing that neither one wants to become so involved that marriage is the only alternative.

I would not want to *hurt anyone*—especially not a husband, not someone who has depended on me and trusted me.

I know that it is possible to have an affair with someone and keep your self-respect and respect for the other party. It is something which we go into because we both want to. We know it cannot last forever—but it will last until, you might say, "the total desires are fed." But don't get "hooked" on anyone.

You may not understand—but I do. I suppose I don't really know what the strong "marrying love" is, but I do know that in some way I have "loved" everyone I ever went with except "the next-door boy." Each person in an individual way—a love for them alone. Try to understand.

A 32-year-old woman reports an experience which occurred when she was 5:

The one thing that has been hard even for me to accept and has handicapped me personally—is the fact that my father and mother separated when I was only five years old. This was something I could not understand because I loved them both and I could not understand them not loving each other. We children, my brothers and sister, were shifted from one place to another. No one really seemed to care. We sort of grew up on our own. My mother was having affairs with different people and it hurt me terribly. I have always looked at other children and thought, "How lucky you are to have a home and someone to love you."

This experience has left me with no confidence in myself. Why try. I feel as though my husband doesn't love me and it is caused from my parents and the terrible experience of not being loved by anyone when I really needed it. It has left me with fear. I am afraid to love.

A 24-year-old woman reports an experience which occurred when she was 24:

I am married and do not love my husband. There is a lot of holding back in expressing my feelings. I have children that I have to consider, therefore I take a lot that has tended to make me suffer physically as well as emotionally.

This is something that I have experienced and still am experiencing. It makes me feel like I am playing a double role, or really fighting a battle between the person I am being, versus the one that I long to be, and that's really *myself*.

A 35-year-old woman reports an experience which occurred when she was 34:

Last winter, my youngest child developed a growth on her wrist which had to be studied for several months by X-ray and examination. After the lump was determined to be a tumor and the doctors recommended surgery we all lived in a limbo between hope and despair. The surgeon said that the operation would take 45 minutes unless radical surgery was necessary. As we sat and waited over 2½ hours for the operation to end, we were truly faced with the realization of our human vulnerability. In the week that followed while pathology studied the growth, we suffered and loved and grew together in a way we would never have believed possible.

When the results were in and the growth diagnosed as benign we were relieved, renewed, and reassured. That painful, horrible week gave us all insight into our need for each other and has been an experience none of our family will ever forget. It was for me the truest taste of life in all its horror and in all its potential for human endurance and growth.

I know now, that never can a single day with those whom we love be taken for granted. Every day is precious because it never happened before and it can never happen again. Our lives aren't totalities, our lives are but a series of days and to be unaware of even a single one is to create a void that can never be filled. We are all human and as human so vulnerable, also as humans so potentially powerful—able to create love and respect with those closest to us or able to exist together as autonomous individuals "going through the motions." To love is to be vulnerable, to love is also to be able to live.

A 30-year-old man reports an experience which occurred when he was 25:

I think my most intense personal experience was the day I got married. As always there are doubts, apprehensions, etc. just prior to one's marriage. I knew that this would have to be a one-time thing with me. Although I knew that this was the girl I really wanted to marry I had some doubts, but more overwhelming was the thought that something might go wrong to stop that ceremony and more than anything else in the world I wanted to get through the ceremony, because in spite of all my doubts I still knew that I was doing the right thing.

My feelings that day were of shock, numbness, and feeling of utter pleasure and anticipating that the girl I had set out to get as a wife, was now becoming my wife. This actually was the happiest day of my life.

[I feel] content—that I have gained a wife.

A 29-year-old man reports an experience which occurred when he was 23:

The most intense experience in my life was when my first wife obtained a divorce. I thought I would never get over it. We had been married about three years and I decided we should move to California. We sold the house, packed our clothes, and left. After about five months I decided I was ready to come back to the south and did so leaving my wife in California with her mother. In about two months my wife called me and said she had applied for a divorce.

Well, at first I thought I would never get over it, but in about six months of feeling sorry for myself I started living and having a good time again. I have remarried and love my second wife more than my first one, although I have tried harder in my second marriage.

A 20-year-old man reports an experience which occurred when he was 19:

A feeling of knowing myself, who I am, what I am, where I am going, through an intrapersonal experience of total empathy with one of the opposite sex. [I feel] fine, new perceptions of life, love, and human fulfillment.

A 21-year-old man reports an experience which occurred when he was 19:

The first time I got intoxicated almost to a point of helplessness I had no control over my movements which to me was terrifying. All things I saw were distorted. Even though my mind was seemingly clear and functioning correctly my body was not responding. To a person who is extremely independent this was a drastic event, to realize that this period of helplessness will pass with time but having to survive the time it takes for it to pass.

This experience impressed upon me the fact that being drunk to the point of helplessness is for the birds. It is an experience which holds no meaning for me and has set up rather strict drinking habits.

A 20-year-old man reports an experience which occurred when he was 19:

A year and a half ago I met my grandmother and grandfather at the country club dance. I asked her to save a dance for me. When the dance did come, it was a fast one. We started jumping up and down, and twisting, having a great time. There must have been a crowd of a hundred people, around us watching. All of a sudden, grandmother looked at me and said, "This is too much for me," and instantly fell into my arms. I didn't know it at the time, but she had died instantly.

The whole thing had a very hard impact on me mentally. After the funeral I almost went berserk. I was continually having dreams, reenacting the whole night, waking up crying. I thought I would get over it sooner than I did, but due to that and other personal problems, I couldn't.

A 19-year-old man reports an experience which occurred when he was 18:

The most intense experience that I have encountered was about one year ago. This was the first time that I engaged in premarital sex. At the time it was something new and exciting but in a short period of time it became my greatest suffering. For something inside of me seemed to die. I wasn't the same person I used to be. I became hard and didn't have feeling for anyone like I had before.

I believe this experience has helped me grow up but the main reason it happened was pressure from society. It was the *thing* to do and people made mock fun at you if they knew your inability to sleep with a girl. Now I have met a young girl that I love very much and wouldn't ever think of doing anything with her.

A 19-year -old woman reports an experience which occurred when she was 17:

For as long as I live, I'll never forget this night. It was an experience that left a deep scar on my mind and has affected my actions and decisions. The street was dark the night I came home from a movie with my date. I wasn't feeling quite well and didn't want to go to a movie but my sister insisted we "double." As the car pulled up to the house I thanked her date who was driving and got out. My friend followed (a little upset at my behavior). Soon an argument started over some small detail (between my sister and me) about my actions. She followed me to the front door of our home, and in order to get away from fighting I turned and walked rapidly down the street—alone. I came to the end of the dark corner, when my date, my sister and her friend came with the car and demanded I get in. This made me angry. I refused, turned the corner, and walked down another dark street. We have a prowler. We've had one for several years. I've seen him twice—he *always* gets away. I heard a voice as I walked and turned and saw him standing ten feet away. I began to run, screaming, but never expected him to follow—but he did. They heard me screaming three blocks away. He grabbed for my dress, but missed. Scared by the lights of an oncoming car he stopped his chase.. I ran into the street if for nothing else than to get hit by a car—*anything* but what was behind me. No one stopped. Six or seven cars *passed*. They actually went out of their way to go around me as I ran down the busy street. No houses were lit, it was late. I ran up to the sidewalk and froze. Suddenly a boy grabbed my arms. I looked up to see it was my sister's date who followed me as soon as the screaming started. I dug my hands into his sides and fainted.

[I feel] tremendously horrified! I do not trust anyone. I fear a boy to get near me. I can't stand to be touched at *all!* in any way even holding hands. This is difficult for me, as I am naturally an affectionate person, thus it creates quite a bit of anxiety. I want someone to care, but no one does. That was proved to me. I'd give anything if that night had *never* happened.

I'm awfully nervous, jumpy, and suspicious, I detest people. Maybe this attitude is wrong, but I just can't see the world any differently now.

A 19-year-old woman reports an experience which occurred when she was 19:

I was going to my room and I heard the stool fall over in the kitchen so I ran to that room. My father was lying on the floor. I thought maybe he had passed out, but he was dead. It took the ambulance an hour and a half to get to my house, the whole time I thought they could be saving my father. They took him to the same hospital my mother was in (she was recuperating from a cancer operation). I stayed in the emergency room for three hours with doctors deciding what to tell my mother.

My father had had his stomach removed five years ago because of cancer. He was not supposed to live more than three months. He lived almost six years. When an autopsy was performed on him not a trace of cancer was found. He died of a cerebral hemorrhage.

I felt in some way I was the cause of both incidents. I lost faith in God and still have lost it to a great degree. I have tried to take over the household since I am the oldest child and have no brothers. I try to shield from my mother any hurt. I really don't even realize what has happened, it seems that my father is gone for awhile and will show up any day now at the house. I am pushing myself to be a success. I'm very concerned for the first time about excellent grades. I get very upset easily because I'm wound up inside. I don't want to become seriously involved with anyone because I'm afraid something will happen to the relationship, though I strive very much to find love and have people show love to me. I put on a big jolly act in front of everyone. This is causing conflict at home since my mother thinks I'm not concerned about anything any more. I am getting to the point that I want to leave home but continue school. For the first time in my life I am fighting with everyone I love. Sometimes I feel like saying "forget it" to everyone and everything. It really doesn't seem worth the struggle.

A 22-year-old woman reports an experience which occurred when she was 19:

[When I was] 19, my father was transferred to another city and since I had a very respectable job, I decided to stay in the city where I was raised.

Being on my own opened my eyes to the world we live in today. While I was growing up my parents sheltered me very much. I actually could not make any of my own decisions and felt many times that I was deprived of having opportunities to meet more people.

Certainly I experienced moments of loneliness and sometimes wished I was living at home, but for the most part I was living "in the world" and could do and please as I wanted.

Today I feel that this experience I had has made me a better person. I think my marriage has worked out better and I can understand the feelings of my husband better. I realize there are all kinds of people in the world, some good, some bad.

I can appreciate other people's ideas even if they don't coincide with my own.

A 19-year-old woman reports an experience which occurred when she was 18:

It will be hard for me to describe, accurately, my most intense experience because it is entirely a mental process. The first of these feelings began when I started college and I find myself falling into these states on either a bright clear day or a stormy day.

At first my eye catches something that attracts me. An example would be a flower or the ocean. Then I just start noticing how beautiful everything is—nature. I find myself stopping to gaze at a tree or stare at the sky.

Whenever anything like this happens I get a feeling of extreme contentment. I don't really think about anything while this is going on, but I catch myself smiling and no matter how many problems I may have at the time, they don't seem to matter. Nothing matters because everything seems beautiful and I am content.

I think that these moments have helped me realize that life is a great experience that is worth anything one might have to pay as long as he has moments, like the one I described, to revive his spirits and refresh him.

A 21-year-old man reports an experience which occurred when he was 10:

> My grandmother died in 1956. She had cancer, and her life for the last few months was very painful. This had a great impact on the family.
>
> My father was very close to my grandfather, who was very old. My father loved and respected this man, who was now left alone in the world. After the funeral my father broke down and cried.
>
> Until this point in life I had not known my father very well. Our relation had not been that of most father-son relationships. This experience made me feel a greater love for my father. I did not know his feelings for people were like this until this time. This knowledge has enhanced my life to the extent that I now can have a better love for mankind.

A 19-year-old woman reports an experience which occurred when she was 12:

> When I was 12 my mother and father separated. I can remember so well what occurred before this happened. It started two years earlier. My father just stopped coming home when I could see him. He would come every night after we went to bed and would leave before we woke. So in a sense I hardly saw him for two years. The greatest impact was when he sat down and told me he was leaving. He lied to me and I knew it then but I said nothing. I didn't realize the extent of his lies until later though. He told me that he was very sick—a nervous breakdown—and he would have to leave before he got sicker. The truth was that he had stolen the family store (in a sense—it's hard to explain) from us. We no longer have any access to it and it had been in my mother's family for many many years.
>
> This experience of mine has made me more insecure. I am more afraid of the unknown—what will people say? How do I tell them? Am I really capable of loving someone? I know one thing—when I do marry someone it will be *for good*—I will make sure of this if I have to wait until I'm 50. I saw, and still see, the pain my mother went through. She can never forget it.

A 20-year-old woman reports an experience which occurred when she was 19:

> My most intense experience occurred when I gave birth to my daughter. I am not speaking of pain or suffering but of a feeling I experienced which can best be described as the most creative moment in my life. The feeling I experienced immediately after she was born upon seeing her for the first time was of such pure ecstasy that I could hardly contain myself.
>
> Actually I had very little to do with the whole process and it seems strange that I should have felt such accomplishment. But having been only the medium through which it occurred gave me an ineffably useful and important

feeling. I feel it is the first thing I had ever taken part in that was of any real value. I also feel that the reason the effect was so stunning to me was or may have been because every part of me physically as well as emotionally was used to its fullest, maximum capacity.

A 28-year-old man reports an experience which occurred when he was 17:

My father came into the room where my mother was fixing a meal. He had been out working and was coming into the house for dinner. My mother was in a nervous anxiety state, with some hysteria in her behavior. She hated my father's presence at the time, but could never directly confront him with her hostility for him. She always used side attacks that tended to be diminishing to him. I of course had to witness their conflicts with each other. I loved both of them and felt pulled to take sides. My father lost his temper, which he does or did often when I lived home, and kicked my mother in the hip, and then slapped her into the wall. She began pleading with him to stop, saying, "Oh please stop, don't hit me again, I'm sorry," etc. I wanted to stop the fight (wasn't really a fight because she never hit back), but I felt powerless to do so. I felt like my mother needed help, but I also felt she deserved the beating and precipitated it when it happened. I also did not want to get involved for fear of having to take sides, so I remained hanging, ambivalent, and indecisive.

It made me feel that open confrontation and conflict, and expression of dammed-up hostility and hatred were about the worst things that a person could let himself do. I learned how to control my feelings and behavior so that I never show my anger to another. Even now I avoid unpleasant situations. I am fearful, and feel that suffering during the years has left its mark on me for life.

A 20-year-old woman reports an experience which occurred when she was 19:

When I married my husband at 18, I did not do so because I loved him. I suppose I did it for the hell of it. After six months of marriage however, this began to change. Now I love him dearly, sort of like he's part of me physically. Perhaps this came about because I came to know and understand him—to value him as worthwhile, consequently to love him. I don't know why I feel the way I do about him, my main concern is to make it last and to nourish it in its growth. Before I loved him, I was not happy, had few desires, and cared little for myself. Now I am happily working toward our hopes and dreams, striving constantly to please him. We never argue, always we are together in any issue.

I feel often that we are one, sharing the same mind and heart. Our communication is so great that words slow us down. I feel as though he really is my better half, making me laugh, making me see those things that are valuable in life, and making we want to live, rather than exist. "When the experience occurred" makes it sound like the past, but it isn't, it's a continuation.

A 24-year-old woman reports an experience which occurred when she was 20:

> Four years ago, while doing my housework, I had a pail of boiling hot water on the floor. I left the room in which I set the water for mopping, and used the bathroom. While [I was] using the bathroom my little girl started crying. Not knowing why she was crying, I paid no attention to her. On returning to the living room, I found her buttocks in the water. She died after becoming infected, two weeks later.
>
> This experience has made me refuse to take a job with children (of any nature). I feel guilty.

A 34-year-old woman reports an experience which occurred when she was 27:

> I think the most intense personal suffering that I have experienced was when my father passed away. I was married and had my own home, but I had a feeling of being lost as if nothing mattered anymore. For about a week I felt as though there was no reason to do anything. Then one morning I started crying and for about two hours I just cried. When I had finished I felt much better.
>
> This experience helped my feelings, after it was over. I accepted my father's death and went on with my life.

A 24-year-old woman reports an experience which occurred when she was 24:

> A few weeks ago my father learned I had been dating a young man, a native of India. My friend, being from Madras in southern India, is dark and could be mistaken by some racist Southern whites as negroid, although he had no features whatever of the Negro race. He is a most sincere and nice young man. Being a narrow-minded white Southerner and a man to react impulsively, my father was ready to get a gun and track down my friend, and kill him. And, if the opportunity had been at hand, he would have. My reaction to this was that he'd have to kill me first and this he said he'd be glad to do rather than let me throw my life away on a "nigger." The thing that bothered me most was not the fact that my father was ready to kill but the reason he possessed for doing it. He knew nothing about the young man except that his skin was dark.
>
> I felt at first genuine hate which later mellowed into dislike and still later, as I reasoned the matter out, compassion and pity that a man with the ability of my father was cheated, by circumstances beyond his control, of the further education that I'm positive would have changed his views. As I observe him today I see that he's at conflict with himself and am happy he made it possible for me to gain a broader education so that such biased opinions would not be handed down further.

A 24-year-old man reports an experience which occurred when he was 24:

I experience more intense pleasure from my two children than anything else. The feeling of love watching them at Christmas or a birthday receiving gifts. The excitement and joy which these things bring. Or just watching them having a good time or trying something new, these are the things which make me feel best. I guess loving them is what I'm saying. This gives me great personal pleasure.

It feels good. It gives my life more meaning. I only hope that they too will experience this same feeling.

A 32-year-old man reports an experience which occurred when he was 21:

The greatest and most intense experience which was bestowed on me was my marriage day. I was hearing every word to its deepest meaning, spoken by the minister, and having the satisfaction of receiving the responsibility of a wife. Being able to love my wife to the fullest extent, to be able to do my best to make her the happiest.

It has given me everything to live for, a reason to use each day. The marriage gives me companionship, someone that I may share my life with.

A 39-year-old man reports an experience which occurred when he was 22:

During the Korean War, I was recalled to active duty. At this time in my life, I had one child who was about seven months old. The night I left to report to duty I experienced one of the most trying moments of my life. As the train pulled away from the depot, separating me from my wife and child, a feeling of complete helplessness, sorrow (or grief) filled my consciousness. No feeling of duty to country or anything else mattered, I was leaving a wife to an uncertain fate with a small child. We needed each other—I was needed and leaving them. Tears welled into my eyes; I almost jumped off the moving train. My need for them was not evident at that time—just they needed me and I was deserting them. A feeling of terrible loss also pervaded, as if I would never see them again.

I feel that this experience has been an important one in my personal growth. It has enabled me to understand and cope with life.

A 47-year-old woman reports an experience which occurred when she was 5:

In thinking back over the many personal experiences which I have had the one which I seem to have never been able to erase is that of my mother's funeral. My mother passed away when I was five years old. Even today after 42 years have passed, I recall each shovel of dirt which covered the body. It's hard for me to believe that a child was allowed to witness such an event.

I have attended very few funerals and I become very emotional when I do so. The "aloneness" I felt when I returned home is indescribable. I still am afraid of facing the reality of death, which of course we all know we will face sometime.

A 26-year-old woman reports an experience which occurred when she was 22:

> What caused the greatest change in my life and forced me to examine myself would have to be the breakup with a young man I had gone with for four years and I met when I was 18 and he was 17. He was a brilliant young man, very sensitive to his own feelings, but relatively insensitive to mine. He was very nice looking, and all the girls flocked around him. However, between his college studies and me he never had time to bother with them. Nonetheless, I was extremely jealous and was constantly accusing him of being "unfaithful." I nagged him, badgered him to take me to certain functions, etc. When I felt he was ignoring me, I picked a fight with him which always hurt him deeply, but brought him around. My faults are endless, but finally after four years the breakup came. The night I knew it was all over, as he turned to leave the house he said, "I love you and I always will. Goodbye." I suffered more I believe over the realization that I was at fault for driving him away, rather than because I had lost him.
>
> I was determined to do everything in my power to correct my selfishness. I am now married, and have a small daughter. I believe that in my marriage I have found happiness, satisfaction, and fulfillment in a most extraordinary way. And the breakup . . . is what has permitted me to come into my marriage with the attitude and values that I have.

A 24-year-old woman reports an experience which occurred when she was 20:

> Right after my husband and I were married about three months we announced we were expecting. Since we had not been getting along too well with my parents, I called and told my mother my husband and I would like to talk to both of them. Things were very relaxed and I had high hopes. My husband and I both explained how we felt that we had not been considered as *individuals* but just as "the Children"—My father laughed and said we were being ridiculous. That ended it. It was as though a very precious opportunity had slipped through my hands. I was void.
>
> [I felt that] something had died. And to this day I feel intense grief because I cannot communicate with my parents and yet I still love them. My mother more than my father—I have very little feeling for him other than just another person—I feel sorry for him. This is an intense feeling because it will remain with me always. I think this incident was the culmination of many years of not being able to communicate.

A 23-year-old man reports an experience which occurred when he was 21:

> My most intense experience was one of both pain and pleasure. This was when our child was born. My wife was given injections to induce labor and we were told the birth might be as much or more than 16 hours from that time. As it was, my wife was in labor only five hours. I stayed with her the full time but was not allowed in the delivery room. The time I spent in the

waiting room was pure hell (upset stomach, nerves, etc.) but there was also great joy when I saw my wife and son in the recovery room.

At times [I feel] like a man—at times scared—always loved. This pleasure is lasting, because I still love my wife and son.

A 25-year-old man reports an experience which occurred when he was 22:

The experience which holds closest in my mind is the relation I had with my wife before our marriage.

It grew from "Boy-Girl" to love in a few months. She was everything I wanted at the time. Possessing all the qualities, warmth, understanding, kindness, and joy.

She was alive, young, happy, and lovely. It came to a point where I didn't have to speak. A look or touch was all we needed. We could sit and feel each other, even doing other things in the same room. Even apart, I could feel her presence or being on every movement and thought I had.

Sex wasn't a game, it was joy, a feeling of total us. Both mingled together for a supreme reason.

Since our marriage went bad, I feel that I have killed something very dear to me.

This made me feel human, more aware of the important things to my life. I also think at the present I may never feel the same again, since our marriage went bad, now and then I strike out at myself for revenge.

A 20-year-old man reports an experience which occurred when he was 20:

When I got married I was very unsure of what I wanted out of life but I thought [marriage] would help me out and would be fun. I had been to college and had decided this was not for me, but I did not know what I wanted to do. I got a job and the next thing I knew my girlfriend had talked me into getting married. I felt like she was the girl for me so rather than take a chance of losing her I married her. Right now I don't know what to do. I keep going in circles. Being married seems to kill anything that I would like to do. It seems like the world is passing me by. Like tomorrow I will be 100 and I will die, and to me death is the end. How do you get out to find yourself if you can't do what you want?

I think I just goofed. My whole outlook on life is different. What am I looking for? According to life I am supposed to be happy with my wife. But I am not. I don't know where or who to turn to. Everyone I have talked to asks why? How do you find out?

In school I know I should study but can't or try to put it off. I can't get my mind clear. I am always thinking of something.

I did all this before I got married but it did not seem as bad. I have 1,000 problems and no way to solve them. Maybe they aren't big but they are to me.

God seems unreal to me now. Maybe this would have happened anyway but not as fast.

A 48-year-old man reports an experience which occurred when he was 22:

> When I entered the army I was already married and I took my wife with me to Texas, where I was to be stationed. My total income was $42 per month. I started gambling on paydays and at first did all right. Then came a payday when I lost my complete pay. I borrowed money from my friends to cover this up; not telling my wife. On the next payday I of course owed most of my pay. After taking care of those debts I gambled the rest of it, and again lost. I then had to go home and let my wife realize my lack of maturity. I was so crushed I did not know what to say. I wanted so much for her to know that it was not that I did not love her, that I did care for her despite the fact that I obviously was not attempting to even take care of her. She threw my empty wallet in my face. I had nothing I could say. I was so ashamed I could do nothing. I cried, sobbing as a baby, until I was completely exhausted. Such shame is a wracking thing for any man to endure. The contempt my wife felt for me was just more salt added to the tears.
>
> My wife had to leave me, temporarily at least; I did not stop gambling right away but after a while I did stop. I have, since that time become very conservative. Possibly this is to avoid ever having to experience this degradation again.

A 20-year-old man reports an experience which occurred when he was 19:

> The experience which has had the greatest personal impact on me and my life is my third back operation. I did a lot of psychological suffering. Having two operations before was hard enough and realizing what I had to go through again was the most painful part. I couldn't walk, I was paralyzed from the waist down.
>
> This operation affected my life in many different ways. For one thing I have lost faith, or should I say all possible belief in God. I thought about this many a night, of how I could possibly lose something so precious but I have. I guess you could say I've lost my self also. I live in pain every minute. I have a tumor which cannot be removed from my third vertebrae. They have operated twice on this tumor. For this reason I'm not a happy guy. I don't think or really care if I'm ever happy again for I've lost all hope.

A 23-year-old man reports an experience which occurred when he was 22:

> The most intense experience that has occurred to me was when my brother was killed in a freak accident. This feeling of hurt is impossible to describe. The only thing that has brought me any comfort is time. This has changed my complete outlook on life inasmuch as I have the impression that this society is rotten. It is impossible to explain how you feel when someone you were right beside, and who spent his complete life just trying to make you happy, is with you one minute and dead the next.
>
> This has made me feel like taking a gun and blowing the person that killed

my brother to hell and back. I think society is rotten. I think that our law enforcement in this town is as rotten and dirty as the lowest tramp.

A 30-year-old man reports an experience which occurred when he was 14:

My most intense experience was when I was in high school at a swimming and diving meet. I won both of the events. After the meet was over, and as I was leaving, a girl, who I always thought a great deal of, came up to me and said, "Isn't there anything you can't do?"

This was the best compliment anyone could have ever given me. It makes me feel good to remember.

11

yes, but have we really achieved encounter?

THE RELEVANCE OF ENCOUNTER TO BUBER'S I-THOU RELATION

A chapter to be read after your encounter group has been meeting for some time and you want a kind of check to make sure you really have achieved what we have been calling encounter—an acid test, as it were, for the human encounter.

Let us presume that you have been meeting with your group for some time. You have begun to feel very much at ease with each other and you look forward to each encounter meeting. Also, when you see each other in the hall, you sense a friend with whom you can share a lot of your personal life. But still, for some reason, you feel a nagging wonder whether your group has really achieved a level deep enough to be called *encounter*. Or maybe you truly believe that your group has achieved encounter, but you would like to be really sure. This chapter was written for this particular point in your encounter journey to provide you with a kind of checklist. This could very well be a major topic in one of your encounter meetings. Have you really achieved encounter?

Although others have talked and written about that deep sense of relation to God, to men, and to the world around them, Martin Buber's particular vision seems to speak directly to us who live in the late twentieth century. It is surely right and just that truths must be reinterpreted from age to age, and what Buber says captures in a beautiful way the quality of that unique event we now call *encounter*. Furthermore we believe that what he has to say can be translated from his philosophic-religious (he rejected the word *mystical*) language into psychological language which applies directly to encounter. He has provided us with at least seven (perhaps more) very specific characteristics of the encounter relation and quality, seven characteristics which your encounter group members may want to use to check the quality of your relations to each other.

Since each person's insights are influenced by and rooted in his life-view and his experiences, we are first going to provide you with just a little background on Buber himself and a little of his frame of reference about the world and all that relates to it.

We do not think this brief excursion into philosophy will be too difficult for most of you, but if philosophy is not at all your cup of tea, skip over to the next section and pick up on page 133 after the asterisks. It is there we begin to list the very pragmatic seven characteristics of the encounter relation.

Buber described that quality of relation we have called *encounter* as the *I-Thou* form of address. Buber's description of the I-Thou relation is the expression of his life as a philosopher, as a theologian, and as a person deeply committed to the Hasidic movement[1] of the East European Jews. Buber was a deeply spiritual person who came to be recognized throughout the world of letters as a pioneer in that realm that bridges philosophy and religion. When still a young man, something happened to him—something so impelling, so extraordinary, that he was compelled to write of it. The product of that vision was a small book entitled *I and Thou*.[2] Though small, this book acquired a significance that made it a classic within the lifetime of its author.

---

[1] Hasidism, in brief, is a movement that has as its focus not the individual *per se*, but the larger community of persons of which he is a part. The communal living of the cloister, the kibbutz, and the hippie crash pad all partake of some quality of this socially-based commitment.

[2] Martin Buber, *I and Thou* (New York: Charles Scribner's Sons, 1958).

I and Thou is a book to be studied, to be sipped, to keep by one's bed, to travel with . . . as are all those works which speak to our hearts.

In *I and Thou*, Buber describes two ways of being-in-the-world, two attitudes, two modes of relating ourselves to all that is: *I-Thou* and *I-It*.

For Buber, the first mode is the I-Thou mode of address. I-Thou is the primary and loving relationship between the person and the *primary being* (for *primary being*—read *God* or *Godhead* or *existence*, or *universe*, whichever is your religious-philosophical bent).

The second mode, I-It, is not a way of relating to others at all, but rather a way of perceiving things that lie outside ourselves. I-It is a way of grasping the universe, of defining our world, of making the world ours; that is, of making it subservient to our purposes; it is a means whereby the world becomes a more useful and comfortable place in which to live. I-It is a way of using things; I-Thou is a way of relating and loving. I-It is a way of understanding things; I-Thou is a way of living.

Let us now attempt to express the I-It mode in "first-person" terms:

I live in a world of objects—beds, tables, chairs, cars, glasses, books, etc. All of these things are valuable to me because I use them. They are useful. I use the bed to make my sleep more comfortable; I use the table and chair to make my eating more pleasant; I use my car to get me where I want to go faster; I use my glasses to make my reading easier. These objects (which are there at hand) are of great utility in making my world an easier, more pleasant place to be. Their value lies in what they can do for me. I appreciate them but I do not love them; I do not have a relationship with them. They are objects.

Objects are in the world of I-It. I cannot have a relationship with my bed. A bed is a thing to be used. It would be absurd to have a relationship with it. It is an object. I do not love objects. I use them. I value them so long as they are useful to me, as long as they serve some purpose. But when they are no longer useful, I will discard them. If my chair becomes too broken down to be fixed, I will discard it. I will get another.

The world of I-It is the world of objects, not of human relations. It is the universe in which *usefulness* and *replaceability* are the basic attitudes.

By contrast, the mode of I-Thou is not of the world of *objects* or of *perceptions;* it is the world of *relation*. A real relation cannot be replaced. Only an object is replaceable. The mode of I-Thou contains no objects, since objects lie outside of ourselves and are things perceived by ourselves.

Only I-It can be reduced to the world of objects; I-Thou has to do with relating to the Other. I-It has to do with the rational use of rational objects; I-Thou has to do with process, with relating, with what is unstable, dynamic, expanding.

In its deepest sense I-Thou indicates our way of addressing ourselves to the *primary being*—profoundly, reverently, lovingly; and it indicates also the mutuality and reciprocity of that relation.

Each person may have his own interpretation of what Buber meant by *primary being*. Some will simply call it God. Others, rejecting the notion of God, will interpret the *primary being* as the universe which is the ground of our being. Still others will admit the *primary being* as the world in which we live—our own known environment.

However we interpret it, *Thou* refers to our way of addressing ourselves to that which we hold sacred. And it indicates also a relation without limits or definition. We cannot make use of *primary being* as we do an object in our environment. Use is not a part of relating, of I-Thou. We cannot grasp *being*, mold *being*, shape *being* to our liking. What is even more essential is that neither can we discard *being* when *being* is not to our liking. We cannot disengage ourselves from our god, our world, our universe. They are there whether we like it or not. To think that we can discard them is an illusion. We can be indifferent to them, but that is only alienation. In some way, then, we must address ourselves to *primary being*, to God, to the world, to the universe. And when we begin this address, we enter into the relation of, into knowledge of, into the process of I-Thou.

In the first-person terms, I-Thou might be expressed in the following manner.

> Thou art beyond my comprehension; yet I know thy being.
>
> I do not perceive thy shape, thy substance, for in that moment that I describe thy attributes, *Thou* transcends even that. I cannot describe or summarize thy attributes. Descriptions and summaries belong to the past; *I* and *Thou* belong to the present, the Here-and-Now. *I* and *Thou* are not confined to time and space. *I* and *Thou* are individuated but not separate. *I* and *Thou* have become, not *we*, but the *United I*.

According to Buber, "the spheres in which the world of relation arises are three." First, our life with nature, which is the realm wherein speech clings still to the nonverbal level of being. *Thou* may be spoken to nature by man but he hears no *Thou* in return—since nature remains below the threshold of speech.

The second sphere in which relation arises is in the life with men. Here I-Thou is possible: Relation exists, and has its being, in the form of address that enables encounter and the "speaking" to each other.

The third sphere of relation, according to Buber, is our life with spiritual beings. Here there is only reverence, the awareness of the holy, the sacramental, that which "does not use speech, yet begets it." Of that realm, Buber says, we perceive no *Thou*, yet "we feel we are addressed and we answer—forming, thinking, acting. We speak the primary word with our being, though we cannot utter *Thou* with our lips."

Since it is in the second sphere—our life with men, with one another—with which we are immediately concerned, we ask now the following questions.

* * * * *

(a) What are the signs of the emerging *I-Thou* mode as it develops in human relationships?

(b) Do these signs apply also in the process of *group* encounter?

Buber makes some definite statements regarding the quality of the *I-Thou* relation. And we shall see now how Buber's formulations (derived primarily from *dyadic* relationships, namely, one person with another) may be applied to the process of *group* encounter. (The italicized words below are Buber's own.)

1. *Relation is mutual.* Relation is mutual—what does that mean? It says that what happens to the *I* in a relationship is also, at this moment, happening to the *Thou.* Relation is a shared process, an empathy, a feeling of being part of what is happening to someone else.

I-Thou in the group situation is no different. What happens in an encounter *group* never happens to a single individual alone, since what affects one person will also, in some measure, affect other members of the group (insofar as they permit themselves to be affected by the present process and do not cut themselves off from the group).

Emotions are seldom one-way streets, whether the emotion be one of sympathy, apathy, boredom, hatred, or love. If we dislike someone, he is more than likely to reciprocate the dislike in time. And if we develop loving feelings for another member of the group, or in a moment for the whole group, that emotion also will find its reflection and expression eventually within the group. Thus dialog can begin! Unrequited love does not exist in an encounter group anymore than unrequited resentment, or hatred.

Buber indicates this mutuality by hyphenating the words into a single unified phrase: I-Thou. Buber refers to the *United I,* in which the *we* is present, without the loss of the individuated *I.* Group members describe their experience of mutuality in terms of "feeling closer," a "family feeling," "having friends"; or of having a sense of "we-ness," or "group-ness."

We are working together learning about each other and at the same time learning about ourselves. I feel like a part of a rather unique family . . . a family that has a real and honest concern about its members. Although these people are really strangers and are now friends, we have a unique friendship. Our conversations and opinions are in an earnest manner. A hello or hi as we walk down the hall is more than a surface thing, it's a shout of honest feeling. It is very hard here to explain this, but I hope you might understand.

I feel that our group is getting very close to each other and that in the weeks to come it will become much closer.

I feel a feeling of not being so alone since we started.

When I first entered this class, I felt that I was not part of the class and that I was all alone. But now as days have passed, I no longer have this feeling. I feel that I am a part of the group. All of the alone feeling has gone. I haven't spoken up in class but I have been deeply touched.

I like the personal atmosphere that surrounds you. These people are my friends. This is a completely new experience for me. I have made many friends and this has made college seem more like a home to me.

2.   *The other is not an object.* When we address a person in relationship we are aware then of his essential integrity and uniqueness: He remains there and is always a being, a *Thou*. When we perceive him in terms of some category we make of him an object, an *It*. There he becomes a "Catholic," a "Jew," a "black man," a "white man," a "tycoon," a "boss," a "teacher," a "hippie," etc.—a something, an "It."

Such stereotyping turns *this person* into *that object*; it effectively dehumanizes him. We then can no longer know him since our labels prevent us from seeing this person's individuality, his personhood. We may perceive his external characteristics, but his essential being— that blend of qualities that makes him uniquely himself and no other— will escape us. Another way to turn a person into an object is to perceive him as an extension of some plan of ours—an *It* that can be of some use to us.

People have expressed their dim awareness and their resentment of their usefulness as objects. The following statements testify to such an understanding, however inarticulate:

She only married him for his money.
He only goes with good-looking girls.
She dated me as long as I owned a fancy sports car.
My aunt likes anyone who has an expensive price tag attached to him.
No one likes me just for myself.

Implicit in these statements is the value of the objectified person, categorized according to his usefulness or function—his money, his looks, his car. Also implicit here is the idea that if that objectified person should lose his money, or his looks, etc., he would no longer be of value. If the first three statements, incidentally, have a familiar ring, it is because they reflect the adolescent misapprehension of the quality of love. Some adolescents grow older, but do not grow into the deeper understandings of the human relation. If they base their marriage upon the other's function or usefulness—wealth, looks, dancing ability, etc.—the marriage is in jeopardy once one or both have lost their value: when the wife is no longer young and pretty, when the husband no longer cares for dancing at night clubs.

Another way to dehumanize a person is to prejudge him, to make a snap decision about his personality, and then to "relate" to that person in accordance with this prejudgment. A group member will confess having had a different impression of someone before the encounter group. After encountering, however, he no longer sees the person as *It* but as *Thou*, divorced from his original perceptions.

> There is the fact that probably nine out of ten people in the group are people that, under normal conditions, you would never even talk to; yet in the group atmosphere you are able to discuss and gain insights and understandings about them and yourself.
>
> My attitude toward several of the people in the class has changed because I have been able to listen to them and talk to them.
>
> I can honestly state that I feel there is a genuine sincerity to the purpose the instructor wishes for us students to feel for the course. I was not sure of this sincerity at first, maybe because of the difference in this course from any other I have ever taken. I cannot truthfully say that I am more open in my thinking of other people because of this course but I have begun to try. I am beginning to look at people more as individuals than as a mass. I may not get any further than that, I do not know. But for me that is an improvement.
>
> I feel I have gained a greater understanding of myself and others. More of a willingness to try to understand others.

3. *The primary word* I-Thou *can be spoken only with the whole being.* The person who addresses another as *Thou* does so with his whole being: his guard, his mask, his defenses are slowly dropped so that he lives in this revealing and the other may know him. And since I-Thou is mutual, the other now also reveals himself and is known. Both may be vulnerable in their unguardedness, but because they are I-Thou, they are united in their mutuality and trust in each other. It is a relationship both enter (*Thou* can never be unrequited), and in which both are submerged. There is then no holding back since the partners have transcended the rules of pastimes and games, of rituals and individual egos—all is now new, untried, a mystery revealing and unraveling itself, as *I* and *Thou* begin to know each other and themselves.

Because they address each other with their whole being, there is contained in their address a *sacrifice* and a *risk*. One sacrifices his mask, the *form* of himself which is at the same time not himself. And the other also takes a risk—he gives himself whole and withholds nothing. When members of an encounter group partake even in small measure of that event, they become more open and less guarded with each other. They speak of the experience as being able to talk about personal problems; as being surprised at their own utterances; as being themselves.

> Our group to my way of thinking is a very honest and open one. Everyone expresses their feeling without being afraid of being laughed at.
>
> Our class is very open, each individual brings his problems out on the floor and we try to solve them.

My first reaction to the group was that we were making a big thing of nothing, but after seeing how our people open up and really say what is inside them I think it is most beneficial to all. I really wouldn't have believed that the group would reveal such personal problems until I heard it myself.

I feel that I have progressed remarkably well and that I have opened up a great deal. Of course, I still have a long way to go but I feel sure that if the progress continues it won't be long before I really get with it.

My group session to me is a place where I can give the real me a chance to come forward. The way I can do this is because I am relaxed and trusting when I am with the members of the group.

Some of the students are glad to have a group of people who they can feel free to say anything to.

4.   True beings are lived in the present; the life of objects is in the past. And in the future. We can exist laden with ghosts of the past, and frightened of things yet to come. Or we can meet each moment as it comes, unburdened of childhood fears, insecurities, guilts, prejudices—open to the possibilities of the future. Group encounter members reveal this feeling of being in the present as a feeling of hope where there was dread, as feeling worthy rather than insignificant, as feeling filled with a sense of aliveness, joy, greater sensitivity to their surroundings, and more openness to their environment.

I think I have come to feel free and more that I am as good as the next person. Because of this course I can talk to others and I'm beginning to look people in the face. I feel that this is a big step. I haven't been able to do this before.

I have found I speak more freely to everyone. I am not afraid to say what I think. . . . I am beginning to find myself, who I am and what I am . . . . I feel better inside also. I feel like a person.

I believe that I've become more of a person and more of an individual . . . and this feeling makes me much more confident and secure about my actions and what I say.

I am much more like an individual and I am beginning to have confidence and belief in my decisions and myself.

These remarks also reveal a distinctive awareness that "I am more of a person." Buber notes this effect when he distinguishes between the person who makes of himself an *individual* separated from other individuals and the person who knows himself as an "I" being and co-existing in shared community with other beings. The individual *I* is ego, self-important, "puffed-up," conceited. The *I* of I-Thou is that of relation to other men and other beings in the world. In each of the student quotations above, the student stands in relation to others, sharing a commonality with others, feeling worthy and of value but also feeling the worth and value of others. The *I* in each of these is not the individuated *I* but the I-Thou relation, the one that partakes of the *United I*.

5. *The relation to the Thou is direct.* Nothing intervenes between the *I* and *Thou.* Thus we do not plan what we will say to the other; it just happens. Nor do we play games and pastimes with other members of the group. Nor do we bring in anything extraneous. We deal with what is of the moment with the person it involves. We do not interpret how something will appear to the other person. We talk directly to him, not through someone else. If we wish to ask someone a question, we ask *him*, not the group leader. If we disagree with someone, we disagree with the person, looking at him, confronting him. When *I* and *Thou* talk, we talk of relevant things. We do not use speech to avoid the relevant matter because it is painful or embarrassing.

> We don't seem to worry about how the others will react to what we say. We just say it.
>
> I've said things to other members in my group I never thought I would be able to say to anyone—even my wife. And I know that they held my words in confidence.
>
> I never have to think what I'm going to say. It's really wild how we talk when we're together.

In time, then, irrelevant matters drop away—because the relationship is direct, without barriers. The painful, the hurtful is not avoided but is dealt with. Feelings of love and caring can also be expressed without fear of rejection, without embarrassment. Embarrassment and fear drop away, for these are unnecessary and extraneous emotions. Pain and suffering are not blocked out; rather we allow ourselves to suffer pain for we know that it will bring new growth, new understanding of *I* and *Thou.*

An example of the effects of directness: let a group member (no matter how quiet) be absent a time or two, and the other group members feel the effects of his absence. He is not swallowed up in anonymity. His absence directly causes a longing for his presence in the other group members.

6. *Every real relation with a being or life in the world is exclusive.* When we love someone deeply, all others are seen in comparison with the beloved. We can't help making comparisons between the one we love and others of the same sex. And generally speaking, all others fade in significance. So too, there develops among group members a relationship which excludes other individuals. For example, sometimes a member wants to share his new-found joy in the group with another friend or with his spouse, and he brings her to a group meeting or two. He discovers something then that he had not realized before: that what has developed among the group members is an exclusive relationship in which his friend or spouse does not belong. The friend or spouse has not lived through those shared moments of pain, suffering, tenderness.

The exclusiveness of the group does not mean that the friend or spouse is forever locked out. It means rather that the friend or spouse must grow into the membership in the group community through lived moments of suffering, anguish, tenderness, etc., by actual participation rather than by merely hearing what happened in the group.

7. The Thou meets me through Grace. Or to put it another way, the I-Thou relation lifts the being beyond sensual impulses. Desire, lust, even anticipation are dissolved in that moment. (We hear, do we not, a faint echo of the no-desire of the Buddhists?) The moment becomes sacred. At the moment of meeting, *Thou* transforms the *I* and the *I* transcends. It is not a one-way process, for at the moment of meeting, both are irreversibly changed. There can be no going back, for even the past has been changed. To use Buber's words, *the memory itself is transformed.*

An event which has the power not only to change the present and the future, but the past as well, is something more than the ordinary power of man and his machines. It is extraordinary, an unworldly event.

If this experience is so far above the ordinary events of everyday, how can we speak of it in everyday words? Of course we cannot. And that is precisely the mark of the encounter moment. After the event occurs, it becomes difficult to talk of it. We may struggle to find the right words, hint at it, talk around it, even point toward it . . . but ultimately we know it cannot be spoken of and we fall silent. It is inexpressible, like the name of Yahweh. This inability to put into words what lies beyond words, this sense of helplessness with the language, has, however, been described:

> Last term I realized just how unique this experience was. It is so hard to put down on paper the feeling and ideas about encounter.
>
> The feelings and reactions I have toward encountering other people are very hard to put into words or to convey to any person other than myself.
>
> I tried to tell someone what had happened to me. All I could say to him was that it was the greatest thing that has ever happened to me. I still can't explain it. I'm not even sure what happened exactly.

Another girl, rather literate and sensitive, wrote:

> It "means," not in a sense of definition,
> but in a sense of emotion.

We are reminded here of the Archibald MacLeish poem that asserts, "a poem must not mean, but be."

But if students cannot put into words what happened to them they are at least aware that they have changed:

> Human encountering means getting involved with someone else in conversation. Through this conversation, two people come to know each other

and themselves better. They understand each other and themselves and come away from the experience changed in some way.

In similar vein, an inarticulate black student wrote:

> When you encounter someone, they become a part of your life. In some way they change your life because you become a part of them and they become a part of you.

They have described the change as generalized, as applying to other persons in their environment:

> I just dig people a little more, all people. I have a feeling of trusting all people a little more. It's funny.
>
> I think I have changed through the way I see people. I used to judge people a lot.
>
> I respect them for who they are, not for what I want them to be.

Students experience the feeling of change as deep and immense, as bigger than themselves, and as making them somehow a little better than they were before. In other words, their reactions remind us of the vivid language of the literature of religious experience.

> I feel I am standing on the threshold of something big.
>
> I think I am a better and happier person because of my friendship for [this person].
>
> I feel a much more fullness to my life.
>
> I feel I have achieved more of a deeper feeling about things.
>
> When I am seriously participating in an encounter I believe I become a very different person than most people see.

We are not making a case for a new religion. On the contrary, let it be clearly understood that encounter is not a religion, but as discussed by V. F. O'Connell[3] a transient phenomenon of a secular age. It is a method by which men can be with each other in a world that is presently dominated not by a sense of religion but by a sense of the machine. It is a method by which men can talk with each other and help each other to address God until each person can address God without help.

---

[3] Vincent F. O'Connell, *"The Self and Others: Growth Groups and Personal Growth."* Unpublished paper delivered at Conference on Personality, University of Florida, January, 1969.

12

styles of leadership

Just as all groups are different in their makeup, so are all group leaders in their approaches—and we would have it no other way! For group leaders share in the deepening self-awareness of encounter group members, and their leadership style is a manifestation of their own individuality.

Each individual in a group cannot be other than he is (although he can change himself from one lived moment to the next) and so it is with the group leader. In the beginning, therefore, as a group leader you may find yourself *imitating someone you admire,* and you may imitate and incorporate more of him or her than anyone else. The time will come, however, when you will not so much *become* yourself as a group leader, as you will emerge in the mode, the style, the being-in-the-world which expresses your essential self.

We turn now to the intent of this chapter, which is to present ourselves in our different styles of leadership so that you may begin to see how we are different from each other. In this way we hope you will recognize more readily that a style of leadership (when it is authentic) is an expression of a "total person," that is, of that individual's style of life in its strengths and limitations.

The contrasts in our leadership styles and even the way we have chosen to write about them may be startling to some readers. April's style is sure and comes from a firm foundation; many readers will say to themselves, "I would feel comfortable with her as the leader of the group." She is willing to take on much responsibility and one feels with her the strength of her experiences. She is solid, firm, to be trusted. Terry is not the opposite of April, but he is different. His openness may frighten some readers. One is intrigued with the idea of a meeting with him but there seems to be risk involved—and a deep, underlying question "Is he real?"

In writing about these styles we have been as "real" as we know how to be. We have tried to communicate ourselves in two very different ways. We know that readers will react to us in different ways. We hope this chapter will help you to know us better, but more importantly, we hope you will understand our central mesage regarding leadership style: *You must be your own self in a group; you cannot be someone else.* We do not describe ourselves in order for you to imitate us; we describe ourselves (risk revealing ourselves) in order to celebrate our differences and to encourage you to come to know and accept your own unique style.

We come to groups to learn to facilitate our growth and in so doing we learn to facilitate the growth of others as well. In that sense all of us are group facilitators and all of us have unique styles. If we thus "stand for ourselves" and admit our individuality as group leaders in this chapter, perhaps we will have pointed the way for you to stand for yourself as you emerge with your own method of being a group facilitator.

I, LEADER: APRIL O'CONNELL

Responsibility. In the first place I am active in any encounter group I lead; particularly in the opening meetings of the sequence, and *at the beginning and end of each meeting.* I am active because I feel responsible for what happens in a group. I believe terrible things can go under the guise, the aegis, of group encounter. I believe I have witnessed things that send the same kind of shivers down my back as I get when I read the Grand Inquisitor scene in *The Brothers Karamazov*. I am not willing to let such scenes take place *with my knowledge*. I do not believe that a group *per se* is necessarily protective of human dignity. On the contrary, sometimes people will do things under the license of mob psychology that they would never do alone. I am unwilling to allow anyone for whom I take responsibility (which is synonymous to me with *leadership*) to be damaged by the group. This is one article of my faith as a professional person.

Rules. But that means therefore, that I set rules, and that certain things are permitted and other things are forbidden. Of course, the group members also invent rules. For example, they may all decide together on a certain procedure. One group decided (along with the rules I set) that we could not discuss religion, race, the national elections, or local wars, to prevent the group from becoming mired down in the hostility and anger which had happened several times previously when these topics were brought up. But the group then found, to its embarrassment and (eventual) amusement, that it had stopped talking— we had boxed ourselves in!

The rules I set are thus not concerned with *subject matter*, for that is how the "boxing in" syndrome takes over. My rules have to do with behavior. The three rules I begin with are (1) confidentiality; (2) sensitivity to other members of the group; and (3) direct communication.

Confidentiality. I begin always by asking for a pledge of confidentiality. This request is necessary mainly in the beginning, for once a group feeling is established, confidentiality then becomes one of the living experiences of the group's awareness of itself. Furthermore, the group members soon find out that it is difficult, if not irrelevant, for them to try to convey to an "outsider" what goes on within an encounter group.

Sensitivity to Others. The second rule I establish is the rule of politeness and courtesy. This may seem to some to be a limiting of group process (which it is) and an attempt, for example, to prevent anger or the working out of repressions (which it is not). I have found that a group can handle anger (which is warm) and hostility (which is cold) just as they can the various expressions of tenderness and love in its own due time. But a group which does not control itself in consideration for others will accomplish little except bloodletting, or maybe thrill-satisfaction. I consider both of these to be more appropriate for the bullring or the football field.

I also take up here the factor of leadership sensitivity: unless the group leader is aware of the criss-crossing currents of group dynamics, individuals with hostile feelings or unworked-out aggressions tend to dominate the group. Because of the sheer power and energy of jealously, hatred, and fury, the more tender emotions of love and affection, consideration and warmth are often submerged and prevented from appearing. Mob rule is just such an instance of the strength and force inherent in hate and hostility. Some persons have actually told me that they have never been in an effective group meeting that hasn't exhibited hostility. My wonder, at that moment is, "What kind of a person is the group leader?"

To understand the rule of politeness and courtesy, the reader will need to know what I mean by it. The best definition I can offer is "deep awareness and consideration for the being of another." I have never forgotten an "encounter" group of many years ago in which a group member turned to a fat and very shy woman and said, "I hate fat people." The woman said nothing (indeed, she could not) but she never came back to the group. Did it do any good for the person to make this savage remark? Did it in any way help him to vent his hatred? Obviously not, for when he came to understand his underlying sickness (as revealed in the remark he made) the woman was gone, and it was too late for him to undo the damage. Since he could not withhold his feelings about fat people, then he may not have been ready to encounter. He may have needed psychotherapy instead. Hatred such as exhibited by this individual needs special attention and I will not let anyone unleash his hatred for long in my encounter groups. Instead, and very simply, the "hatred" itself is discussed and the group is made aware (including the person toward whom the hatred is directed) what is going on.

This is, incidentally, how I now handle situations of hostility. In this particular incident, as I recall, no attempt was made to salvage the victim (her feelings or her person). I was younger then and made no attempt to intervene since I was seduced by the "permissive" philosophy of the group.

An obvious question can now be considered: How can we deal with a person's aversion to fat people if it is not expressed? The answer is so intimately tied up with the dynamics of group membership that it may be overlooked. In the course of events, and if the group is successful, the group begins to establish a bond of relation with each other (a spiritual communion, if you will), what Buber called the "United I" relation. Even the man who hates fat people will be caught up in the tide of this love and caring for all the group members and to some extent, at least, this will include the fat lady. The aversion has already been dealt with then to that degree. Meanwhile he is learning a nonhating mode of behavior, and to express his hurt and fear in a nonhating way. As a result of the enforced "consideration," group members find that they begin to understand someone in the group that they had not understood before, and will often express (without causing hurt or hostility or offense) their previous feelings of distrust, dislike, suspicion, etc. (Sometimes it is expressed by the person more to understand himself than to enlighten the other.) The "I hate fat people" becomes in time, "You know, when I first came into this group, I hated fat people. But I found you to be different from what I thought you to be." He has, so to say, considered her further . . . he and she are changed. And in that moment, too, we can ask the speaker to explore his aversion to fat people—what associations, or unfinished business, or signal reactions does he have in regard to them? That is the real issue.

Now the question that needs to be asked is: Is this approach helpful to people with negative hostile, sadistic, etc. feelings toward others? Let me first ask another question. Does a person have to act out his neurosis or psychosis? If we follow that question to its logical absurdity we will end up with the premise that the best way for a person to cure his murderous feelings for someone is actually to murder him! At least in fantasy! Some group leaders follow this method in theory (the acting out of a fantasy murder) and so we have many techniques which utilize role playing and psychodrama. But another way to approach a person's murderous feelings is to have him examine introspectively the possibilities that can result from his murderous feelings. (And even closer to the bone—*what has already happened* to him because of his murderous feelings.) In that way, he can alter his behavior without acting it out either actually or in fantasy. I have never been convinced that the boundary line between our actual and our fantasized worlds exists at all. Surely, it doesn't exist in our dreams, or for the madman, the poet, and the lover. I would be careful therefore not to permit a person to act out such terrible deeds—even in fantasy.

Now to return to the first question: Does learning a new type of behavior actually do any good for the person with aggressive feelings? Let me answer it this way. I have been working in a junior college in a small Southern town. Many of my students in encounter groups are white and black students who have never experienced close association with each other, and never in a classroom situation. They come with feelings of dislike, fear, suspicion, discomfort, and, in some cases, outright hostility. In other words, they express a wide range of prejudices and emotions that are indicative of people who do not know each other. Although another encounter leader might encourage or allow active expression of antagonistic feelings that underlie prejudices (in an effort to break down group barriers), I do not. But I have watched these students break down their barriers *at their own pace* and *in their own way* as they work in the group, in which they must be at least civil to each other, even when they cannot yet be courteous. Some of the reactions expressed by these students later are:

I wasn't exactly prejudiced against Negroes but I was a little afraid of them. They aren't as different as I thought.

I am less afraid to talk with white people than before.

I don't know if I like Negroes any better than I did, but Johnnie Brown is O.K. in my book.

I have one more comment regarding the belief held by some therapists, group leaders, counselors, etc., that it is "good" in some way for a person to vent his hostile feelings against another. I suppose if we were committed to regarding the world as a hostile environment, and if hostility were an essential ingredient to survival, then I could agree. For we need to consider the fact also that allowing a person to express hostile and aggressive feelings actually reinforces that behavior. I prefer, therefore, to have the group explore other ways more in spirit with cooperation and consideration. And if we allow complete freedom for feelings of anger and hostility we do not allow the hostile person to examine and explore for himself these other modes of being.

Some persons, for example, "sexualize" their feelings; that is, they interpret their experiences and the behaviors of those around them through a screen of sexuality. For example, a girl gives a man a smile of gratitude and he interprets the smile as "seduction." There are of course many other modes of experience through which behavior can be interpreted and distorted: anger, hostility, sabotage, etc. It seems to be symptomatic of our time and era to screen our feelings of love and tenderness through a web of suspicion and fear. In this regard, I know of several persons who are made so uncomfortable by their feelings of tenderness for other individuals that they defend themselves by becoming angry and then turn their anger on those for whom they had felt the tenderness and love the moment before. It is easier for these persons to handle anger than to manage their feelings of love. Generally speaking, such persons feel ashamed or helpless (and thus vulnerable) when they experience bonds of caring that come with tenderness and love and that overwhelm them. For these people especially, I deem it imperative that they experiment with and become accustomed to other modes of experiencing and expression, to other ways of being-in-the-world than their conditioned responses of resentment, hate, rage, impotence, etc.

Direct Communication. We live in a world of noise, especially those of us who live in cities. Noise is generated from the streets, from the factories, from our homes, and, alas, we also contribute to the uproar. We contribute to the "noise" in our environment when we make meaningless statements to each other. Much of what passes as "polite conversation" at teas, or conferences, committees, meetings, even the casual conversations we have with friends and acquaintances are often nothing more than pleasant "noise" (Berne calls it *back-stroking*) which is comforting because of its lack of information ("No news is good news!").

"Hello."

"How are you?"

"Fine, thanks."

"Same here."
"Nice day."
"Sure is."
"See you later."
"Right-o."
"Bye."
"Bye."

As Berne notes, such a conversation is a pleasant but noisy pastime, in which the essential and only bit of information relayed is that nothing much has happened, everything is unchanged.

The whole issue of language (how our words create a world) has been the concern of the area of general semantics, and students of this discipline have been studying the ways people communicate with each other. It often comes as a surprise for the naïve student to realize that people do not always speak their minds and hearts, but actually manipulate their language so as to camouflage their motivations. Not only do we prevent other persons from knowing what we really mean; we prevent ourselves from understanding what we really think and feel. Thus our speech may communicate our ideas and thoughts effectively, or very ineffectively; it may clarify the issues or obscure them; foster creativity or inhibit a new discovery; reveal our intentions or camouflage them; finally it may build or it may sabotage. We have spent so much of our lives, however, engaged in language that confuses, obscures, sabotages that eventually we do not hear it. In effect, we have become deafened by it.

One aspect of encounter that is fundamental for me is the sensitivity to what a person is saying. In encounter we listen to what is really going on, that is, to the language that is being used, and to the "noise" in the communication as persons attempt to speak to each other. As we learn to distinguish between what is "noise" and what is "information," we also begin to recognize what prevents persons from knowing each other; and what situations help to promote meeting, encounter, etc. Those things which prevent persons from knowing each other in group encounter are the same things which prevent us from knowing each other in the world outside. We can therefore begin to identify those elements in our environment which are destructive to us, and which have been destructive to us *without our realization*. For example, one sentence that signals danger to me is, "I'm only telling you this for your own good." Many an unkind, hostile, manipulative demand follows this sentence.* I seek ways, therefore, to help

---

*I am reminded of the novels of C. P. Snow. When the officials of Cambridge wished to sabotage a man's promotion or even entry, it was generally done under the excuse of "the best interest of the college" or even more incredibly "for the man's own best interest." In one college where I have worked, the magic phrase went something like "In the best interest of the students" or "I am only thinking about the students in this issue." "The students believe this to be the right course of action for them," or some such. Thus, the first person to come up with this kind of sentence rated the first "down" (to use football jargon) of the discussion.

the group members establish clear communication with each other (and with themselves) and to eliminate the noises which confuse, and the camouflage which screens out the real motivation.

One way is to make a rule that the group members talk to each other rather than to each other through me. This sounds easier than it actually is. Group members tend, in the beginning to talk to each other through the authority of the group leader. We have been programmed to do so in school from kindergarten to college in which we were taught to raise our hands to speak, and in which class discussion is interpreted as directing remarks to the teacher (even when the remarks are meant for a classmate).

If we proceed with leader-oriented discussion in an encounter group, what results is not open and free exchange among the group members, but a series of private conversations between the "leader" and the "student" with each student waiting his turn to speak. That can be one method of classroom teaching, but it does not belong in the encounter group since it works against the openness and exchange that encounter demands. Thus I insist that each person directly address the person he is speaking to or about. I remain in a dual role: group member, but also (to the best of my ability) guardian. Since I am (by definition) the group leader, I take on the responsibility of helping the group members enter into relation with each other with the pronouns *I* and *You*.

There can be much resistance to talking directly to another person in a beginning group for the members bring their old habits into this new situation. If a group member makes a remark to me starting with "But he said . . . ," I interrupt him and ask that he speak *to* the person he is talking *about*, by addressing him with the pronoun *"You."* He often becomes flustered at this point, and will frequently protest that he was really talking to me, or try and convince me that what he has to say about the person cannot be said to him; that his sentence has no relevance to that person, only to the rest of the group or me; that it would be ludicrous or embarrassing to talk to the person directly, etc., etc., etc. But *as Perls has emphasized,*[3] if he is talking to me about someone else he is *gossiping* about that person to me, openly gossiping, yes, but nevertheless still gossiping about that person to me, and with my consent. If I allow it to go on, I accept gossiping as an adequate method of communication. I do not. I do not permit gossiping in a group.

If members are allowed to gossip about each other, and if they are not encouraged again and again and again to talk to each other of their differences or misunderstandings, the group gets into a lot of noise (what Berne calls *uproar*) out of which we can get only a jumble: "But he said. . . ." "No, he didn't say that; he said. . . ." "I think you are both misunderstanding. . . ." "I think what he meant by

[3]Frederick S. Perls, *Gestalt Therapy Verbatim* (Lafayette, Calif.: Real People Press, 1969).

that statement. . . ." And so on and so on, until no one, not even the *person being discussed* can really remember what was said originally. And if we were to take a closer look at all those "He said . . ." sentences, we would discover that the sentences reflect more of the interpreters' own perceptions, misperceptions, distortions, and projections than any real understanding of the speaker's original sentence.

What happens when a person uses the pronoun *you* instead of *he*? First, he is beginning to talk directly to the person in the group and not gossiping about him. This simple procedure can eliminate much of the noise that goes on in a beginning group in a relatively short time. Second, the speaker is taking his first step in going forward toward the understanding of another, since he is now speaking *to* rather than *about*. Third, there is less chance of semantic tricks and games; namely, methods that cut each other up. Finally, he has begun to explore at last genuine communication rather than gossip. And it does one more thing. It begins us on the path of I-Thou relation.

Thou (and *thee, thy, thine*) is a translation of the familiar form of address which is no longer used in English (save in certain circumstances). Other European languages, however, have retained this usage, and although it makes the structure of the language more complicated, it lends a nuance that is now lost to English. The use of *Thou* in other languages indicates that the person being addressed is sacred in one's life, that the pronoun *you* which we use to all others, even those who are strangers to us, is not special enough to use with this person. In English, we use it now only to address our God. *Thou* signifies that we place the Being (in this case, God) in such relation to us that all our actions, thoughts, and words are conceived and directed to that Being in reverence. To do otherwise would be to blaspheme.

We have not only lost the use of *Thou* in English but we have also gone a long way in eliminating *I* as well. We say, for example,

"It's nice to have you back in the office" instead of "I'm glad to see you."

or

"The children are supposed to keep their rooms clean because you never know when someone is going to drop in."

instead of

"The children are supposed to keep their rooms clean because I never know when someone is going to drop in."

In the first sentence above ("It's nice to have you back in the office"), the speaker finds it much less anxiety-provoking to use the impassive and impersonal pronoun *it* than to say *I* (am glad to see you . . .). In the second example, the person does not just eliminate the *I* altogether, she projects her feelings of anxiety on the listener by using the generic *you* form. To say that the use of the generic *you* is simply a form of speech does not explain the need to use it in our language.

It is too much to expect an instant transformation in our everyday language, but at least in encounter groups we can use language as it is meant to be used: to reveal and express our feelings rather than to camouflage or distort. We do not hide behind the impersonal pronoun *it* or the generic *you* form, any more than we hide behind the impersonal authority of *we* or *everyone* or *science says.* For all these forms of speaking are only a way to avoid saying "Here I am; this is what I think; and this is where I stand." When I talk from and for myself, I allow you to come forward also to talk from and for yourself. We can stand thus in I-Thou relation. There is *no one*, and *no thing* between us.

I have told you my three rules, and the rationale behind them. There are, in addition, some things which I find helpful as a group leader and I share them with you in the hope that they may also be of some use to you as a beginning encounter leader or member.

Helping the Quiet Group Member to Speak. As in any classroom situation or committee session there are often a few verbal, outgoing individuals in encounter groups. These are the persons who are willing to take a risk; they possess that delightful spark of spontaneity which enables the group to come forward toward encounter, for they are eager themselves to risk something as they come forward in the path of self-knowledge. In the group, they are often the persons who give more easily and from whom the others in the group draw strength and encouragement. (I say *often* because there are some verbal people who participate from a need to dominate and who must command attention from others. These people have a difficulty to be worked through eventually.)

In most encounter groups there are also those who have difficulty in participating verbally. The eager participators mentioned above I have only to react to, for they enter the encounter process with open and unsuspicious hearts. Once given only a little direction, they need "leadership" hardly at all. The nonverbal member is the one I consciously give more attention to, for he needs attention (that is, strengthening and encouraging from the group leader) if he is to become a part of the group. (By the way, it is this person who is often very perceptive of group dynamics, and who can, when he finally is able to surmount his timidity, be an asset to the group, because of his learned ability to listen and see what happens.)

Incidentally, before I discuss what helps the shy person to come into the group on a verbal basis, I would like to mention that I never insist that a person be made to speak; only that he be mindful of the three general rules of conduct when he does. The key to the participation of the person who is inhibited verbally is to provide a warm and inviting environment that makes it safe for him to venture forth in a new kind of behavior. In most instances, after a time, a nonverbal person can be a fully functioning part of the group process, that is, unless his support is so damaged that he cannot risk any more of himself within the group.

Those who are eager to participate but still too shy to blurt out their feelings spontaneously or who do not have enough support to compete with the vigor of the early participators, are actually already involved in the group process on a nonverbal level (they are following the conversation closely, are the excited listeners to whom the early participators talk) and have those signs of expectation and excitement that mark them as ready to enter the group on a verbal basis. What are those signs? There are many, but I will mention only a few: a sudden leaning forward toward the speaker; an inclination of the head; any new sudden move which indicates a change and increase of attention; a nodding or a biting of the lips, or a slight smile. These are a few of the signs of "moving into the group." There are, of course obvious signs of disagreement: anger, indignation, etc. Thus, for example, I watch also for a crossing of the arms, impatient kicking of the feet, frowning, finger tapping, etc. These people are already responding "somatically" and are only holding themselves back from responding verbally.

It takes little to encourage them. Sometimes, it is only a matter of looking in their direction and they speak out. Or it may be an encouraging gesture which supplies them with just the little support they need to speak. With just the support or active interest of the leader or another person in the group, they come forward eagerly and often prove to be the most sensitive to the group needs. It is their sensitivity, in fact, that holds them back, because they perceive the risk involved in group encounter.

I have discussed, so far, two apparent types found in encounter groups: the early participator who gets the group into the process of verbal participation; and the mildly inhibited person who, with some minor support and encouragement, can speak out in the group. There is still a third sort of group member—the deeply withdrawn—who will need firm and continuing encouragement; and I maintain an ongoing alert to see when he may be ready to venture out of his silence and withdrawal. Insofar as he is withdrawn, he requires more than an invitation—he requires a *calling forth*. Sometimes he needs many such callings, for he may be deaf to the invitation being extended to him, or he may be confused by the fact that someone in this world (perhaps the only one in the world) is calling him. Or he may interpret it as "being picked on," etc. Such a person lives more in his fantasy than in reality and the calling forth is an invitation to participate in reality.

It is not easy for him to give up his fantasy world and engage in the world of reality without continuing help and support.

How do we call such a one forth?

First, by noticing the person and by commenting on his visible reactions in a supportive and interested way:

> "Jane, you seem to agree with what John's been saying."
>
> "John, do you find that to be true in your experience?'
>
> "Andy, does that speak to you?"

Sometimes, such a sentence is all that is needed to release the flood of words which has been dammed up inside of the person; a response which needed only this here-and-now calling forth to break the inhibition. Of course, the individual may need encouragement many times before he is able to volunteer on his own. To come out of his withdrawal and to allow himself (his "inside self") to be seen by others and to be known by others can be a frightening experience for such a one—I believe we need always to remember that!

There is, finally, the fourth kind of group member, one who is unable to do much more than be an attendant observer in the group. He stays withdrawn in spite of the many attempts and invitations and callings forth either by the leader or another member of the group. On occasion, and this always surprises me, these people sometimes "come alive" when we notice their lack of verbal interaction in a supportive and interested way.

> "We haven't heard from you, John, and I, for one would like to. What's your reaction to what's been going on?"

If the person demurs by saying he has nothing further to add that hasn't already been said, then I ask him to contribute to the group by telling us with whom he most agrees, or with whom he has most identified during the meeting. This maneuver (and it is only a technique) often serves to give the person some foundation upon which to lay his small offering. He may be so insecure that he cannot contribute of himself, but he may be able to underline another's response. I prefer, by the way, not to take a "punishing" attitude toward these withdrawn people, for that only compounds their feeling of isolation. The individual may then be able to contribute at least the following kinds of remarks:

> "Well, I've been very interested in what Bob's been saying."

in which case, I can then ask him in what way and so encourage him to elaborate further.

Or he may say:

"Sally's problem is similar to mine. Not exactly, but something like it."

In this he has at least given me a clue, a signpost by which he may be guided forward another inch. True, it is not the great stride of another group member, but for him an inch is a mile. At any rate, I can follow up the clue he has given me and ask him, "In what way is your problem different from Sally's?" And with this (if I have gauged his support correctly) the person may find it easy to speak to this difference. Or of course, he may decline at the moment to go into it. In the latter event, I always support that decision and move on to another. I always affirm the person in his choice.*

There is still another category of individuals the group leader needs to know. This is a very general category, I realize, constituted mainly by the people who are destructive to the group process. Each group leader probably has his own pet list but the following is mine:

First, there is the *saboteur*. Any teacher will recognize him at once. He's the one who crosses his arms with the "I-dare-you-to-try-to-teach-me-something" attitude. He's the one who, after we have gone over something several times in class, says, "I don't understand!" His gambits are legion "All right," we say in all innocence. "What don't you understand?" or "Where did I lose you?" We hope this time he will give us a clue. Instead he gives us more sabotage!

"Nothing! I just didn't understand anything!"

In the encounter process, this person sometimes has a very interesting symptom: his foot waggles. A lot of people wag their feet (which sometimes just indicates impatience) but the saboteur wags his foot very conspicuously, very energetically, and very aggressively. When we ask if he would like to share his thoughts (he's putting his energy and attention into his feet rather than into his mouth), he says, "Oh, I'm not thinking of anything!" Sometimes, he will not even give us the benefit of a verbal reply: he may just shrug and remain within his zone of conspicuous silence. Sometimes by discussing his need to sabotage, or the wall he is erecting between himself and the group (particularly toward the group leader, as symbolic of the entire group), he is able to stop the need to compulsively sabotage. But more often, and particularly if he is a skillful saboteur, he will enlist the aid of the group against the group leader until they tire of him, that is to say, get wise to his game. This, by the way, is the one particular difficulty in which I may overrule the agreement regarding gossiping. For gossiping about him is the one thing the saboteur cannot countenance for long. He

---

*Sometimes, though, the individual is unable to state his real choice. And if I suspect this to be true I may say something like this: "I hear you saying one thing with your words but I also hear you saying that you would like to go into this but you are afraid to. Would you like me to encourage you? Sometimes people feel *yes* and *no* at the same time. Is that how you feel now?"

becomes, in spite of himself, involved in the group—in order to head off the counteraction and to take control of the group once again.

Second, there is the *hostile individual.* I have discussed him already to some extent at the beginning of this chapter ("I hate fat people"). Now I wish to discuss the differences between anger and hostility. Hostility is cold, cutting, the calculated lack of involvement that can really damage someone. It can take any of a number of forms: "one-upmanship"; a "cut"; a nasty comment disguised as a joke; the "I'm only telling you this for your own good" routine; the squelch; etc. Hostility says, in effect, "I look at you as an object—I'm not involved with you!" And in this is the essential damage—the consignment to nothingness! Anger, on the other hand, is quick, springs up like a flame (hot and uncalculated), and is aimed at a person, not at an object. It says to that person, "Stop it!" "You're hurting me!" Or "Don't do that!" But always anger is a call for involvement—which hostility never is.

The hostile individual is easy to spot, in many instances on the basis of his "cool." Sometimes, he masquerades, however, as someone who is interested in the welfare of others. Then he is harder to detect—for then his essential coldness is disguised. His weapons are so sharp that it may take some a few moments for his victim to realize he has been "cut." There seems to be one unmistakable outcome with this individual: We come away from him generally hurting, not knowing exactly where, or when, or how we've been hurt. At least, not in the beginning. After a while, however, we begin to experience a dread at seeing this person even though we are confused by it. This person, we tell ourselves, is very intelligent and sharp to talk to; or perhaps has an engaging sense of humor; or maybe he keeps the atmosphere of the group from becoming tedious. Still and all, we sense a reluctance within ourselves to proceed in his direction, or to engage him in encounter. We feel on guard; unsure of our footing when he is around; edgy and tensed up. When this happens, it is wise to look around for the person shooting hostile darts.

Third, there is the *observer.* He won't participate on any level other than the visual. He plays the "Peeping Tom;" that is, he participates at a distance. His manner says to the group, "I have no problems— I'm just here to see what makes people tick!" but with the implication that he has only to learn how others have messed up their lives; his own is fine, just fine! Sometimes the observer acts the *very kindly observer* who is glad to "listen and relate" to the other group members. After a while, however, a pall seems to come over the group, and the members find themselves unable to reveal themselves any longer. They become secretive and on guard. When that difficulty happens, look for a "Peeping Tom"—and discuss his hindering of the group process.

Finally, there is the *"coax-me-a-little"* person. He acts as if he is guarding a secret which he will reveal if the members just coax it out of him. Sometimes, this seemingly reserved and modest person ends up by receiving the attention of everyone in the group during the whole meeting—meeting after meeting after meeting. People ply him with questions to which he answers little more than *yes*, or *no*, or *sometimes*. And the game becomes ludicrously like Twenty Questions. There are sometimes variations, of course. One is "I'm just a little mouse!" and the other group members all take turns as her protector from some alleged attacker.

*   *   *   *   *

The Use of Here-and-Now. One of the characteristics of an encounter group is the focus on the here-and-now experience of the group. Here-and-now has been discussed by the leading existential philosophers and psychologists of our day and I urge the reader to study these people's works for an in-depth treatment: Buber, Heidegger, O'Connell, and Perls.

Most groups come to the here-and-now aspect on their own; that is, they come to the realization that what is relevant is not the past, but the present: not to talk about another person, but to talk about one's present feelings about him; not to "discuss" topics, but to confront head-on the day-to-day problems of living. They find out eventually that an event in the past is essential only if it has relevance for the present. In that respect I recommend Herbert Otto's approach, which he labels the DUE (Depth Unfoldment Experience) method. He requires each person in the group to reveal some event or influence that has contributed to the kind of person he is at the present moment.

Focus on the here-and-now does not imply ignoring past experiences. (I limit not the subject matter—but the behavior!) On the contrary, I find revelation of past experiences helpful to the group when it assists the members to grow toward the here-and-now actuality. Such growth is accomplished by using certain sentences that emphasize the *here* situation. That is, we work toward the lived moment of the here-and-now, the moment when the individual can be here and be now—integrated in this time, free for this moment from the ghosts of the past and the spectres of the future.

At the beginning of each meeting I find the following questions useful in moving the group toward the here-and-now moment.

"Where have we come from?"
"What is the atmosphere in the room now?"
"What seems to be happening in our group?"

During the course of the meeting, a sensitive group member may experience something "underneath," a countertheme, a cross-current in the group (symptoms: boredom, anxiety, tension) which by being expressed openly will overcome the conflict and so restore the integrative functioning of the group. For example, if an individual is boring *my* nerve centers with his droning voice, I may ask the other members first what they are feeling here and now. (Feeling is always in the here-and-now.) They may reply something as follows:

"I haven't been here for a while. I'm sorry, Jerry, but I stopped listening to you for a while."

"I'm kind of bored."

"I am too. I was beginning to yawn!"

In this way we gain not only the valuable insight that Jerry has been boring the group members (confirming my own here-and-now experience), but also the more important fact of Jerry's own boredom. What does this mean? What other emotion has he been suppressing by his technique of boring himself and others? At the moment, by the way, the change in the group atmosphere has been brought out into the open, and the excitement of the here-and-now lived moment has returned. Something buried in Jerry's past has possibly been brought into the open, re-examined, and dealt with.

Another way the here-and-now is emphasized might appear to encourage anarchy, it involves giving a student permission to leave the group. Sometimes a student is withdrawn during the group meeting, or behaving noticeably different. When I notice this disparity, I recognize that only part of him seems present. Typical responses show that, indeed, such a student's attention is elsewhere:

"I've got a chemistry test coming up next period and I'm worried about it."

"I feel kind of sick today. I had a fever last night but I didn't want to cut your class. You might think I didn't want to be here."

"You're right. I've been expecting a phone call from someone and it hasn't come yet. I wish I were home now in case the call comes through."

When I hear something to this effect, I immediately give the student permission to leave. What is here-and-now for him, the relevant and living moment, is to study for the test he's worried about, to go home to bed, or to wait for the telephone call which is overdue. It is more relevant to his growth that he pay attention to the thing which occupies his energy and thoughts, rather than that he stay. Also, his living but empty body sitting in the chair will do no good for him and will only hinder the remaining group members and the group process.

The student is often taken aback by my suggestion. He suspects (sometimes) that it is a trick, that I'm testing him in some way, that I will let him go now, but that I will punish him somehow . . . later. I am careful not to grow impatient with his suspicions. "No, it is not a trick. . . . I think you need to get accomplished what is bothering you. I will be glad to see you when you return to us next time. No, I do not think you are taking advantage of the situation; on the contrary, I know you will come back with more earnestness of purpose than ever." He leaves, somewhat dazed at the possibility that the institutional, impersonal world occasionally can extend an apparently unsolicited kindness. Do the students then take advantage of the situation? A few do; but the majority of the students soon recognize the real point—they become more self-supporting and take upon themselves responsibility for their attendance, for their adapting to agreed-on rules, and for their participation in the group or class.

Of course, I use the situation to help the student and the group to see how we can become more aware of our here-and-now-needs. And I always wait patiently through the silence that falls on the group when the student leaves—each student there thinking through his understanding of what has just occurred. The event never fails to cause that deep and introspective silence which means something significant is taking place—in the silence it is assimilated and digested.

Each Person as His Own Authority. One of the things that I maintain always is that no one is wrong about himself. He may be "wrong" in the real world of ideas (if that exists) but that is beside the point. I hold that only the individual himself can say what is "right" or "wrong," "true" or "false," "good" or "bad" for him. Freud, the founder of psychoanalysis, insisted on the "rightness" of the doctor's interpretation of the patient. If the patient disagreed with Freud, his resistance only proved the "rightness" of Freud's interpretation. Carl Jung, on the other hand, believed that only the patient held the key to his dreams, and to his symbols, and to his truth. I agree with Jung. I accept the person's self-report of his situation as a valid explanation of where he is here-and-now. Not accepting what a person reports about himself can be a great deterrent for his further revealment. For we are acting, or appearing to act, as if the person is telling a lie. If we constantly look for deeper meanings in what he reports, if we are always alert for hidden meanings which will ultimately prove him to be at variance with his words, we convey the impression to him that somehow he is avoiding, lying, suppressing—in other words, that our interpretation is the right one and that he is resisting it! Further, even if we do not intend it, we subtly convey the impression that the group member is not to be trusted. Such an atmosphere will not provide the kind of safe environment he needs if he is to feel free to explore his world and to grow. Therefore whether a person lies, or does not lie, knows or does not know his own underlying motivation, we begin always in the encounter meeting with the premise that each person knows more about himself than do the rest of us. We do not presume to *tell* him about himself; rather we *ask* him about himself. We start with a premise of trust until the person demonstrates otherwise. We provide him with one place, at least, in which he is free to discover himself and others in safety and integrity.

But what does this mean in terms of the practical situation? It means that I do not allow anyone to say with impunity to another: "You know you are wrong in that!" Nor, "You don't really believe that! You're just saying that!" Nor the even more sophisticated, "You think that consciously, but you're just hiding the truth from yourself!" All these opinions are interpretations of another's "inner process," to which only the person himself (I maintain) has the key. And we need to remember that only he can open that "door" for us. Interpretations are often presumptions and always presumptuous! Of course group members may express themselves regarding what has been said by the person. But the speaker must clearly indicate that this is his own impression, his own thought. "You know you are wrong in that" therefore becomes "It seems to me that you are wrong in that! I believe the truth to be this. . . ." "You don't really believe that; you're just saying that!" becomes "I hear you saying that, but it is awfully hard for me to believe it." But then we can discuss the real issues: the listener's disbelief, and what prevents him from believing.

Thus, we give no interpretations, render no judgments of a person's actions or speech unless we first ask the person's permission, and check its validity with him. Only the person can validate the truth of the interpretation.

Any group member, incidentally, can represent his own point of view. He can say, for example:

"It seems to me that you misinterpreted me."
     or
"My impression is that you feel very much outside the group."

By qualifying their statement as their point of view, their opinion, their impression, both speaker and listener are responding to their own truth.

Emphasis on Phenomenology. Space limitations prevent me from saying more than a few words on this topic but I must discuss it, for it is one of my ever-present wonders. We live in different phenomenological worlds. Since I prize these differences, I seek always to know more about them. Thus I encourage each group member to share "his world" with us. Sometimes this may be the first time the person has ever shared his world with another person. On occasion, it can be the first time he becomes aware that his world is not the same as others . . . that he and I and the others live and share a great variety of worlds. Once such a realization happens to him, he becomes more open to the possibility of changing his style of living, of discovering new ways to grow and to be. I have found the following questions helpful in encouraging a sharing of world outlooks:

"What is your family like?"

"How do you see all of us?"

"What is your world like?"

"How do you see the world?"

The resulting responses eventually open up a multilevel universe.

Then, because part of the validity of what a person experiences as the "real world" comes by way of feedback, I ask the group to respond to a person who has come forward in any kind of revealing and intimate way or who has taken a step in some way: recognizing another's right to be different, working out a prejudice about someone else, expressing warmth and affection for someone in the group, admitting a mistake, or telling about a change in his viewpoint. Whatever growth the individual has made, I ask always that the other group members respond to his revelation in some way if it be no more than a sentence. For when a person has done something brave or growth-producing, or has put himself into a vulnerable position, he deserves to have expended himself into something more than a vacuum: he deserves a human response from his listeners. Some kinds of sentences that are volunteered go as follows:

"Thank you for sharing this with us. I feel much closer to you."

"You know, I understand you better than I have ever understood you."

"I share the same kind of problem and maybe I can tell the group about it now that you have done it first."

Sometimes, of course, a group saboteur will not even deign to make a remark to the person who has opened up. In that event, I insist that he address a remark to the person even if it is "I have nothing to say to you" "or "I pass this time."

I have a memory of one young man who revealed to us the strange circumstances of his childhood. We were very much with him as he went into his journey to the past, and back into the present, and we provided for him a warm and safe environment. When he had finished we were deeply affected and we all responded to him out of the depth of our feelings for him. He listened gratefully, aware that we had been with him, and had been glad for him. But spoken response was not enough for this particular group. They decided to write him letters so that he would receive a very tangible feedback from them. He told me later how much the letters had meant to him.

And last, I always end with a closing—to ensure closure within the group. Each person is invited to say something to "finish off," so that he may leave the group comfortably. It might be something he has been mulling over; it might be a response he didn't have a chance to make because of the activity in the group; or it may just be something he would like to say to the whole group.

I ask simply, "Before we break up, let's go once around the group for a closing statement." I start and end. Each person says something even though it be only, "I have nothing to say," or, "See you next time." But much more often than not, the group members welcome this chance to "finish off," to decompress, as it were, from the rarified atmosphere of an I-Thou meeting to that of the everyday world.

"I just want to tell the group I'm feeling very good today and thank you for your help."
"Marianne, I just want to add that you did a very brave thing."
"I feel that I've been treated unfairly. I'd like the group to stay with me."

If, as in the last sentence, the person's closing statement says that he would like to go back into something, then we do that. For that is also part of the closure experience.

On the last meeting days of the encounter group, I concentrate on closing off the whole group, for we have been with each other in an intimate situation over a period of time and that time is coming to an end. The end of the meetings marks a psychological leave-taking and leave-takings are generally sad events if people have achieved psychological intimacy. And so the persons in my groups explore their feelings of ending, of good-bye, of re-entry into the ordinary world, and of what it means to return to a world without encounter on this intense level.

PERSONAL PHILOSOPHY AND GROUP FACILITATOR STYLE: TERRY O'BANION

I am not sure I can describe to my satisfaction what I do in a group. I don't always *know* what I do. I am not an observer who sits at the edge of the group noting the various movements in the group process. I am not an expert who knows the answers and carefully helps each person come to his own understanding. And I am not a leader, in the usual sense of the term, who knows where the group is going and who assumes most of the responsibility for the direction. And yet, there are times when I take some of these roles for I am seldom all or nothing of anything. My point is that I am not primarily an observer, an expert, a leader.

The person that I seem to myself mostly to be in a group is a *participant–facilitator.* I am *in* the group facilitating the growth of others and my own growth as well. I am not outside looking in, or outside directing—I am inside involved, inside vulnerable. In my part of this chapter I will attempt to describe this person I am in a group and will attempt to relate my style to my personal philosophy—as style and philosophy have developed at this point in my life and as I understand them at this point. In writing this section a part of me wants to order my thoughts and carefully arrange my philosophy on the pages from which would then flow my style. Another part of me wants to ramble through my personal labyrinths and see what sloshes out in print—at the moment rambling fits me best.

Sensitivity. If my style, my way of being in a group, had to be summarized in one word it would be *sensitivity*. I have enough feedback from others and I have enough access to my own knowledge of myself to recognize that sensitivity is a major element of my being in a group. Some faculty members in a group I am co-facilitating at the time of this writing have noted this part of me in their written correspondence:

> I hope that Terry is as resilient as I think he is. If I lose him, too, I'll have to retreat some more and straighten myself out. But then I would retain his naked sensitivity as a goal in my life.

> I see you as a very sensitive and emotional person who is very involved and much more real to me than the first time we met.

> He is both facilitator and member—a most difficult tightwire to walk! His sensitivity to the group enables him to intuitively perceive feelings, which by his very real skill he is able to respond to in a creative, liberating way.

> You feel so intensely, hear so acutely, and give so much of your own being to others that I marvel at your stamina.

> He is good at allowing others in the group to respond to others. Have not yet stopped to analyze how he does this. Perhaps by truly being himself. I think so. "Technique" may not be necessary if a person can hear, feel, respond, articulate.

The process of sensitivity is described well by this last observer of my behavior. Being sensitive means hearing, feeling, responding, and articulating. Most of us are insensitive because we do not hear, we do not listen. To listen we must focus our attention on the here-and-now, concentrate on the individual who is communicating, and at the same time be aware of self and others in the group—a Herculean task. That is often why group facilitators feel drenched and worn—although often peaceful, euphoric, or agitated—at the end of sessions.

I see my person as an instrument for hearing, feeling, responding, articulating. I do not like the mechanical connotations of *instrument*, but in our technological society such illustrations may communicate most clearly. I am a tuning fork in a group waiting for the vibrations of others; I send out vibrations also, because I am not a mechanical, placid, reflective tuning fork. I am a live, squirming person, and it may be that many of the vibrations I hear come back to me in response to my own vibrations. In this sense I may actually "lead" the group, but not with the conscious, determined leading of some group facilitators.

I am a radar screen with a wide range of wavelengths through which the communication of others can come to me. Sometimes I even feel as if the pores of my skin are attuned to the movement of others. My body leans toward a person, my hands reach out, palms open, to catch the meaning. My radar screen scans the group, focusing if necessary, but including as much of the action as I can—spotting a movement here, searching an eye there, touching a hand, looking for new developments, watching reactions, encouraging involvement with a nod of the head or a word or two. The radar screen probably catches little of the available human behavior, but it catches enough, and it teaches others to listen.

I am a finely tuned violin, played by the bow that is the group. When there is pain I often hurt. I sometimes cry. I make guttural noises that come unconsciously from my own pain of being human and from the recognition that there is much pain in living. When there is joy I share in it. I may clap and laugh. I have shouted and cried with others in their joy. I am "beside myself," standing apart from my more usual restrained mode of behavior; I like being beside myself. Again the unconscious guttural noises come out of me to express my joy—I am a primitive puppy romping and playing with the great delight of hearing and feeling the joy in another human being.

These illustrations of instruments are mechanical and cold and perhaps deny the very sensitivity I am trying to convey. Another illustration that one of my friends uses to describe me is as follows:

> You are a primitive sea creature scuttling about the ocean floor, kicking up the primeval mud with your constant-moving feelers. You are an ancient form in touch with some original force, not like the new forms of fishes that move with the tide and the currents, and you scuttle about your business with your secret within you. At any moment you can unfurl a hundred blue antennae that dart out into the deep, searching the dark purple for cause. The ocean is your realm and you listen for the birth of a seahorse, the drop of an anchor, a starfish dying, a pearl growing—you hear everything, and your blue antennae throb with response. You are a crusty old crab with a jellyfish heart.

I don't know what all that means about me, but I suppose in some ways it means I wear the shell of a person although inside I am a caring, sensitive being who responds to others as much as he can.

If I listen I hear. If I hear I feel. Not to feel what one hears is to deny a natural human process. Hearing does not occur only through the ears. Reik talked of listening with the third ear. My third ear has nothing to do with my two physical ears. My third ear is my readiness to listen with my whole being. All of "me" that I am in touch with and can command is directed toward you—What are you saying? All the facets of my being that *feel* are ready to receive your feeling. All my outside feelers and inside feelers are connected and ready. I begin to feel the struggle of your wanting to share with me, not being me, not trusting me, not knowing if you understand what it is you want to share. I feel you struggle and offer support—"I want to understand." "I know this is not easy for you." I lean toward you—I am ready to

hear and feel—I am to be trusted. You share more—I do not retreat—
I do not scold—I seem to want to understand—I seem to know what
you are feeling. The pain grows strong and the tears relieve the pressure inside. I do not run away—I move closer—I touch a tear and say,
"What do they mean?" Your pain wells up again and you share your
agonizing struggle to be human. Your pain touches the feeling of my
pain and I respond with like pain—we share tears. Now we talk some
more, "What does it mean? What am I to do? I care for you. Thank
you. How can we help?"

And so I move through hearing, feeling responding, articulating—
through the process of being sensitive—because for me sensitivity
to self and others is the essence of being human. I don't know how
I came to be sensitive; I only know that it is a major characteristic
of my being that I have no question about. I was not always sensitive;
for a period of about five years I chose to be insensitive, to shut off
my feelings, to be a lump on the face of the earth. This was a period
in my adolescence when all feeling was pain so it was simply better
to have no feelings. Perhaps my experience helps me a little in understanding those who are not in touch with their feelings; I don't know.
I only know that I like me being sensitive, and I hope that I grow to
be an old man with even more sensitivity.

I have described myself as a very sensitive person, and I have noted
supporting evidence of people who know me, and although what I
have described is true it is not always true. There are times when I
am a terribly insensitive clod. Sometimes I am most insensitive to
those who are the very dearest and very nearest to me. I often miss
the vibrations of my family; I do not respond to the need of a graduate
assistant who works with me 20 hours a week; I fail to feel the crush-
ing pain of a co-facilitator; I sit amid anguish with a vacant, empty
stare into the nowhere of my being. Sometimes I am too tired—too
worn out from being sensitive—to feel anything more; sometimes I
am too ensnarled in my own tangle of problems to be aware of others;
sometimes I fear involvement and withdraw; sometimes I am so insensitive I am not sensitive enough to know why. I do not mind inconsistency in myself; on the contrary I value it as one measure of my
humanness. When I am terribly insensitive, however, there is something
in me beyond inconsistency, and I need to understand these dynamics
of my behavior. I wish I could pull it together here; readers and writers
expect closure. I am working on my bifurcated behavior; I hope understanding comes.

Self-Disclosure. Many effective facilitators will not allow themselves
to become involved in the group as a participant. They might be very
involved in their *role* as facilitator, but they do not share themselves
as other members share. It is difficult, if not impossible, for me to be
uninvolved in the group. I want to be involved. I want to be sharing
in the human action that occurs in a group. I want to experience others.

I want to experience myself. I come to a group to facilitate the growth of others, but I expect my own growth to be facilitated as well.

I have discovered some important things about myself as a facilitator: (1) when I am open and honest in the group others tend to become more open and honest; (2) when I am able to share the existential sadness and loneliness that are much a part of me, others are encouraged to be in touch with the wells of their being; (3) when I tell others in a group who I am I come to know myself better and I become known to others; usually I begin to care for myself more and others begin to care for me.

When I am open and honest about myself in a group others tend to become more open and honest. In a group honesty leads to honesty, openness leads to openness. When I am able to be honest and open with my feelings toward others in a group it helps others to be open and honest with their feelings. Since most of our daily living is within the framework of structural and routine behavior regarding our relationship with others ("Hello, how are you today?" "I'm well, thank you, and how are you?" etc.), it is sometimes shocking at first to experience the honesty and openness necessary for the group's survival.

In one session a female faculty member was describing the nonsense she had to put up with from the administrators of her college. She described how she and several other faculty members would get together and talk at great length about the conditions in her college: the janitors didn't keep the wastebaskets emptied, there was a shortage of supplies, there were no paper towels in the restrooms, etc. Since this was a group of college faculty members they understood these conditions and sympathized with her plight. Encouraged, she talked on and on and kept absorbing the sympathy of several members of the group. In a few minutes she had become the person she was back on campus and was "bitching" her head off with the encouragement of her friends. It was difficult to intrude on her show, she was really going, but I finally communicated to her: "Jean, I see you sitting in the teachers' lounge right now and really enjoying playing one of your favorite games, bitching at the administration. Why don't you do something about those conditions instead of bitch about them all the time? If you aren't careful you may become an ugly old bitch yourself—is that what you want to be?" Some members of the group were shocked at my statement and a woman next to me gave me a motherly slap on the arm in reprimand. There was a great deal of immediate syrupy smoothness to placate poor Jean "who isn't that way at all!" and much gentle reprimanding to make me shut up. Then I became quite angry: "Damn it! Don't you hit me and try to make me shut up. All of you were sitting here letting Jean bitch her head off and to what good end? Be honest with her, and don't you jump on me when I'm being honest." There was a lot of static and confusion until Jean said: "Wait a minute! Wait a minute! Wait a minute! I want to hear more of what he was saying." We learned a great deal about honesty and openness at that point and moved on to helping Jean look at herself in a good health-engendering group climate.

Experiences of being open are not usually this dramatic. In the first meeting of a day-long encounter held recently I asked the question: "Where are you in your life now?" A number of people responded at fairly intensive levels to the question during the next several hours. Early in the afternoon someone turned to me and said, "We don't know anything about you. You haven't shared anything with us about yourself. Where are you in your life now?" This person really wanted to know me so I took the question into myself, and it found a hollow spot that quickly filled with tears. I explained, through my tears, that I was not at a very good place in my life now. Later that day one of the other co-facilitators asked members of the group to write down their impressions of the first day's experience. The following account refers to this incident of self-disclosure and affirms the point that openness leads to openness:

> On the first day when Terry cried, I was embarrassed, and it was for me a funny experience. I had already realized that the people who were able to plunge in at a deep emotional level were the ones who were most free and open, most truly human. Terry's tears reinforced this for me and permitted me to reveal my personal feelings just as freely. I think I will have no further embarrassment with students who cry as they reveal themselves.

When I can be myself others are encouraged to be themselves. I believe that all people want to be open and honest, that all people want to share themselves with others. All of us would probably like to be completely known by at least one other human being. When we can become known in part by a number of people in a group some changes begin to occur in our lives. If I am willing to risk being known, others take risks, and together we choose new directions for fuller living.

When I am able to share the existential sadness and loneliness that are much a part of me, others are encouraged to be in touch with the wells of their being. An important part of my philosophy has been that man is basically and totally alone in the universe. Regardless of how much we want to relate to others and care for them, regardless of how much we want to be absorbed in the being of our concepts of god, we must still return to the awful realization that we live inside ourselves, alone. No other person or being is likely to enter our one last locked room—if the last is entered we create another to peer out at the new creature who has entered what we thought to be the last room.

There is strength in such a philosophy. We know that we have to depend upon ourselves; in the final reckoning we must turn to the sources of our own inner strength for survival. At the moment of death we are alone in feeling the last breath of life course through our lungs; there is no one to share that experience with us. There is also hope in such a philosophy for it means we are the determiners of our being and that we can invent the life that we would like to live. A poet has told us that we are the masters of our fate, the captains of our soul. The human encounter provides an opportunity for us to invent ourselves anew.

There is strength in such a philosophy, but there is loneliness and fear as well. We are usually raised within the comfort of a family whose members attend to our needs, and most human beings are raised with some concept of a god to provide comfort or strength of some sort. In our early adolescence, when we first begin to feel our aloneness, we are often frightened. College is a time when this experience usually becomes most acute, and one of the major purposes of this book is to help college students learn of the loneliness of others and to come to ways of living with their own loneliness.

A human encounter group can provide a safe environment for the sharing of our loneliness and can help us to come to understand and accept it. One member put it this way:

> How many poets—how many writers—have said over and over that man enters the world alone, stands alone, dies alone? This has always bothered me because I don't like being alone (although I don't like being too crowded either) but here, now, I have a contentment with loneliness. That's where I am now—alone. But I'm not dripping with loneliness—the group has given me a sense that there is support behind the aloneness of making decisions, the aloneness of functioning as I can where I can.

> This mood of near-euphoria will not always last—I know that, but, driving home, I began to think of myself as one of those circular jigsaw puzzles with an intricate pattern. Monday and Tuesday put together more of the interlocking pieces. The pattern begins to show: loneliness, yes—but more of a pattern now—more wholeness is emerging. It doesn't matter so much any more—so I'm always going to be slightly aloof, accepted but not truly very, very close. Alone, yes—but with all the strength of the group's lovingness behind that aloneness.

Loneliness becomes accepted for this group member, and it is not difficult to bear because others recognize where she is and care for her. Perhaps that is as much as we can do for each other as human beings—we can care for each other and we can communicate our caring: "I recognize where you are, my friend, I live there, too. Perhaps when it becomes too frightening we can hold hands until the night passes." When I am able to share my living in this world with others they do not feel so inhuman, and they are able to share their experiences, too.

When **Terry** revealed the deep sadness which underlies so much of what he is, he made me think of the most moving motion picture I've ever seen—"The Parable." I've admired him since our first meeting; today I loved him and lived briefly within his fear for a moment, our real selves touched and tonight I am emptied of some of my fear—it dissolved in his tears.

The most single rewarding experience of the day, in my opinion, was Terry's tears. Now I feel so close to him because deep down inside I did sense similar agonizing pain—the realization of existential vacuum. I admire Terry for his courage and gentle humanness. How I wish I could myself let go as Terry and feel emotional as April.

In a way you seemed to be a little "unreal" in a way in which I cannot pinpoint—perhaps this is my hang-up, however. Then when you talked to us about yourself in regard to your constant searching and striving, I felt as though you shared as much of you with us as is possible for you, because you might be unsure. Therefore, this was real for me and I appreciated you because I (as well as all others probably) am constantly striving, pondering, growing, etc., in my being.

When I tell others in a group who I am I come to know myself better and I become known to others; usually I begin to care for myself more and others begin to care for me.

I want to be known by other people—known as fully as I can be. I don't want to be an object for other people: a professor, a group leader, a teacher, an author, a speaker. I don't like categories and stereotypes that limit me in the perception of those who are in contact with me and, therefore, in the process of coming to know me. I have a doctorate; I have been a dean; I am now an assistant professor. I don't like the title of Doctor, Dean, Professor; others use these titles to harness me as if I were some societal ass dancing on my hind legs to fulfill their expectations of a role.

I am Terry—with all my foibles, considerable strength, numerous weaknesses, growing, fearing, loving, hurting, hoping. I want to be known and accepted on the qualities of my personhood. I know that who I am as a person cannot be separated from who I have become as a doctor, dean, or professor; but I don't want to be known primarily through those roles to others. I don't want those roles to dominate and restrict me for myself—I don't want to address myself with titles when I talk with me. I want access to my more basic humanness. If I allow others to diminish my humanness by coming to me only through the titles and the roles I may get too comfortable—I may meet myself in the same way. What a pathetic old man I would become if I sat in the corner of my own inside room addressing myself as "Dr. O'Banion."

The human encounter group is one of the best opportunities any of us will have to come to know ourselves and to become known by others—such knowing will lead to accepting and caring. Such knowing led me to a point of integration following a recent session and I wrote it down in this way:

> *Babblings of a Man Going Sane.* When I care for others I am the best that is in me. Inside me where I touch myself most there is a peacefulness that comes from caring. The *I* in me that really controls me knows that the caring is good for me and allows me to feel that goodness. From that peacefulness comes both relaxation and radiance; my intensity to live my nonlife becomes less important and there is a smile behind the eyes that betrays the secret I have with me.
>
> Because I may be new to caring it does not come easy for me. When I first feel the caring for another I am the best that is in me. The complexities of being human in the world soon intrude, however, and the *Me* that I have also become confronts me with old fears that have grown smooth with my constant fondling. I hug these fears in defense of caring, for too much caring would make me become what we can become, and that would mean giving up *I* and *Me*. The old fears hide in these questions: Do you love others because you do not love yourself? Does your loving come from fullness or emptiness? When you are full of love why do you cry? Why is your love so intense? Is your loving perhaps a way of asking for attention and response? Do you really know anything about love?
>
> Caring confirms my being, but it is also painful and frightening if it does not occur within the parameters of my known experiences. I have much to give; I need much; I do not wish to impose artificial limits on my range of giving and needing. The human in me will out and find its being confirmed in caring. If caring is limited, the being of my human must also be limited. I will not limit my being; I have a frightened courage to experience the consequences.

Sydney Jourard has done more research on self-disclosure than any other behavorial scientist, and he suggests that it is a major factor in mental health. (See Bibliography for *The Transparent Self and Disclosing Man to Himself.*) I hope I can convey to the reader that for me self-disclosure is not a technique that I have discovered "works" for me in a group. I was doing it before I knew what it was. When I discovered Jourard's research and learned about other facilitators who functioned as self-disclosers I was much encouraged and pleased to have my own style confirmed. Sharing myself has always been a part of me, and wanting to be known by others is a motivating force in me; it feels good to know how to accomplish these personal aims and to have a word that tells me what it is.

Encountering. My developing style as a facilitator has moved me far from a former stance as a passive reflector of feelings. I now move much more intensely in a group, moving out to others, reaching out for them, grappling with problems, in short; I purposively *encounter* others in a group. *I go out to them.* I assume responsibility as a group member for *going out to* another human being.

All of us live behind barricades, tough-constructed shells—our own private hells—heavens, too. I believe that every human being wants to come out from behind the barricades—to become known to himself and to others, to enter into a shared relationship of caring. Human beings will come out under a variety of circumstances and for various purposes. For myself I have discovered that I reach others best if I am willing to make the first efforts to go out to them.

I sometimes frighten people with my reaching out—they are suspicious of such early engagement. Others respond immediately, and we generally move along rapidly in developing a climate of cohesiveness and trust for more encountering, for more reaching out between other members.

Sometimes I push a little too much, urge too strongly. I do operate from a sense of urgency—we walk this way only once—every opportunity missed for growing is just that—an opportunity missed. I know human beings cannot be forced into growing, cannot be pushed beyond some limits of tolerance. But I do believe that many are willing to be urged, that many will work as hard as they can, that all have great capacity for growth. And I cannot sit by and fail to communicate my feelings to others in this regard. So I encounter—I go out to them: "I see you struggling. How can I help? What do you want to work on here? I don't accept that. That's nonsense! I fear you. I have much *aloha* for you. Put your palms to mine—all on top of the table, it's safe. You're beautiful! Hug me. Why do you keep playing your parlor trick of attacking? You are sitting on the edge of tears; can you share them? Isn't that a great feeling—jump up and down with us in the middle of the room so we can all enjoy it. Take off your shoes; you can touch my feet." I don't know if these few experiences help convey any feeling of the encountering process or not. I am trying to communicate that it is not a passive role; it is an active role and it involves risk.

Encountering always involves risk: you may miss the target, hurt someone, project your own problems. But I am willing to take risks; I believe that living is risky and that risk taking should become a part of our healthy response patterns to being in the world. If we risk and fail that is not the end of the world. Not to risk can be a more demoralizing failure.

In a group, risking is quite safe if couched in terms of caring, trust, confidence. We care enough to "try this on and see if it fits." That's being risky, being unsure but feeling that you are on to something in understanding the relationship with another. Taking a risk means we have enough faith in the strength of the other person to be able to discard our communication if we are wrong and enough faith in ourselves not to be diminished by the rejection.

Here is the response of a person I encountered in a recent morning session. She wrote to me that evening:

> I love you! Just now, after washing the supper dishes, I sit listening to the benevolent rain and feeling so at peace with myself and with my world and with my God—even though days to come will inevitably bring frustrations, griefs, tensions—the memory of today will be there for me to take out and look at. I can still feel the arms of the group about me—my shoulders are shaped by their warmth. This joy I had to share with you, *who reached out for me* through the obstacle course I had built. Thank you, my dear friend, and God bless and keep you.

Reaching out can be risky but if we move from a center of genuine caring for another, I believe we will communicate in an enriching way. One person noted this in my behavior: "Overriding all your actions in your role within the group is your concern for others. To me this will always cover any other sins of action a person will commit."

There are many other dimensions of my behavior that reflect my facilitator style and many other aspects of my personal philosophy that have not been discussed here. I believe I have discussed the most important dimensions of my style as it presently exists. I hope to be ever changing, and I am sure my style—my way of relating to others—will change. Perhaps the following descriptions of my style by group members indicate some other dimensions of my behavior and suggest ways in which I may develop myself further:

> The way I perceive Terry's style in a group is that he seems to have no style! This is a real compliment to you since style connotes something artificial to me. You delegate authority and responsibility, make very subtle suggestions, and are so finely sensitized that it is perfectly smooth: *natural*, in the ultimate sense.

Earlier this person had said of me: "Terry presented many pictures to me—more bad than good I'm afraid. This was disillusioning to me." Later she goes on to say:

> Now I perceive Terry as a very wonderful person who has so much that he gives—(and a lot!). I am still awed. I hope so very much that we will continue what we began. I still confess, however, that I am confused. But I do know Terry is a unique, wonderful person who can skillfully (even standing on his head, blindfolded) facilitate encounter groups—groups, crowds, and, yes, even an individual.

Another person writes:

> We are very much alike so that I would delight in your sincere warmth and ability to concentrate your attention on an individual to the point where you convince that individual that he is truly a delightful, totally unique person.

And finally another group member sums up many of the things I have been trying to say:

> To look for the best in every person in the group, to offer the loving support to one who is wounded, to guide without dictating, to perceive the hidden meaning in what a member of the group is trying to say—to do the necessary business without being curt or officious, to listen with his heart is to be the man we call Terry.

It is not easy to write about one's self in this way. I am obviously biased in my perception. I have not been immodest; written feedback from group members has made me brave in my communication. I am sure I have been selective in using that feedback and in talking about my style in my own language. I honestly believe that the picture I have presented of myself as a facilitator is true for the greater part. But I know, and those who know me well know, that I do not function at all times in all places as the effective person presented. *I often fall quite short in reaching my goals of effective participant-facilitator.*

At the time of this writing I am seriously questioning and exploring my own patterns of behavior in hopes of making some changes. I am a member of a group along with some staff members and graduate students, and we have a most effective facilitator to help us. I have begun to explore some aspects of my behavior that were once prized in the past and now have become dust in my mouth. I am learning that the everyday experiences available to me have been overlooked; relationships with my wife, with my children, in my home have taken on a new freshness. I am learning to place some limits on my need for success and approval. Life is marvelously confusing and unsure, and I am still inconsistent. But I feel a deep strength in myself, a strength that will help me address myself in meaningful ways to the questions that help me focus on the future: How can I love tenderly and wholly? How can I die gracefully? Finally, I am hearing with Van Dusen that while I am my brother's keeper, I am also my brother.

13

let us
now talk
of life
and death

A dialogue between April O'Connell and Terry O'Banion in which they encounter each other in their significant differences—and the deepest encounter of all.

TERRY: We've talked about some of our ideas and feelings for a while now. You talked about the only thing there *was* to talk about, which was life and death.

APRIL: That's the only real subject there is. Everything else is bits and pieces of it, of life and death, I mean. And I don't even want to say that—life is actually one subject and death is another. Our existence. It's *how* to live and *how* to die, or how *not* to live and how *not* to die.

TERRY: Yes, yes. I've always wanted to. . . . You know there are a lot of courses like this one, maybe—in which we help people learn how to live—in fact some courses are even titled "Preparation for Life," that sort of thing . . . and I've always felt that we needed a course maybe "Preparation for Death." It may be that we can't talk about one without the other. Would you be willing to tell me how you feel about death?

APRIL: I think death is the most beautiful thing there is. That is to say, it makes *life* beautiful. If there were no death, and if we were not conscious of it, each moment along the way wouldn't be that beautiful. It's just like the future—if we really knew the future, there would be no future! If we could predict, we would have no future, we would just be re-enacting the present. If there were no death, life wouldn't be that *valuable.*

This isn't a very new idea—this is very poetic, they keep talking about this, you know. . . .

TERRY: Well, but what about *you*—is that how *you* feel—that really life has meaning only because it's something that you *lose*?

APRIL: *Yes*, because I have this feeling that I want to pass the test that life has given us.

TERRY: What does *that* mean?

APRIL: Well, it means that if we don't come along this way again, you know, if we don't come around life again, this is our *only opportunity*—to become the most that we can become. Wow! It's like never having another chance. And if the end is all right, for example, and if we don't pass the test on our first go-round, or whatever it is, and we are really reincarnated to come back, I *don't want* to come back this way. I want to get as far as I can in this life!

TERRY: Yes, I see—you're not going to put it off—

APRIL: That's right! There's an old story about some people who asked a great teacher, "When is the time to repent?" and he answered, "The day before you die." And someone else said—I'm not sure whether it was Voltaire, or who, "Live each day as if it were your last, but also as though you have eternity before you." Make the most of each minute! That's what the threat of death does. What does it do to you?

TERRY: It doesn't really change—it doesn't really make me more living, I don't think. I don't really have any poetic feelings about it; it doesn't lift me; or make me want to live more fully today, because I know I might die tomorrow. It doesn't *really* affect my behavior very much—in other words, I don't think it really even affects very many people's behavior. I think death is something many people don't think about; they hide it away from themselves.

APRIL: Yes, I think you're probably right.

TERRY: Yes, but I'm really asking about *you,* and not how *other* people feel. If it does this to you, that's what *I'd* like to know.

APRIL: Terry, would you be shocked if I told you I feel like a prisoner in my own skin?

TERRY: No, I don't think it would really shock me—but I'd like to know more what it means.

APRIL: Yes, *what it means*—this is something I've said to people very often, but I often feel that this is really not my home and that I'll be delighted to go home.

TERRY: Home?

APRIL: I don't experience life as the best that there is. To live is a burden—and I feel much as though I'm in a chrysalis, and I can't wait to become that butterfly.

TERRY: Will death be, then, that opportunity? Or maybe I should shoot at you a straightforward question: "Do you believe in life after death?"

APRIL: It's a hard question to answer, because I—I don't believe in life as we know it after death. I believe that there is a purpose to life, and there's a *purpose* to life that leads to the logical conclusion that life was *for* something and *toward* something.

TERRY: So, therefore, death is not an *ending,* for you?

APRIL: No, it's a beginning, a consummation devoutly to be wished.

TERRY: Mm-hmm.

APRIL: Does it scare you?

TERRY: No, no! I think it's the end of a lot of things which scare people. I think it would be the idea that death is a *beginning* which a lot of people want to hear. That's really what most religions have taught.

APRIL: It seems to me that all science has been saying is that there is *order,* that the universe is not chaotic, that it is orderly—and then, we turn right around and say, "But life was an accident." It seems so.

TERRY: Yes, but order—we bring order to the universe with the human mind. I don't know whether that means that the *universe* is orderly. I think it means that our minds, somehow, we call orderly, and our understanding of the universe, it seems, would then make the universe orderly. It's actually the human mind that makes it orderly.

APRIL: The atoms are orderly.

TERRY: Our minds perceive the atom as being an orderly thing.

APRIL: Oh! I see what you're saying!

TERRY: Right, it's my mind that calls it order—so I have to bring it right back to human nature again.

APRIL: Good, you make me think.

TERRY: It's not that I could go to the universe and say, "Ah! the universe is orderly, therefore I am more than human." But it's my mind that tells me the universe is orderly in the first place, so I am the one who brings order to the universe. I don't know whether that's order or not.

APRIL: I like that!

TERRY: So, the argument, you know—How far back do we go? Who made man? Who made the earth? Who made the universe?—which is really a cause and effect argument, has never had any meaning for me.

APRIL: You point up something which I should have said, but I didn't—actually, a belief in life being purposeful is not something which we can prove—or disprove—by logical, scientific evidence. It must be . . .

TERRY: A human thing—a human hope.

APRIL: Well, you can call it hope, or you can call it faith, or you can call it like the Indians in Taos do—knowledge. I would say, Terry, this is the difference between immediate knowledge and indirect knowledge which is a philosophical concept. To me, there's a purpose to life—when I acquire knowledge, I feel as though I don't need proof of it, as though I had proof of it. The knowledge itself proves itself. I feel it in every cell of my being. That's how I believe in love.

TERRY: I think there's good evidence that so many people have felt it that—

APRIL: I like the computer joke—all little philosophers, or the ultimate computer: all philosophers, sages, and scientists send all the relevant information into the memory banks of a computer, and they ask the ultimate question of it—"Tell us if there *is* a God." The machine rumbled and roared and tapoketa-poketa'd, and out came a little slip of paper which said, "There is *now*."

TERRY: Would you talk some more about death? I think the question that interests me most is, *Is there something beyond death*? And secondly, How can you die? How can man die gracefully? And I think the second question is related, probably, to the first. It's related to how you feel about what opportunity there is, and probably colors a great deal how a man can die gracefully. Tell me some more about what is behind or beyond death, for you.

APRIL: Let me go back—because I'm not sure—let me go back to the other question you asked, which is the easier one for me to answer: How does a man die gracefully? I think this is the most *beautiful* question in the world, and I'm glad you asked this, because I believe I know—I know that some people, the people who are really more self-enlightened, and who have progressed furthest on their spiritual journey, can choose their manner of death—can say, "Now is the time to die, and this is how I will die." And they retained their faculties so that they can be in possession of their death. They haven't resisted death. They didn't resist being born, they didn't resist living, and now they're not resisting death. And this is what I pray for—and when I say pray, I mean all deep thoughts are prayers, all deep ardent desires are prayers, just as I believe that whatever we *really* want we will get and therefore let's not wish by accident for a sausage on the end of our noses like the fairy tale. So, what I would like is a happy death—I can use the word *happy* for the first time in connection with death, which is interesting. I would like to be able to leave life in such a way that it was part of my life. I didn't fight it. These sages in the world can say, "Well, it's time to die."

TERRY: To savor the experience of death, for you, would be almost I suppose, a culmination.

APRIL: I'm not sure I like the word "savor" death—but that I die rightly—I say goodbye, and I prepare for the next life. I say goodbye for the people after me, so that they can live. Mourn me a little, if they want to, in their sadness, but go on.

I had a conversation with my grandmother about six or seven years ago. She's an old Russian-Jewish woman, who came over here when she was 21 and was a real peasant—and I said to her, oh, she was complaining that all the relatives and her close friends are dead and she has a lot of *tsouras*—which means worries and woes, and life is painful for her now, and she said, "I should be dead." And I said to her, "Don't die yet, grandmother, I still need you. Stay awhile yet." And then, last fall, when I went to see her, I told her that I was ready for her to die—she'd wanted to know. And it was so *good* that I could talk to her like this! This is how I would like to die. I think what a shame that we can't die in this way, all of us; that we die accidentally, or by some tragedy, the unforeseen death—the Catholics have some expression for this, in which they ask, "Save us from an accidental death," because Catholics want to receive the last *viaticum*—which means "with you on the way."

How does that strike you?

TERRY: Well, I think it's a very *compelling* philosophy, a very attractive idea, and sort of makes a part of what's going to happen comfortable for you, for most people are frightened. In our society, you know, we never talk about it, so I am intrigued with your ideas. It sounds like it embodies some of the really important deeper aspects of some religious groups, without all of the tin drums and blaring noises that accompany death sometimes in religious groups.

APRIL: I want to say something to you, Terry. I think you're a "gooder" person than me. I know that we've kind of joked, and you've teased me about my religious streak, you know, and I've teased back about what you resented—about my labeling you as a humanitarian— I think that was a good criticism, a good resentment, and it made me stop. It seems to me that what I've wanted to say to you was maybe my need and feeling to be religious come from a deeper sense of saying that I have a lot farther to go than most people in terms of right and wrong, and fullness of life, and understanding. I've watched you do things with people and I've thought, "There's a step that I must take."

TERRY: Are you saying that you feel you're *deeper in sin*? Like the Protestant way of looking at that—a long way to grow up. I hope you really don't feel that way.

APRIL: I'm sorry, but I do. I have a great sense of sin. I recall the first time I read T. S. Eliot's *The Cocktail Party*, in which the girl Celia talks about having had a great sense of sin, and she hopes that it's her, personally, because if it isn't her, then it's the whole world, and she'd much rather have it be her. I have to get jolted by other people in my own smugness.

TERRY: We *all* need that! I suppose I was really having difficulty understanding about what I'm saying here—the idea is compelling and so forth. I have honestly rejected the idea as not being very meaningful, well not really being a very good idea. And it's not a good idea for *me*— this is what I'm saying, but I'm also being awfully smug and saying it's not very good for you either.

I have a very deeply ingrained biased feeling that I have an idea about death that is probably nearer to the truth, and at the same time thinking that the truth isn't important here—we'll never know what it is—but it seems that understanding and accepting other people's ideas give me a very smug idea about death.

APRIL: What is your smug idea?

TERRY: Well, I think that man is ultimately and completely *alone*. That he is all there is—I think there may be possibilities of other life somewhere on other planets; in fact, I'm quite certain there is—but I don't know what that means for us, now, because we don't know what it is. But, here on this planet, I think that man is ultimately and completely alone. All that he really has is *other human beings*. I think that's all that exists. And, for me, death is a cessation of being, and there's a kind of immortality if you're interested in immortality at all. There's a kind of living after dying to this extent: that man is built of, made up of, a structure that never ceases because matter never dies—it takes on new forms—and as I am matter—

APRIL: As we have ordered the universe in our perception—

TERRY: Exactly, as I have brought order to this, I have an order to my physical being that has no relationship as I perceive it, between other matters. So that dying means the dissolution of one form— human-beingness—and becoming other forms, so that I can feel immortal, you see, in terms of my body becoming the fertilizer for trees, or hopefully, I have always thought it would be beautiful to die in water, so that I could be more useful in terms of supplying nutrients to a living thing. Because my form ceases to be "living" in the definitions we have brought to order, and called this "living" and that "nonliving." For me, "living" and "nonliving" are man-made concepts. If I am willing to accept, and relate, and act as if I were a living being now, death would probably mean changing from one state to another, and un-living—I don't know what it is because I haven't experienced it yet, and probably won't experience it, because "experiencing" again is a man-made concept. So I don't know what dying means at all. All I know is that it means a cessation of my current being. It doesn't frighten me. I have no expectations beyond the border. No expectations whatso-ever, of any kind of continuation. I think that's a foolish idea, a foolish, man-made thought that somehow was invented because life is lonely, and we have been busy inventing sops for the future—I don't think there is any future beyond death.

APRIL: I got two reactions—one is, way back you said that my theological point of view is what most of mankind believes—Do you really believe this? Or maybe that most of mankind does not believe this? That maybe they use it as a "sop" as you put it; as a hope and a defense against the ultimate end. Because, if most of mankind be-lieved as I did, they wouldn't be afraid—I'm not afraid. I'm somewhat afraid of dying—I hope it's not by cancer—that's why I say I hope for a *happy* death—I hope it's not accidental. See, I think that a lot of people today will consider me old-fogeyish and will consider you like the enlightened Renaissance man.

TERRY: I don't think so, because I don't think people believe this way; not even the wild-eyed, radical students have this kind of concept. I think they feel like there's some kind of other being of some sort, and probably have ideas about being joined in ultimate love of some kind. You know, not the pearled streets of heaven—I don't think any-one believes that any more—perhaps a few—but I don't think most people believe that. But I think they still believe in some kind of ultimate reality—some absolute truth—that has some relationship to their being, and therefore a relationship to their dying.

APRIL: So you reject all absolute truths?

TERRY: Well, that gets me into making an *absolute*, you see. I've kind of said it for myself, like this: *that the only truth there is is that there is no truth.* And I add something very quickly to that—that's what I used to say—the only truth there is is that there is no truth, *and THAT may not be true.* I'll hold this one for a while and see if it has any meaning for me. So far, it *has* had some meaning.

You know, an interesting thing about ultimate reality or absolute truth is that even if there were such a thing—even if I entertained the pos-sibility of ultimate reality and absolute truth—again, I have to come back to my humanity in this: it is—my humanness—my mind—that is understanding it. So, again I still would be limited to *my* perceptions of absolute truth. Even if absolute truth came and spoke to me in a vision, a burning bush, or whatever, *you* might interpret the burning bush differently.

APRIL: Oh, yes, I can agree with you finally on one point.

TERRY: So absolute truth doesn't have any meaning you see.

APRIL: Supposing, for example, that there is a god—I don't care what you make of him—and he talked to you and he talked to me, I think we would interpret how he talked to us in our own way; we would limit our interpretations.

TERRY: Man does create god—

APRIL: In his own image—

TERRY: Well, most of the time in his own image. Our primitive conceptions of god—they look like the people.

APRIL: The thing is, does then, what you believe or don't believe influence every waking moment of your life?

TERRY: I don't know about every waking moment, but it certainly has influenced us. It means that I have, at this moment, I have to assume that I am alive and functioning, and I can't think of any better reason to be here than to love and be loved. So perhaps I just make the assumption that this is the best possible way to pass the time while I'm here. Does it mean that I'm going to raise love to a deity?

APRIL: That's a *good* statement. Loving is not enough.

TERRY: I'm going to make this assumption and go with it. And I've had some experiences with it—love is good; it makes me feel *good*. I would really choose love as a major reason for being and I'm going to try to get love, and I'm going to try to love. And when I die, I'm not going to suddenly come out of a cocoon and be in the midst of love, or more loving. I am just going to cease to be, because that's it—that's where I start feeling smug because it's become a very narrow idea, in which I've become almost dogmatic that that is an absolute truth. Which is kind of strange for me to become dogmatic, because I'm usually not; but I suppose if I believe in it as strongly as I do then I am.

One thing I've done is to will my body to a medical center, and my eyes to an eye bank; and even got my mother to do this. I also tried to convince some friends of the feeling that it would be useful—even after death—and there's a kind of immortality in that. I certainly want this—I guess it's a part of my wanting to be loved. I need for people to know me and to remember me. I wrote a little poem once called *Epitaph*—it was really about suicide—let's see, it went: "I cannot live without you, so I choose to die. I, who believe in no meeting place after death, perhaps in the still of the night you will have a thought of me, and that will be immortality enough." After you've gone, that some people can think of you—*knowing that now is the goodness*. And I know that this is true, or will be true, already, you see. I can sit back and look at the people I've known, and I can know now that I'm loved by some of them, and that I'll be an absence in people's minds.

Or, the other part of immortality—is that I will have *affected* people— so that ideas that I have spawned and created will continue to grow— that gives me a good feeling! That validates my being, and I don't need the validation of afterlife, to know that this life has been good.

APRIL: I read someplace that, to a person who doesn't believe in life after death, this world is opaque, and the other is ephemeral. And to those who believe that there is something beyond life, that life is real, and this life is transparent. That this life is not solid, and has little substance. I think this kind of represents our points of view here. I hate to say points of view because it doesn't represent me. It's not a point of view and it's not a belief. It's something I live with day in and day out—it's a part of me and a part of my skin, or my heart.

TERRY: If it's not a belief then you can't discard it.

APRIL: Right, I cannot discard it. I could no more discard it than I can pick up a cockroach. I hope some day I can get to the point where I can pick up a cockroach and say, "This, too, is life, and is related to me in some way!" Although I'm better than I was. I remember in *Androcles and the Lion* the heroine—I forget what her name is—is talking about why she couldn't put incense on the idol; she's a young Christian and she's going to be thrown to the lions, and the young Roman who loves her, who's trying to get her to do it even if she doesn't believe in it, and she says she had a pet mouse once and that she could no more put the ashes into that idol than she could pick up the mouse. It's just not physically her. So *I* could no more discard this than I could discard the fact that my name is April O'Connell. My name *is* April O'Connell. And I am living—I believe I am living.

TERRY: Is it something that was part of you when you were born, or is it something that you have come to know? Have you felt other ways and discarded them? Have you *chosen* this way? Was this always a part of your being?

APRIL: That would be more apt. I came from parents who were atheistic, although they had come from different religions, and so I didn't get a lot of training; in fact, I recall that my mother talked about —I came home from school one day, and I said, "What is Santa Claus?" and she said, "That's the spirit of Christmas. It's a thing that has been made up by people, but it's not real." This is how she interpreted things. She wanted "reality."

And I came across the concept of god somewhere, and it seemed so right, that I can't remember when, in the forming of my consciousness, that I accepted it. Then, of course, our society doesn't believe in this sort of thing. I went through the intellectual college rebellion against religion, and I'd had indoctrination into so many—and found people fighting it. Oh, for example, in Bergman's *The Seventh Seal* at one point, the knight is sitting there and saying that he has witnessed rape, and murder, and disease, all in the holy name of God; and I was troubled by this, and I had a terrible reaction that this was not it, you know, the kinds of things that church people do belie all this. But it didn't matter how much I protested, I felt like the hound of heaven was following me. And that it was something that was always there—all I had to do was face it, and now it seems to me that a lot of us are not what we should be—whether we be Jews or Christians or Moslems—we aren't as we should be if we were really acting out all these things. But that's no reason to say that they're not doing the best they can. I think I've come to use the term that this world is the kindergarten of God, and it's *we* who make the division, and it's *we* who misinterpret, and it's *we* who see through a glass darkly. And, finally, I couldn't resist any more, then the hound caught up with me. I couldn't rationalize my way out of it. When I went into psychology, I felt that you can't prove scientifically this feeling that I have, or that other people I know have. It's much the same experience as when you pick up the phone saying to yourself, "I bet that's so-and-so." And you haven't heard from so-and-so in a long time, and it *is* so-and-so. You say, "I'm sure there was thought transference." And yet, we could rationalize it away and be cynical. All I know is that because of this, because there's a part of my being that influences everything I do, and when it doesn't, then I have sinned. That is to say, I have lost the light, you know, I have forgotten; and when I re-remember it everything clears up again. Oh, yes! How stupid I was, I'd forgotten for a while. . . .

And it's not a death-bed religion, because it's when I'm depressed that I lose the sense of God.

TERRY: It must be a good feeling to have a firm thing to have with you.

APRIL: It's a firm thing, and it's a *good* feeling, but it makes everything that I do unimportant. I, for example, want no immortality here. I would like, in contrast to you, I would like as soon as I die that the waves come in and wash away my footprints, because what I do here is of no importance, but what my *soul* does here, oh! that is *so* important! I almost didn't want to be in this book because of that. I don't want to leave a mark, a footprint here. I'm still nervous about it.

TERRY: I would, I would, because this is the only place there is to leave a footprint.

APRIL: Oh! I agree with that. I came across something wonderful: this earth is as good a place as any place to love.

You can't love from the grave, you know, right. You can't put your hands around somebody in the grave—and, for some strange reason, I also believe that, so you know, I can appreciate it. Boy, this is a darned good place to love! And it's a darned good place to argue, because arguing is love. An argument can be a very intimate thing and a very loving thing—that's what I meant a while back when I said, "Love isn't always enough." If you love somebody strongly enough, you will argue with him.

TERRY: Well, it's for sure that you wouldn't argue with anyone you didn't care anything about.

APRIL: A student of mine, Robert Pratt, once said that fighting could be a very intimate thing, and that was a very beautiful concept he gave me—and shared with the class. And I believe that, because I love my children enough to care for them, and caring sometimes means to spank the hell out of them, to help them in their behavior—nobody *else* ever will! And for this reason, I disagree with a lot of psychologists who say, "If you have a child from the day *one*, and just set a good example, and provide a wonderful, marvelous environment, he will become the best person possible." No, I haven't had a child from day one, as all my children are adopted, but I am not so sure that the concept is right at all. My husband had a friend once who was about to do something very terrible—about to destroy somebody else, or try to destroy somebody else and he would have destroyed himself too. And my husband drove 100 miles down to see him to tell him, "You're wrong, Alex." And Alex replied, "If you were really my friend, then you would support me whether I was right or wrong." And Vin (my husband) said: "If I am your friend, I will tell you when I believe you're wrong."

TERRY: The most terrible thing is that most people go through life without any kind of encountering at all; and encountering is an affirmation that someone at least *cares*—and encountering may be negative and painful.

APRIL: A *good whack* on the rear end is a darn good encounter!

TERRY: Right! It's that people care—it shows they do. The terrible thing is that no one wants to get involved; the terrible thing is *not* to be involved; not to have someone *fuss* at you. Many people just need that, because it affirms their being. I'm struck by the *need to have people affirm our being*, and that people will affirm our being only if they care. And this can sometimes occur in not very pleasurable ways —I'm thinking of a friend of mine who was a teacher when I taught in the public schools of South Florida—and I—for some reason, he meant something to me, but he hurt, he was always on my back about something, and so the way I had to handle it was never to speak to him until he came around; until he finally noticed it and it got to him. What I would do is I wouldn't talk to him, ever; when he came to the faculty lounge, I'd get up and leave; if I saw him in the grocery store, I'd go down another aisle; if I saw him on one side of the street, I would literally walk to the other side of the street.

APRIL: Did you *really*?

TERRY: Yes. In fact, I did it for about three months. I was saying to him, "You are hurting me, and I care for you or I wouldn't care"— if I didn't care for him, he wouldn't or couldn't hurt me.

APRIL: In like manner, you once did this to me.

TERRY: Well, I wouldn't speak to him; I'm not sure about doing it to you. I wouldn't . . .

APRIL: You spoke to me gruffly and rudely for one whole week, and you shook my sense up when you did this. I remember being terribly hurt at the time! You *shook* me, so that I had to stand up on my own feet, and not lean upon you.

TERRY: Mmmmmm.

APRIL: You shook me loose from my dependence on you—I was going through this thing, you know, that you were my boss, and I needed your approval. And you said, "I'm not going to give you my approval," because you didn't give me your approval, by goodness, you gave me your disapproval for one *whole* week in *every single manner*, until I was just knocking off one wall onto the other! You actually made me stand up—by myself! And what a loving thing for you to have done, Terry. *I'm glad.*

TERRY: I appreciate that. I made this guy do it also, because he wouldn't have kept bugging me if he didn't care for me, too. And finally it stopped—finally, we called a truce, and he re-encountered me. About 10 years later, in fact it happened this year, about five weeks ago, he was invited to a party I attended, and we really touched each other—realized that here was a person whom I cared for very much, and he cared for me. And we talked about that experience we had, 10 years ago, when I couldn't speak to him—*would not* speak to him— because I cared for him. Does that make sense, what I'm trying to say?

APRIL: Yes, but I suddenly have something else that's beginning to make sense to me. You and I have struggled through the last dialog—why it was that we didn't get closer—we admired each other —two people, and interested in things like this—why didn't we get *closer*? Terry, could it be that your mode of existence is so different from my mode of existence? My mode of living, your mode of living, are so *different* that we won't be able to share our world and have a complete soul-sharing type of thing. And that we'll have to just every so often just wave at each other—"Oh, well how are you doing on your journey?" "And here's where I am now"—and be willing to say that this is all that you and I will ever be able to do. But to value it . . .

TERRY: Yeah. To value the other person—yes, that has meaning for me. I think I only get very involved with another human when his world or his *way* is similar to mine.

APRIL: This wise man I know said that there are many paths up the mountain and that there isn't just one way.

TERRY: But I travel daily, personal paths of people when they are more similar to mine, which, you know, is a way of saying that "We understand people who are more like us!"

APRIL: Than different, right!

TERRY: And it may be that people who are quite different we never will—well, we can only touch the edges.

APRIL: Somehow, I feel very close to you, now. I feel it's okay; this may be the way it is, and it will *content* me! That whole thought makes me happier—if we can say, well if this much—I know you've been close to some of the others on the staff, and it will content me that every so often our spheres can touch because I have a real respect for what your sphere or world is.

TERRY: And I have a very healthy respect for yours—a tremendously healthy respect for your sphere—it's one that probably will never—you know, run in . . .

APRIL: The maps won't cover very much!

TERRY: That's a good realization for us to come to, I think.

APRIL: Yes, personally, for you and me.

TERRY: Yes—because I remember saying very early in our meetings that—almost about the second or third meeting—I said, "April O'Connell, you're going to be a very significant person for me." I said that to you in the hall—do you remember that? "A very significant person in my life." And you *have* been a significant person, but not in the way that I thought it would be—because on our first meeting, I thought, "Well, now, here's a person who is similar, understands, has a similar outlook . . ."

APRIL: Or who's suffered like yourself.

TERRY: Yes, well maybe who suffered similarly—but we're very, *very* different people, very different.

APRIL: How very nice to come to that conclusion. And to *like* the difference, and to say, well, all right, we'll never share this kind of tremendous closeness, that you share with others, or that I share with others, but I have a wonderful, *wonderful* recognition of you as a person, and valid—I like that *very* much.

TERRY: It's a kind of affirmation I seldom get, because as soon as I see that people's spheres are not similar to mine it becomes more difficult to encounter them.

APRIL: I think this is true of me. In *My Fair Lady*, the hero says "Why isn't a woman more like a man? Why isn't a woman more like me?" I think this is a very important thing—that each person recognize that he has his *mode* of living—and that's why I don't like all these rules about mental health and how to be successful, because what is good for someone else may not be valid for you. Each person must ferret out—I don't like the word *ferret out*—must *soul-search* himself, to find out the most important things. The two most important questions I was ever asked were: "What is most important to you?" When I was asked that, the answer was very quick—some of the things I've talked about—and then the person said to me, "What are you doing about it?" Oh, and I felt as though I'd been kicked in the stomach! I thought, "Oh, my God, I've let so many years go without doing something!" And I ask each student, and I can't answer this for him, what he is doing.

TERRY: The motivation for encountering other people may be just the human need to find people who affirm our ideas, our feelings, our mode—maybe that's the whole motivation behind encountering—not just to love and be loved, but to discover people who are on the same path with you, so that you don't feel lonely being there.

APRIL: That's a lovely thought! I like that. But then, of what value is it that you and I recognize that our paths and our spheres are different? That also is an affirmation, and brought me a lot closer to you because of the recognition that we are quite far apart. Maybe just that *sudden understanding* and that was kind of beautiful and kind of a jewel.

TERRY: Yes, just the good feeling of *knowing*.

APRIL: Ah, yes, that's it! And I really believe, too, that there are some common kinds of ways of feeling and being. Oh, you know, we joke about astrology! But it may be that there are some 12 basic modes of living. And Spengler and Vernon, Lindsey and Allport said there were six or seven basic types; and somebody else said we have so many specialized traits—127 at the latest count of Cattell, wasn't it? I mean, how far off are these? What does it mean—that we're political, or religious? Spengler says: political, religious, aesthetic, economic, persuasive, and social service types. They could be subdivided or grouped together again. Maybe it's important for each person to find out *his* mode: This is who and what I am.

TERRY: *Yes*, I think this is what we've been meaning here when we talked about how to be a human being—this really is: *How, for you, to come to know your humanness is to come to know your mode, your way of being, rather than to let* others *tell you who you are*. It is *to know from within* which is *your* way. And so that you can even begin recognizing it and touching it in others, because I have a kind of feeling that there's a nonverbal communication between people in terms of their modes of living, and that I can pick out my kinds of people, in groups, or from groups.

APRIL: This has all kinds of implications—what if this is the real problem between parents and children?

TERRY: No wonder they don't understand them.

APRIL: "Here, I've been brought up to believe in these kinds of things, and do these kinds of things, and here you are doing *that!*" Yes!

TERRY: Or, when a young couple marry, they haven't really had this kind of sensitivity to their own being. Maybe they're sensitive to something *else*, like sex, or money, or physical beauty; and are not sensitive to their own mode of being and haven't learned to be sensitive to others' modes of being.

APRIL: So they may have married the *wrong mode*—for the wrong reason! One of the marvels, for me, is that four of my children are so unlike me. I appreciate them in their *own* mode.

TERRY: That's what *you and I just did*. We each appreciated the other in his own mode—and we're not at all saying that what a man needs to do *is to find his own mode*, and then go out and contact people with the *same* modes. We're not saying that. We're saying *it's beautiful to know your own mode—yes, so that you can discover people who are similar*, and probably have some very good encounters and contacts with them; *but it's also good to appreciate the contrast* when it does happen, among the different modes when you encounter them.

annotated
bibliography

The following bibliography is not meant to be representative of the field of social science; nor does it attempt to include all the important authors of the humanistic movement. What we have tried to do is to list some books which, through our personal experience, we know get enthusiastic reactions from students. It is thus first and foremost aimed toward student interest and as adjunct reading for a course in personal growth and for human encounter groups. Because it is a book list for students, we have, wherever possible, listed the paperback edition so as to keep it within the students' price range.

PART I: BOOKS WHICH DEAL WITH HUMANISTIC AND EXISTENTIAL PSYCHOLOGY AND PHILOSOPHY.

Bugental, James F. T. (ed.), *Challenges of Humanistic Psychology.* New York: McGraw-Hill Book Co., 1967. (Paperback).

A book of readings which include most of the authoritative names in the humanistic movement, among them: Hadley Cantril, Thomas S. Szasz, Colin Wilson, Hubert Bonner, Hobart F. Thomas, Carl A. Whitaker and John Warkenten, Herbert A. Otto, James V. Clark, Carl R. Rogers, Abraham H. Maslow, and others. An excellent overview of the humanistic movement.

Fromm, Erich, *The Revolution of Hope: Toward a Humanized Technology.* New York: Bantam Books (Grosset and Dunlap), 1968. (Paperback).

Fromm agrees with many sociologists and psychologists today that Technological Society seems to be reducing its members to the level of the machine in which they experience themselves as dehumanized and—like the machines they have invented—victims of a sick society. Unlike others, Fromm sees greater possibility of restoring man's social system to man's control. He denounces our present craze (fad, fashion) of "hopelessness" and thereby takes issue with such existential writers as Herbert Marcuse (*Eros and Civilization*) and presents a pragmatic methodology for solving our dilemma. The student may want to read some of his earlier works as well: *The Art of Loving, Escape from Freedom, The Heart of Man, Beyond the Chains of Illusion,* and *Man for Himself.*

Jourard, Sidney M., *The Transparent Self.* Princeton, N.J.: D. Van Nostrand Co., Inc., 1964. (Paperback).

This book, more than any other, made popular and actual the term, *self-disclosure.* As Jourard describes it, because we are afraid of rejection, hurt, or criticism we hide behind various masks which prevent us from knowing one another. "But such protection," says Jourard, "is purchased at a steep price. We are then never able to be truly ourselves to someone else." The choice is ours: Shall we wear our masks or shall we reveal our true faces? A *must* background reader for Chapters 4 and 5 of this book. If this book speaks to the reader, he will want to read Jourard's newer book: *Disclosing Man to Himself.*

Maslow, Abraham H., *Toward a Psychology of Being.* Princeton, N.J.: D. Van Nostrand Co., Inc., 1962. (Paperback).

If we want to know the fully functioning, psychologically healthy person, let us study *him* rather than the psychologically disturbed, proposed Maslow. And this is just what he did. This book contains the results of his research; namely, that self-actualized (fully functioning) adults are altruistic, dedicated, self-transcending, spontaneously creative, etc. This book answers the students' needs for a model of the healthy personality in the area of self-growth. Maslow also describes psychologically the "peak" experience which has been variously identified by others as related to the mystic experience, sartori, joy, etc.

Otto, Herbert, *Group Methods Designed to Actualize Human Potential*, 2nd ed. Chicago, Ill.: Stone-Brandel Center, 1967.

Otto has devised a number of programmed exercises to help beginning "do-it-yourself" encounter groups get started. These exercises emphasize *positive experiences* so they are relatively safe for beginning leaders to use for experimentation.

Perls, Frederick, *Gestalt Therapy Verbatim*. Lafayet, Calif.: Real People Press, 1969. (Hardback).

This book is composed of actual transcripts of this creative genius' insights and work with people in the encounter situation. While few of us would ever be a Perlian leader, some of his techniques (shuttling, fantasizing, dream-interpretation) are easily grasped and can be used by sensitive practitioners. This is a book primarily for the professional rather than the student.

Psychology Today, December 1967, *Vol. I.*, No. 7., 16–41.

This magazine devotes several articles to the encounter phenomenon, Esalen, and applications (such as race relations). The Carl Rogers article, in particular, is an informal exposition of the encounter group as a family situation.

Rogers, Carl A., "The Process of the Basic Encounter Group," *in* F. T. Bugental (ed.), *Challenges of Humanistic Psychology*. New York: McGraw-Hill Book Co., 1967. (Paperback).

Another explication of the encounter process by Carl Rogers, who pioneered the "client-centered" approach to human growth. He describes his encounter group facilitations and readers may find it interesting to compare Rogers' style of leadership with those of Terry O'Banion and April O'Connell.

Other equally noteworthy books by Rogers include: *On Becoming a Person; Person to Person: The Problem of Being Human;* and *Freedom to Learn.*

Schutz, William C., *Joy: Expanding Human Awareness*. New York: Grove Press, 1967. (Paperback).

Schutz regards *joy* as the feeling that comes from fulfillment of one's potential—both physically and psychologically through overcoming of the psychological obstacle emotions of guilt, shame, embarrassment, fear, failure, success, retribution, and through physical exercises and disciplines: sensory awareness and techniques for self-discovery, fancy free association, group fantasy, acting-out group games and techniques, psychodrama, and nonverbal touch-and-trust techniques. As a listing of encounter methods this book may be a resource of encounter techniques.

Sohl, Jerry, *The Lemon Eaters*. New York: Simon and Shuster, Inc., 1967.

The author, a journalist and science fiction writer, wrote this "true-to-life" story of an encounter marathon supposedly based upon his own experiences. Actually, the book tends to present a good story rather than an actual encounter weekend. It does, however, give the reader some idea of encounter by illustrating the drama that unfolds when one psychologist and 12 people get together to establish a deeper level of communication with each other.

PART II: BOOKS WHICH DEAL WITH THE INTENSE PERSONAL AND PSYCHOLOGICAL PROBLEMS THAT MAN "IS HEIR TO."

Berne, Eric, *Games People Play.* New York: Grove Press, 1964. (Hardback). New York: Grove Press, 1967. (Paperback).

As a supplement to Shakespeare's thought when he stated . . . "All the world's a stage," Berne describes the different parts one may choose to play while living. *Games People Play* is a very enlightening book describing much of human behavior and one which no student of human relationships should be without. He discusses the three social levels of game involvement—parent, child, and adult, as well as the "strokes" of social intercourse. He describes one hundred and twenty human games with an analysis of their strategy as a football coach would when describing plays.

Camus, Albert, *The Myth of Sisyphus and Other Essays.* New York: Vintage Books, 1959. (Paperback). New York: Alfred A. Knopf, 1955. (Hardback).

Suicide as a possibility is impossible for anyone to understand except perhaps another fellow-despairer. Perhaps nowhere in literature and social science has suicide been made so understandable to those of us who have never experienced a wish to die. Camus concretized for us the "ultimate alternative" as a legitimate answer to a life that seems to have no meaning. One of the most moving, disturbing, yet coldly impassioned treatises on the subject of suicide.

Cohen, Sidney, *The Drug Dilemma.* New York: McGraw-Hill Book Co., Series in Health Education, 1969. (Paperback).

This book was written to be used as an informative aid for those counselors of youth or for youth, themselves, who indulge in drug usage. Cohen offers a relatively unbiased report on the history, classification, effects (both physical and psychological), complications, detection, and treatment of the different types of drugs. He calls drug usage "chemical roulette" and attributes truth to the fact that the majority of users are youth because youth is more impulsive, curious, and idealistic than is the older generation, and as one grows and matures he represses these traits. Cohen has a good definition of the generation gap, ". . . the distance between the parents' forgetting and the children not knowing."

Goffman, Irving, *Stigma: Notes on the Management of Spoiled Identity*. Englewood Cliffs, N.J.: Prentice-Hall, Inc., 1963. (Paperback).

A stigma is a bodily sign which indicates a blemished person. In previous eras it was burned on to the person, as punishment, who then was forced to avoid public places. Goffman uses the word *stigma* to indicate the physical disability itself which causes the individual to conceal it from public view: such as homosexuality, stuttering, mental illness, dope addiction, deafness, prostitution, scars, amputation, mental retardation, Jewishness, racial ties, etc. This book will sensitize the college student to the embarrassments and fears that stigmatized persons suffer from and the methods they use to keep from being discovered.

Green, Hannah, *I Never Promised You A Rose Garden*. New York: Signet Books, 1964.

This is a novel about a sixteen-year old girl who lives in two worlds: reality and madness. It is not only a brilliant exposition of the internal battle of the psychotic, it is (in our opinion) a literary and psychological masterpiece.

McNeil, Elton B., *The Quiet Furies: Man and Disorder*. Englewood Cliffs, N.J.: Prentice-Hall, Inc., 1970. (Paperback).

This is a primer of the major neurotic and psychotic disorders ranging from the mildly neurotic to the psychotic, from dope addiction to severe alcoholism. It is an excellent introduction both for psychologically näive students and for students who have some preliminary knowledge of psychological disorders. The disorders are presented in well written case history style and the whole book has been beautifully illustrated.

Rechy, John, *City of Night*. New York: Grove Press, 1963. (Paperback).

Homosexuality is a "problem" area: problematic for the homosexual who must then hide it in the "straight" society; and problematic also for the non homosexual who is confused, frightened, and horrified by it. The author presents the plight, the aspirations, the doubts, the double-life, the masquerade in beautifully literate form. The homosexual is treated neither as a "case study," nor as a "demi-god," nor as a "pervert"—rather he is seen as a human being cast in this mold but who lives it in many ways. Although fiction, it seems to us a more valid explication than the traditional case study approach.

Rubin, Theodore Isaac, *Lisa and David*. New York: Ballantine Books, Inc., 1961. (Paperback).

This is a love story involving two severely disturbed adolescents. The setting is a residential treatment center for exceptional children. Rubin describes life and therapeutic treatments in such an environment, awakening the reader to two facets of human therapy—one, that which medicine and counseling offer; the other, that aid which is derived through a relationship in which two people are sincerely interested and involved in the welfare of each other. Through their attraction to each other, both David and Lisa succeed in breaking down the barriers of communication between them and, eventually, with those of the "outside" world.

Simon, Anne W., *Stepchild In the Family*. New York: Pocket Books, Inc., 1965. (Paperback), New York: Odyssey Press, 1964. (Hardback).

Once upon a time, stepparents existed mostly in fairy tales. The stepmother was traditionally pictured as wicked, ugly, jealous, cruel, and the stepchildren as the innocent victims. Today one child in nine is a stepchild, although generally now through divorce and remarriage. This book will provide insight and relief for stepparents and stepchildren alike as they read the misconceptions and problems (inherent or otherwise) in this relationship.

PART III: BOOKS FROM THE AREA OF SCIENCE WHICH ARE RELEVANT TO AND EASILY READ BY THE NONSCIENCE MAJOR.

Ardrey, Robert, *The Territorial Imperative*. New York: Dell Publishing Co., 1966. (Paperback).

Animals seem to exhibit ownership behavior as though they have instinctive "territorial rights"; i.e., they lay claim to a certain domain and then guard it ferociously, heroically, against all intruders. Ardrey describes this behavior as it appears in the evolution of species up to and including *homo sapiens*, which seems to him to account for man's aggressive violence with his neighbors whether it be on the football field or the battleground. Will we be able to recognize and channel this aggressive energy into more constructive avenues so as to achieve a permanent peace? He poses the question but it is we who have to answer it.

Hall, Edward T., *The Silent Language*. Greenwich, Conn.: Fawcett Publications, Inc., 1961. (Paperback).

We speak with more than just words. In fact, even when we say nothing at all we speak and are spoken to all the time. The way we treat time and keep appointments, how we relate to others with formal or informal reference, how we laugh, sit, stand, dress, all these things speak volumes to others in the same social setting. But these signals are changed from culture to culture. And in this era of international relating, we should know the "silent language" of other nations and cultures for progress in all areas of human relationships.

Hayakawa, S. I., *The Use and Misuse of Language*. Greenwich, Conn.: Fawcett Publications, 1962. (Paperback).

General semantics is the study of the way language can be used to promote understanding or to confuse understanding. It is the whole area of "language habits." Semanticists believe (with much justification) that with proper training in language usage, problems can be better defined, executives can become more skilled in dealing with others, students can be taught to clarify their thinking, and (by eliminating prejudices) distorted views can be avoided. The founder of general semantics, Alfred Korzybski, believed that the skilled use of language would lead to the dissolution of many personal and social problems. This book of readings presents a wide range of areas in which the principles of general semantics apply.

Lorenz, Konrad, *On Human Aggression*. New York: Harcourt, Brace & World, Inc., 1966.

Lorenz hypothesizes that the basic features of human behavior are inherited from man's nonhuman ancestors: human "morality" may in fact have its roots in the innate presentation and recognition of appeasement gestures. Aggression is a major facet of human behavior necessary for the formation of a stable, complex society by a gregarious animal such as man. Aggression may be expressed individually or by groups. A certain form of group aggression is called militant enthusiasm and in man is expressed in a species specific fashion such that Lorenz maintains it is ". . . a true autonomous instinct: it has its own appetitive behavior, its own releasing mechanisms, and, like the sexual urge or any other strong instinct, it engenders a strong feeling of intense satisfaction."

Morris, Desmond, *The Naked Ape*. New York: McGraw-Hill Book Co., 1967. (Hardback). New York: Dell Publishing Co., 1969. (Paperback).

If you really take a good look at man, says Desmond Morris, you have to see him as the most fully developed of the primates: a vertical, hunting, weapon-toting, territorial, neotonous, brainy, Naked Ape—a primate by ancestry and a carnivore by adoption . . . a new and experimental departure from his progenitors and, like many new models, he has a few imperfections. Although culturally civilized, he is genetically *still a primate*—and his animal nature causes him problems.

The chapter on the sex of the Naked Ape is probably one of the most interesting chapters on human sexuality. The whole book is worthwhile reading.

Standen, Anthony, *Science Is a Sacred Cow*. New York: E. P. Dutton & Co., Inc., 1950. (Paperback).

Does the scientific approach seem to you the answer to the problems of society? Does the realm of the scientist seem awesome and mysteriously inhabited by intellectual giants? This book, written by a scientist, will give you another slant. In humorous and cultured fashion, he strips the scientist of his aura and reveals him as human, fallible, and even as you and I.

PART IV: BOOKS WHICH SAMPLE SOME OF THE SOCIAL PROBLEMS OF OUR TIMES.

Boorstin, Daniel, *The Image: A Guide to Pseudo-Events in America*. New York: Harper & Row, Publishers, 1964. (Paperback).

Boorstin has created a new term in the area of communication, *the pseudo-*

event. A pseudo-event is not real; it is a preplanned, blownup news item. It is not so much a reality as an illusion of a real event designed to satiate our demand for sensation. A pseudo-event is contrived more to make head-lines than to report real events. He applies this term to the many facets of our mass media which he says cause us to be inundated with phony, exag-gerated, sometimes fictional "News" stories. He levels his criticisms at our newspapers, our magazines, our television, our advertising and travel agen-cies, publishing houses, movies, etc., with the result that the very media we have invented to enlarge our vision have now become "deceivers" and "obstructors" to our vision.

"There is a crime of deception being committed in America today and each of us is the principal."

Erickson, Erick, *Identity: Youth and Crisis.* New York: W.W. Norton & Co., Inc., 1968. (Paperback).

A well-known psychoanalyst, Erickson has devoted much of his clinical re-search to the area of children and adolescents. He considers one of the major developmental tasks of youth to be that of identity. He sees the acting-out, confused, self-conscious behavior of the adolescent as sympto-matic of "identity crisis." Although identity has been a factor of human development for longer than we know, *now more than ever* the adolescent seems to be behaving in even more bizarre ways both in achieving a distinct identity divorced from that of his parents and in purposely avoiding identity by "dropping out."

Friedan, Betty, *The Feminine Mystique.* New York: Dell Publishing Co., 1963. (Paperback).

Another aspect of "identity crisis" (see Erickson above) concerns the girl-woman-wife-mother. After World War II, says Betty Friedan, the American woman was sold a bill of goods of the joys and creativity of "house-wifery." It became apparent that society had relegated her to a position more in keeping with the prewoman-suffrage era than to the decade of the sixties. This overemphasis on her mother–wife role served to diminish her as a person of worth in her own right. She makes a plea for a new concept of womanhood, freed from the restrictions of previous eras.

Griffen, John Howard, *Black Like Me.* Boston: Houghton Mifflin Co., 1960. (Paperback).

This book gets enthusiastic responses from college students. It is the story of a white man who turns himself black and learns, first-hand, what it is like to be "black"—it is to be hated, humiliated, ridiculed, reviled.

Harrington, Michael, *The Other America: Poverty in the United States.* New York: The Macmillan Co., 1963. (Hardback). Baltimore, Md.: Penguin Books, Inc. (Paperback).

This book is a very readable (albeit factual) book about the poor in America. The highest recommendation we can give to this book is that our college students are enthusiastic in their praise of it. It really "turns them on" to the plight of our poverty stricken millions.

Hoffer, Eric, *The True Believer*. New York: Harper & Row, Publishers, 1966. (Paperback).

Eric Hoffer is the justly respected ex-longshoreman-turned-philosopher-and-commentator of the political scene. In the light of the present surge of mass movements and frenzied political demonstrations, this book is truly timely and insightful. He describes the fanatical revolutionary as a "true believer" who seeks causes to worship and to die for. He is, says Hoffer, the "mortal enemy of things-as-they-are" and ready to die for an impossible dream. He has profound understanding of the character, and mind of the fanatic—a man who will join any cause at peril to his life, the lives of his family and friends . . . or yours.

Packard, Vance, *The Pyramid Climbers*. New York: McGraw-Hill Book Co., Inc., 1962. (Hardback). New York: Fawcett Crest Book, 1967. (Paperback).

Packard has been commended for his vivid portrayal of businessmen's experiences and tactics as they travel the road of social mobility. He relates the upward sweep of young executives to the task of climbing a pyramid—the apex of which is aptly titled the "bitch goddess, Success." He describes the ascent as, ". . . assaulting the slippery, crevice ridden slopes" as "they learn the secret love of negotiating difficult passages. They sharpen some very special traits, such as maze brightness, which help them survive and advance." Packard elaborates on the climb by describing the "Screening, Grooming, and Pruning" processes, "the Well-Packaged Executive"; certain "Strategies and Incentives," as well as presenting "Hazards and Harrassments," of the hopeful thrust upward.

Riesman, David, Nathan Glazer, and Revel Denney, *The Lonely Crowd*. New Haven, Conn.: Yale University Press, 1961. (Paperback).

Have Americans lost the national character that once defined them as "rugged individualists," and "pioneering?" Riesman *et al.* suggest we may have. There has been, he says, a transition in our national character to "other direction" in which the goals are that of conformity to expectations of others, rather than to a set of values that come from within.

Scheuer, James H., *To Walk the Streets Safely*. Garden City, N.Y.: Doubleday & Co., Inc., 1969. (Hardback).

Congressman Scheuer draws a picture of crime and crime detection in the United States today. He discusses the obsolescence of many police methods of coping with crime and points toward a new concept of law enforcement and a new breed of law enforcement agent. He presents a practical program for both national and community action based on the hard and behavioral sciences. No matter what your opinion of his program, this is a committed man!

Shostrom, Everett L., *Man, the Manipulator*. Nashville, Tenn.: Abingdon Press, 1967. (Hardback).

A manipulator is a person who exploits and/or uses himself and others as "things" in self-defeating ways. Thus, Shostrom defines manipulation and describes the ways in which children and parents, lovers, teachers and students, husbands and wives do this to each other. An excellent supplement to our chapters and to Maslow's "self-actualization" concept; easy to read and pragmatic in approach.

Stampp, Kenneth M., *The Peculiar Institution: Slavery in the Ante-Bellum South*. New York: Vintage Books, 1956. (Paperback).

A highly literate, graphic, but easily read series of descriptions of what it meant to be a slave, for those who want some understanding of the development of "Black" character types—"The Uncle Tom," the violent militant, etc.

PART V: BOOKS WHICH ARE CONCERNED WITH SOME OF THE SPIRITUAL, ETHICAL, AND RELIGIOUS CONCERNS OF MAN.

Buber, Martin, *I and Thou*, 2nd ed. New York: Charles Scribner's Sons, 1958. (Paperback).

This book became a classic in the lifetime of its author so powerful was its message regarding Man's relation to his world and all that relates to it. It is philosophy, it is theology, it is poetry . . . above all, it is a book to be treasured. Chapter 11 discusses this book in detail.

The student may also want to read other books by this same poet-philosopher-theologian: *Between Man and Man, The Eclipse of God*, etc.

de Saint-Exuppery, Antoine, *The Little Prince*. New York: Harcourt, Brace & World, Inc., 1943. (Hardback).

This classic is a fable for adults and, like *The Prophet* (see below), should be part of the reading experience of every college student. The Little Prince is a wanderer from another planet and through his innocent, curious, and alien eyes we learn to see our civilization in a new way.

Fletcher, Joseph, *Situation Ethics: The New Morality*. Philadelphia: The Westminster Press, 1966. (Paperback).

In an age in which traditions, beliefs, and mores are breaking down, Fletcher offers an alternate ethic. He outlines a methodology for decision making in which each man takes unto himself ultimate authority for right and wrong. He is not suggesting Ayn Rand Ethics; on the contrary, he grounds his methodology on "agapē, the love of which only God is capable, but which every man must endeavor to emulate." Any act, however (abortion, lying, adultery, murder), could be right, depending on the circumstance.

index